# SCOTTISH CASES ON AGENCY

# SCOTTISH CASES ON AGENCY

BY

ENID A. MARSHALL,
M.A., LL.B., Ph.D., Solicitor,
*Reader in Business Law*
*at the University of Stirling*

EDINBURGH

W. GREEN & SON LTD.

ST. GILES STREET

1980

First published in 1980



ISBN 0 414 00657 7



TYPESET BY EDINBURGH UNIVERSITY
STUDENT PUBLICATIONS BOARD

PRINTED BY LINDSAY & CO. LTD., EDINBURGH.

# PREFACE

THIS collection of Scottish cases is a shortened and revised version of a typescript collection with the same title which has been used in conjunction with a course on the Scots law of agency at the University of Stirling since 1977.

On this topic within the mercantile law of Scotland it is, of course, appropriate, and on account of the comparative paucity of decisions in the smaller jurisdiction, essential, that reference be made also to English cases. It seemed, however, to the author that most Scottish cases were being unduly neglected because of the existence of, and reliance on, inexpensive English textbooks and casebooks dealing with the subject, combined with the absence of sufficiently illustrated inexpensive textbook or casebook from the Scottish standpoint. It was a desire to close part of that gap which prompted the compilation of this collection.

The Notes annexed to the main extracts have for the most part been devoted to the inclusion of shorter treatment of additional Scottish material. To have also, or instead, included therein short accounts of comparable English cases would have been an unjustifiable duplication of material already easily accessible elsewhere, at the expense of an increase in the size and cost of this publication.

For the assistance of the many students who now come to the study of Scots law unequipped with a knowledge of Latin, a glossary of Latin words and phrases used in the book has been supplied in the Appendix.

A casebook is no substitute for the reading of law reports themselves, but, judiciously used, it can ease the pressures of library space and shortages and of students' limited studying time. To read selected extracts from judicial opinions is preferable to what may in practical terms be the only alternative — reading no opinions at all.

I record my thanks to Professor J. Milnes Holden and Julian S. Danskin, both of the University of Stirling, for comments which they made to me on the typescript version, and I am greatly indebted to the latter for more than ordinary assistance in the correction of proofs.

October, 1980. ENID A. MARSHALL

# TABLE OF CONTENTS

PAGE

*Preface* . . . . . . . . . . . . . . . . . . . . v
*Table of Cases* . . . . . . . . . . . . . . . . . vii

CHAPTER 1—INTRODUCTORY

Influence of English law . . . . . . . . . . . . . 1
Agency distinguished from mandate
*Copland* v. *Brogan* (1916) . . . . . . . . . . . . 2
Agency distinguished from sub-contract
*Smith* v. *Scott & Best* (1881) . . . . . . . . . . 3
Capacity
*Tinnevelly Sugar Refining Co. Ltd.* v. *Mirrlees, Watson & Yaryan Co. Ltd.* (1894) . . . . . . . . . . . . . . . . . . 8

CHAPTER 2—CONSTITUTION OF THE RELATIONSHIP

Express appointment may be proved by parole evidence
*Pickin* v. *Hawkes* (1878) . . . . . . . . . . . . 10
Implied appointment
*Barnetson* v. *Petersen Brothers* (1902) . . . . . . . . 10
Ratification must be timeous
*Goodall* v. *Bilsland* (1909) . . . . . . . . . . . 14

CHAPTER 3—CATEGORIES OF AGENT

Special agent distinguished from general agent
*Morrison* v. *Satter, &c.* (1885) . . . . . . . . . . 17
Factor who is a mercantile agent distinguished from factor who manages an estate
*Macrae* v. *Leith* (1913) . . . . . . . . . . . . 18
Stockbrokers
*Glendinning* v. *Hope & Co.* (1911) . . . . . . . . . 20
*Del credere* agents . . . . . . . . . . . . . . . 22

CHAPTER 4—AGENT'S IMPLIED AND OSTENSIBLE AUTHORITY

Ostensible authority not to be qualified by private arrangement between principal and agent
*Hayman* v. *American Cotton Oil Co.* (1907) . . . . . . . 25
Wife's *praepositura*: necessaries
*Buie* v. *Lady Gordon, &c.* (1827 and 1831) . . . . . . . 26
Wife's *praepositura*: reliance on husband's credit
*Arnot* v. *Stevenson* (1698) . . . . . . . . . . . 29
Family business: ostensible authority to receive payment and grant receipt
*Gemmell* v. *Annandale & Son Ltd.* (1899) . . . . . . . . 30
General agent has no implied authority to borrow money
*Sinclair, Moorhead, & Co.* v. *Wallace & Co.* (1880) . . . . . . 31
Commercial traveller's ostensible authority to receive payment
*International Sponge Importers Ltd.* v. *Watt & Sons* (1911) . . . 34
Salesman's implied authority to take orders
*Barry, Ostlere, & Shepherd Ltd.* v. *Edinburgh Cork Importing Co.* (1909) 36

Partner's statutory authority after dissolution of firm
*Dickson* v. *The National Bank of Scotland Ltd.* (1917) . . . . . . 38
Shipmaster has no implied authority to make unnecessary deviation
*Strickland and Others* v. *Neilson and MacIntosh* (1869) . . . . . 40
Architect's ostensible authority to employ surveyor
*Black* v. *Cornelius* (1879) . . . . . . . . . . . . 42
Implied authority of solicitor: appeal to higher court
*Stephen* v. *Skinner* (1863) . . . . . . . . . . . . 43
Implied authority of solicitor: repayment of loan
*Peden* v. *Graham* (1907) . . . . . . . . . . . . . 46
Agent's implied authority to employ solicitor depends on circumstances
*J. M. & J. H. Robertson* v. *Beatson, M'Leod, & Co. Ltd.* . . . . 48

CHAPTER 5—DUTIES OF AGENT TO PRINCIPAL

Express instructions: agent liable for value of lost goods
*Gilmour* v. *Clark* (1853) . . . . . . . . . . . . . 50
Express instructions: agent not entitled to commission after breach
*Graham & Co.* v. *The United Turkey Red Co. Ltd.* (1922) . . . . . 52
Skill and care: agent liable for damage caused by negligence
*Stiven* v. *Watson* (1874) . . . . . . . . . . . . . 53
Skill and care: solicitor
*Free Church of Scotland* v. *MacKnight's Trustees* (1916) . . . . . 56
Accounting: unexplained deficiency
*Tyler* v. *Logan* (1904) . . . . . . . . . . . . . . 59
Relief
*Milne* v. *Ritchie, &c.* (1882) . . . . . . . . . . . . 61
Fiduciary position: must not purchase principal's property for himself
*M'Pherson's Trustees* v. *Watt* (1877) . . . . . . . . . 62
Fiduciary position: agent not entitled to recover hypothetical loss on purchase of principal's stocks and shares for himself
*Cunningham* v. *Lee* (1874) . . . . . . . . . . . . 65
Fiduciary position: no secret profit allowed
*Ronaldson, &c.* v. *Drummond & Reid* (1881) . . . . . . . . 68
Fiduciary position: agent's interests in conflict with those of principal
*Lothian* v. *Jenolite Ltd.* (1969) . . . . . . . . . . . 69
Fiduciary position: confidentiality
*Liverpool Victoria Legal Friendly Society* v. *Houston* (1900) . . . 72

CHAPTER 6—RIGHTS OF AGENT AGAINST PRINCIPAL

Remuneration: *quantum meruit*
*Kennedy* v. *Glass* (1890) . . . . . . . . . . . . . 74
Remuneration: contract to pay commission not proved
*Moss* v. *Cunliffe & Dunlop* (1875) . . . . . . . . . . 76
Remuneration: payment excluded by proof of contrary custom
*Leo Dinesmann & Co.* v. *Mair & Co.* (1912) . . . . . . . . 80
Remuneration: whether agent has earned it: shipbroker
*Walker, Donald, & Co.* v. *Birrell, Stenhouse, & Co.* (1883) . . . . 81
Remuneration: whether agent has earned it: solicitor
*Menzies, Bruce-Low, & Thomson* v. *M'Lennan* (1895) . . . . . 84
Remuneration: whether agent has earned it: estate agent
*Walker, Fraser, & Steele* v. *Fraser's Trustees* (1910) . . . . . . 87

Reimbursement of outlays
*Knight & Co.* v. *Stott* (1892) . . . . . . . . . . . . . . . 91
Reimbursement of expenses properly incurred
*Drummond* v. *Cairns* (1852) . . . . . . . . . . . . . . . 92
Relief from liability incurred to third parties in proper execution of agency
*Stevenson* v. *Duncan* (1842) . . . . . . . . . . . . . . . 95
Retention and lien: factor
*Sibbald* v. *Gibson* (1852) . . . . . . . . . . . . . . . 98
Retention and lien: auctioneer
*Miller* v. *Hutcheson & Dixon* (1881) . . . . . . . . . . . 104
Retention and lien: stockbroker
*Glendinning* v. *Hope & Co.* (1911) . . . . . . . . . . . . 106
Retention and lien: solicitor
*Paul* v. *Meikle* (1868) . . . . . . . . . . . . . . . 106


## CHAPTER 7—THIRD PARTY'S RIGHTS AND LIABILITIES


Principal named: general rule: agent not liable to third party
*Stone & Rolfe Ltd.* v. *The Kimber Coal Co. Ltd.* (1926) . . . . 110
Principal ascertainable: general rule: agent not liable to third party
*Armour* v. *Duff & Co.* (1912) . . . . . . . . . . . . . . 112
Principal named: general rule: agent not liable to third party: foreign principal
*Millar* v. *Mitchell, &c.* (1860) . . . . . . . . . . . . . 113
Principal named: exception to general rule: agent voluntarily undertaking personal liability
*Stewart* v. *Shannessy* (1900) . . . . . . . . . . . . . . 120
Principal named: exception to general rule: custom: alleged custom not proved: agent not liable
*Livesey* v. *Purdom & Sons* (1894) . . . . . . . . . . . . 125
Principal named: exception to general rule: interest conferring on agent title to sue third party
*Mackenzie* v. *Cormack* (1950) . . . . . . . . . . . . . . 128
Principal undisclosed: agent known to be an agent: agent's failure to disclose principal: agent liable to third party
*Gibb* v. *Cunningham & Robertson* (1925) . . . . . . . . . . 134
Principal undisclosed: agent known to be an agent: principal suing third party: third party not entitled to plead compensation of debt due to him by agent
*Matthews* v. *Auld & Guild* (1873) . . . . . . . . . . . . 136
Principal undisclosed: agent contracting ostensibly as principal: principal, on disclosing himself, has a title to sue the third party
*Bennett* v. *Inveresk Paper Co.* (1891) . . . . . . . . . . 139
Principal undisclosed: third party's election to sue principal or agent: third party held to have elected to sue principal: agent not liable
*Ferrier* v. *Dods, &c.* (1865) . . . . . . . . . . . . . . 142
Principal undisclosed: third party electing to sue agent: agent entitled to counter-claim against third party
*A. F. Craig & Co. Ltd.* v. *Blackater* (1923) . . . . . . . . 147
Principal not a legal person: agent personally liable to third party
*M'Meekin* v. *Easton* (1889) . . . . . . . . . . . . . . . 153
Breach of warranty of authority: agent liable to third party
*Anderson* v. *Croall & Sons Ltd.* (1903) . . . . . . . . . . 157

CHAPTER 8—TERMINATION OF THE RELATIONSHIP

Expiry of the time for which constituted
*Brenan* v. *Campbell's Trustees* (1898) . . . . . . . . . . . 166
Death of principal
*Life Association of Scotland* v. *Douglas* (1886) . . . . . . . . 168
Insanity of principal
*Wink* v. *Mortimer* (1849) . . . . . . . . . . . . . . 170
Bankruptcy of principal
*M'Kenzie* v. *Campbell* (1894) . . . . . . . . . . . . 178
Revocation by principal
*Galbraith & Moorhead* v. *The Arethusa Ship Co. Ltd.* (1896) 182
Discontinuance of principal's business
*Patmore & Co.* v. *B. Cannon & Co. Ltd.* (1892) . . . . . . . 184
GLOSSARY OF LATIN WORDS AND PHRASES USED IN THIS BOOK . . . . 190

# TABLE OF CASES

(Page numbers in bold type indicate a main entry)


PAGE

ANDERSON *v.* Croall & Sons Ltd. (1903) .......... 1, **157**
Armour *v.* Duff & Co. (1912) .......... **112**
Arnot *v.* Stevenson (1698) .......... **29**
Auchie & Co. *v.* Burns (1822) .......... 92

BAIRD'S TRUSTEES *v.* Lord Advocate (1888) .......... 6
Bank of Scotland *v.* McNeill (1977) .......... 11
Barnetson v. Petersen Brothers (1902) .......... **10**, 168
Barry, Ostlere, & Shepherd Ltd. *v.* Edinburgh Cork Importing Co. (1909) .. **36**
Batchelor *v.* Pattison and Mackersy (1876) .......... 51
Bennett *v.* Inveresk Paper Co. (1891) .......... 118, **139**
Bickerton *v.* Burrell (1816) .......... 145
Black *v.* Cornelius (1879) .......... **42**, 51
——— *v.* Laidlaw (1844) .......... 46
Bowie's Trustees *v.* Watson (1913) .......... 46
Brebner *v.* Henderson (1925) .......... 123
Brenan *v.* Campbell's Trustees (1898) .......... **166**
Brett (A. R.) & Co. Ltd. *v.* Bow's Emporium Ltd. (1928) .......... 80, 89
Brown *v.* Inland Revenue (1964) .......... 60, 64
Brydon *v.* Muir (1869) .......... 23
Buie *v.* Lady Gordon, &c. (1827 and 1831) .......... **26**

CAMPBELL *v.* Anderson (1829) .......... 169
Christie *v.* Ruxton (1862) .......... 107
Collen *v.* Wright (1857) .......... 158, 162, 163, 164
Copland *v.* Brogan (1916) .......... 2, **2**, 55
Craig (A. F.) & Co. Ltd. *v.* Blackater (1923) .......... 110, **147**
Cunningham *v.* Lee (1874) .......... 22, **65**

DICKSON *v.* National (The) Bank of Scotland (1917) .......... **38**
——— *v.* Nicholson (1855) .......... 180
Dinesmann (Leo) & Co. *v.* Mair & Co. (1912) .......... **80**
Drummond *v.* Cairns (1852) .......... **92**
Dudley Brothers & Co. *v.* Barnet (1937) .......... 90, 91
Dunbarton County Council *v.* George W. Sellars and Sons Ltd. (1973) .... 7

FEARN *v.* Gordon & Craig (1893) .......... 50
Fenwick *v.* Macdonald, Fraser, & Co. Ltd. (1904) .......... 111
Ferguson and Lillie *v.* Stephen (1864) .......... 13, 168
Ferrier *v.* Dods, &c. (1865) .......... **142**
Findlay (Liquidator of the Scottish Workmen's Assurance Co. Ltd. *v.* Waddell (1910) .......... 109
Firbank's Executors *v.* Humphreys (1886) .......... 165
Frame *v.* Campbell (1836) .......... 57, 59
Free Church of Scotland *v.* MacKnight's Trustees (1916) .......... **56**

GAIRDNER *v.* Milne and Co. (1858) .......... 101
Galbraith & Moorhead *v.* The Arethusa Ship Co. Ltd. (1896) .......... **182**
Gemmell *v.* Annandale & Sons Ltd. (1899) .......... 24, **30**, 36
Gibb *v.* Bennett (1906) .......... 88
—— *v.* Cunningham & Robertson (1925) .......... **134**
Gilmour *v.* Clark (1853) .......... **50**
Girvin, Roper, & Co. *v.* Monteith (1895) .......... 117, 142
Glassford &c. *v.* Brown &c. (1830) .......... 96
Glendinning *v.* Hope & Co. (1911) .......... 19, 20, **20**, **106**
Goodall *v.* Bilsland (1909) .......... **14**, 45
Graham & Co. *v.* The United Turkey Red Co. Ltd. (1922) .......... **52**, 70, 71
Grand Empire Theatres Ltd. (Liquidator of) *v.* Snodgrass (1932) .......... 107

HAMILTON *v.* Forrester (1825) .......... 29
Hamilton (Ranking of) of Provenhall's Creditors (1781) .......... 19, 107
Hart *v.* Frame (1839) .......... 57
Hayman *v.* American Cotton Oil Co. (1907) .......... 24, **25**
Hill (The) Steam Shipping Co. Ltd. *v.* Hugo Stinnes Ltd. (1941) .......... 144

I.T.C. *v.* Pemsel (1891) .......... 56
International Sponge Importers Ltd. *v.* Watt & Sons (1911) .......... 24, **34**
Irving *v.* Burns (1915) .......... 164

JACOBS & CO. *v.* Archibald M'Millan & Son Ltd. (1894) .......... 84
Johnston *v.* Little (1960) .......... 132

KENNEDY *v.* Glass (1890) .......... **74**, 90
Knight & Co. *v.* Stott (1892) .......... **91**
Knox & Robb *v.* The Scottish Garden Suburb Co. Ltd. (1913) .......... 62, **51**

LAIDLAW (JAMES) AND SONS LTD. *v.* Griffin (1968) .......... 150
Laing *v.* Taylor (1978) .......... 132
Lavaggi *v.* Pirie & Sons (1872) .......... 137
Life Association of Scotland *v.* Douglas (1886) .......... **168**
Lindsay *v.* Craig (1919) .......... 121
Liverpool Victoria Legal Friendly Society *v.* Houston (1900) .......... **72**
Livesey *v.* Purdom & Sons (1894) .......... **125**
London, Leith, Edinburgh, and Glasgow Shipping Co. *v.* Ferguson (1850) .......... 186
Lothian *v.* Jenolite Ltd. (1969) .......... 53, **69**
Luxor (Eastbourne) Ltd. *v.* Cooper (1941) .......... 91

MCIVOR *v.* Roy (1970) .......... 132
Mackenzie *v.* Blakeney (1879) .......... 96
M'Kenzie *v.* Campbell (1894) .......... **178**
Mackenzie *v.* Cormack (1950) .......... 1, 105, **128**
M'Meekin *v.* Easton (1889) .......... **153**
M'Pherson's Trustees *v.* Watt (1877) .......... **62**
Macrae *v.* Leith (1913) .......... **18**, 22, 107
Manson *v.* Baillie (1855) .......... 76
Matthews *v.* Auld & Guild (1873) .......... **136**
Meikle & Wilson *v.* Pollard (1880) .......... 108, 109
Meier & Co. *v.* Kuchenmeister (1881) .......... 143

Menzies, Bruce-Low, & Thomson *v.* M'Lennan (1895) .................. **84**
Millar *v.* Mitchell, &c. (1860) .................. 2, 23, **113**, 142
Miller *v.* Hutcheson & Dixon (1881) .................. **104**
Milne *v.* Harris, James, & Company (1803) .................. 37
——— *v.* Ritchie, &c. (1882) .................. **61**
Morrison *v.* Statter, &c. (1885) .................. **17**
Moss *v.* Cunliffe & Dunlop (1875) .................. **76**, 84, 90

North (The) of Scotland Banking Company *v.* Behn, Moller, & Company (1881) .................. 37

Patmore & Co. *v.* B. Cannon & Co. Ltd. (1892) .................. **184**
Paul *v.* Meikle (1868) .................. **106**
Peden *v.* Graham (1907) .................. **46**
Pickin *v.* Hawkes (1878) .................. **10**
Pollitt (1893) .................. 179
Pollok *v.* Paterson (1811) .................. 171

Rederi Aktiebolaget Nordstjernan *v.* Salvesen & Co. (1903) 1, 158, 159, 160
Rhodes *v.* Forwood (1876) .................. 185, 186, 187
Robertson (J. M. & J. H.) *v.* Beatson, M'Leod, & Co. Ltd. (1908) ...... **48**, 51
Robertson *v.* Ross (1887) .................. 109
——— *v.* Foulds (1860) .................. 45
Robinson, &c. *v.* Middleton (1859) .................. 97
Ronaldson, &c. *v.* Drummond & Reid (1881) .................. **68**
Royal Bank of Scotland *v.* Skinner (1931) .................. 33, 165

Salvesen & Co. *v.* Rederi Aktiebolaget Nordstjernan (1905) ...... 159, 160, 164
Shepherd *v.* Campbells, Frazer, and Co. (1823) .................. 169
Sibbald *v.* Gibson (1852) .................. **98**
Simons *v.* Patchet (1857) .................. 162
Simpson *v.* Kidstons, Watson, Turnbull & Co. (1913) .................. 57, 58
Sinclair, Moorhead, & Co. *v.* Wallace & Co. (1880) .................. **31**, 165
Smith *v.* Scott & Best (1881) .................. **3**
S.S. "State of California" Co. Ltd. *v.* Moore (1895) .................. 187
Stephen *v.* Skinner (1863) .................. **43**
Stevenson *v.* Duncan (1842) .................. **95**
Stewart *v.* Shannessy (1900) .................. **120**, 135
Stiven *v.* Watson (1874) .................. **53**
Stone & Rolfe Ltd. *v.* The Kimber Coal Co. Ltd. (1926) .................. **110**
Strickland and Others *v.* Neilson and MacIntosh (1869) .................. **40**

Teheran-Europe Co. Ltd. *v.* S. T. Belton (Tractors) Ltd. (1968) .................. 119
Thoms *v.* Bain (1888) .................. 45
Thomson & Gillespie *v.* The Victoria Eighty Club (1905) .................. 154
Tinnevelly Sugar Refining Co. Ltd. *v.* Mirrlees, Watson, & Yaryan Co. Ltd. (1894) .................. **8**, 154
Tomlinson *v.* Liquidators of Scottish Amalgamated Silks Ltd. (1935) ...... 93
Trojan Plant Hire Co. Ltd. *v.* Durafencing (Northern) Ltd. (1974) ........ 5, 24
Trollope & Sons *v.* Martyn Brothers (1934) .................. 91
Turnbull (Alexander) & Co. Ltd. *v.* Cruickshank & Fairweather (1905) .... 55
Tyler *v.* Logan (1904) .................. **59**

URQUHART *v.* Grigor (1857) .................................................. 45

WALKER *v:* Somerville (1837) .................................................. 183
Walker, Donald, & Co. *v.* Birrell, Stenhouse, & Co. (1883) .................. **81**, 90
Walker, Fraser, & Steele *v.* Fraser's Trustees (1910) .................... **87**, 90
Watt *v.* M'Pherson's Trustees *et e contra* (1877) .............................. 64
White *v.* Munro, &c. (1876) .................................................. 83
Wink *v.* Mortimer (1849) .................................................. **170**
Withington *v.* Tate (1869) .................................................. 46

## CHAPTER 1

# INTRODUCTORY

### *Influence of English law*

NOTES

1. Both in Scotland and in England the law of agency is for the most part common law, and English cases are frequently relied on where no Scottish decisions are available.

A typical instance of this approach occurs in the opinion of Lord Moncreiff in *Rederi Aktiebolaget Nordstjernan* v. *Salvesen & Co.* (1903) 6 F. 64, at p. 76:

"In the absence of Scottish decisions the pursuers rely upon . . . cases in English law. . . .

"Those decisions no doubt are not binding upon us, but on a mercantile question like the present it is desirable that as far as possible the same rule should be applied in both countries."

2. The English influence is particularly strong where there is a series of English cases:

"I cannot resist the authority of a whole series of English cases on a branch of commercial law in which there is no difference between the law of England and the law of Scotland" (*per* Lord Stormonth-Darling (Ordinary) in *Anderson* v. *Croall & Sons Ltd.* (1903) 6 F. 153, at p. 156), and where the relationship of the parties concerned is seen as being the same in the two countries, *e.g.*:

"It was argued to us that the English cases were an unsafe guide. . . . But there can be little doubt than an auctioneer's functions and duties are substantially the same in Scotland and in England and that in each country the same relationship exists among the seller, the buyer and the auctioneer. Accordingly, although the English definitions of the interest which confers a title to sue are couched in somewhat unfamiliar terms, I can see no reason for thinking that that interest is any different in the two countries" (*per* Lord Justice-Clerk Thomson in *Mackenzie* v. *Cormack*, 1950 S.C. 183, at p. 188), and in the same case Lord Mackay (at p. 191) referred to the English law of public auctions as "completely settled" and advocated that the law ought to be the same in Scotland.

"The English law of public auctions and the specific question of the position of an auctioneer towards the bidders having now been completely settled, is there any ground whatsoever, or any suggestion of any principle, or any authority within Scottish *dicta*, for endeavouring at this stage and at this time of day to set up the Scottish law in opposition to the earlier settled and unshaken English law?"

3. Occasionally the Scottish courts have declined to follow English decisions, *e.g.*:

In *Copland* v. *Brogan*, 1916 S.C. 277, where an argument had been used that the defender was a gratuitous mandatary and that both English and Scots law (differing from the civil law) recognised a distinction between the responsibility of such persons and that of agents receiving remuneration in respect that gratuitous mandataries could be made liable only for gross negligence, Lord Justice-Clerk Scott Dickson said (at p. 282):

"With regard to the English authorities which have been quoted, I have difficulty in accepting them as being in conformity with the law of Scotland, and I do not agree that the same rule of law as applies to gratuitous obligations under English law can be held as applying in this case. According to Bell's Principles, there is an obligation on the depositary to 'keep the thing with reasonable care,' and the editor of the last edition of that work states that reasonable care in the case of a gratuitous depositary means 'such care as a man of common prudence generally exercises about his own property of like description.' "

4. See also Note to *Millar* v. *Mitchell, &c.* (1860) 22 D, 833 (p. 117, below).

*Agency distinguished from mandate*

**Copland v. Brogan**
1916 S.C. 277

B., a carriage-hirer, had been in the habit of acting gratuitously as a messenger for C., a schoolmaster.

On one occasion C. asked B. to cash three cheques for him at a bank in a neighbouring town and bring back the cash to him. B. received the cash at the bank, but failed to pay it over to C. There was no evidence of how the loss had occurred.

*Held* that B. was liable to pay C., since in executing the mandate B. had failed to execise reasonable care.

SHERIFF ANDERSON (at p. 279): "There is not a very large body of authority in Scots law on the subject of gratuitous mandate, which is the legal category in which this case must be placed. The Roman law imposed upon a gratuitous mandatary *summa diligentia*, the highest form of diligence. But it is doubtful if Scots law has followed this rule. Erskine lays it down that a gratuitous mandatary is only liable for such diligence as he employs in his own affairs — Ersk. III. iii. 36. But I think the law is more accurately expressed by Bell, when he states the standard to be that the mandatary is bound to show reasonable care such as a man of common prudence generally exercises about his own property of the like description — Bell's Prin. sec. 218."

LORD JUSTICE-CLERK (SCOTT DICKSON) (at p. 282): "According to Bell's Principles, there is an obligation on the depositary to 'keep the thing with reasonable care,' and the editor of the last edition of that work states that reasonable care in the case of a gratuitous depositary means 'such care as a man of common prudence generally exercises about his own property of like description.' Now, the packet having gone astray while it was in the defender's custody, the *onus*, in my opinion, rests on him to explain how this happened or at least to show that he exercised the necessary reasonable care. Here the explanation given did not, in my opinion, sufficiently discharge the defender of responsibility for the loss of the packet. . . . On the defender's own statements, and on the other evidence in the case, there is enough to shew that the defender, in executing his commission, did not exercise the care which a prudent man would have taken with regard to a valuable packet of this kind. . . . It is right that I should add that there is nothing to warrant any imputation of dishonesty on the part of the defender."

NOTES

1. The Second Division recalled the interlocutor of the sheriff.

2. "Mandate" may be defined as "a bilateral gratuitous consensual contract by which one empowers another to act in some respect on his behalf," and "agency" may be defined as "a bilateral onerous consensual contract whereby one party, the principal, authorizes another, the agent, to execute business on his behalf for reward" (David M. Walker, *Principles of Scottish Private Law* (2nd ed.), pp. 701 and 703).

### *Agency distinguished from sub-contract*

**Smith v. Scott & Best**
(1881) 18 S.L.R. 355

S. & B., contractors for certain waterworks including the construction of a bridge over the Esk, were approached by Cameron who agreed to do that part of the work for £40 less than the schedule price.

Cameron obtained stones from Smith, the tenant of a stone-quarry, telling Smith that he was the foreman of S. & B.

Cameron deserted the work and disappeared, leaving Smith unpaid. S. & B. declined to pay Smith, on the ground that they had already paid Cameron for all the work done and material supplied by him.

*Held* that, as S. & B. had taken no steps to prevent Cameron from being considered their foreman and as a belief to that effect had become current in the district, there was no sub-contract and S. & B. were liable for Smith's account.

LORD JUSTICE-CLERK MONCREIFF (at p. 357): "It appears that the alleged sub-contractor . . . was at the date of the alleged contract in circumstances utterly bankrupt, to the knowledge of Scott & Best, who were the principal contractors for the construction of the waterworks at Forfar. It also appears that he came to ask Mr Best for a job — whether he could give him a job to keep him off the streets. . . .

". . . They went over the estimate for the work connected with the bridge at Justinhaugh; and this bankrupt says to Mr Best — 'I will do that work £40 cheaper than you contracted to do it for.' . . .

"Now, the question, in the first place, is, Is that a sub-contract?... According to the statement we have of the verbal agreement, payment was not to be given until the end of the work. We know that certain payments were made in the course of the work, but on what footing those payments were made has not been cleared up in the least degree. . . . But whether the parties intended a sub-contract or not, of this I am quite clear, that these contractors (Scott & Best), as honest men, knowing the circumstances of this man to whom they paid their money — knowing that he had no means of meeting any demand except the money they entrusted to him if they chose to pay him before the end of the contract — were in duty bound to see that their instalments were properly applied, and I cannot, from anything I find in the case, come to the conclusion that they must be relieved of the liability they incurred.

"Now, that is the general view I take of the matter, and it appears to me that it is greatly corroborated, first, by the correspondence that took place in regard to this affair, and secondly, by the admitted and uncontradicted actings of Cameron himself.

"In the first place, it was not a pure sub-contract. That is quite clear, because material was to be furnished to Cameron by the defenders themselves. The contractors were to furnish the cement, and I rather take it from the look of the accounts that that was a very material item in the furnishings that were to be made. . . . We find Mr Best writing to Mr Main on the 12th September 1879 — 'Say to Cameron the bridge is to be built in lime, which I will order.' So that not only were they to furnish cement, and make a certain allowance for it, according to their own statement, but they considered they had the power, after the completion of the contract, to alter the material to be used and to furnish it themselves.

"In the next place, it is clear that Cameron represented, not only to the pursuer, but to all and sundry, that he was only the foreman or a foreman of the defenders, and that it was on the footing that he was such that the goods were to be furnished.

"So standing the case, I think . . . that the credit of the defenders was interposed to those actings of Cameron, and that they did not take the necessary steps, knowing the circumstances in which he stood, to see that the money they paid him was honestly applied. I do not think that the sub-contract in point of fact, in its proper sense, is proved. . . . I am satisfied, also, that the defenders were not entitled to allow Cameron to go and order goods, and take no precautions for the application of the instalments paid to him, because they must have known that if any one of the parties dealt with had known that it was a sub-contract he was acting upon they never would have trusted Cameron and supplied him with the stones.

"Those are the grounds on which my opinion rests. It would be a matter of law that if this was a complete sub-contract the sub-contractor would be liable to those from whom he got supplies, and the principal contractors would not be liable. That would be conceded at once. But I think, as I have explained, that the proof is insufficient to warrant any such conclusion. I am of the opinion that in the circumstances the sub-contract could not have been completed, or, at all events, was not completed with this man; and that it was not fair dealing, as regards those he came in contact with, to give them the means of forming the opinion that it was not on his credit but on the credit of his employers that they were to rely."

NOTES

1. Contrast *Trojan Plant Hire Co. Ltd.* v. *Durafencing (Northern) Ltd.*, 1974 S.L.T. (Sh. Ct.) 3.

McAlpine Ltd., the principal building contractor on a site at Balduvie Toll, Dundee, gave the job of erecting certain fencing to D. Ltd. as sub-contractor. D. Ltd. instructed Arkle, an independent contractor who had a work force at his disposal, to carry out the fencing work. D. Ltd. gave Arkle the necessary fencing materials and lent him one of its vans which had D. Ltd.'s name painted on its sides.

Arkle went in this van to T. Ltd., a plant hirer, and after introducing himself by presenting D. Ltd.'s business card, hired a dumper and an excavator from T. Ltd. The manager of T. Ltd., by telephone, obtained confirmation from McAlpine Ltd. that D. Ltd. was in fact sub-contractor for the fencing on the site and that Arkle was in charge of the fencing work being done by D. Ltd. there. The manager also telephoned to the sheriff officer for Dundee who confirmed that D. Ltd. was credit-worthy.

D. Ltd. later ratified the hire contract for the dumper and paid the hire charges for it, but repudiated liability for the charges for the excavator on the ground that it was unnecessary for the job and had been hired without authority.

T. Ltd. raised an action for payment against D. Ltd. claiming that by giving Arkle one of its vans and by allowing him (even inadvertently) to have one of its business cards D. Ltd. had so acted as to bring him within its ostensible authority to hire plant.

*Held* that Arkle had not acted within either the actual or the ostensible authority of D. Ltd., that his actions had not been ratified and that accordingly D. Ltd. was not liable.

Sheriff W. G. Stevenson (at p. 5): "On the evidence the pursuers failed to prove that Mr Arkle was either a servant or an agent of the defenders. Equally there was no corroboration of the defenders' evidence that Mr Arkle was an independent contractor of labour engaged by them. Accordingly, I am unable to say on the evidence exactly what the position of Mr Arkle relative to the defenders was.

"In this position at the hearing on the evidence the solicitor for the pursuers submitted that the only question for decision was whether the alleged hire on behalf of the defenders of the said excavator by Mr Arkle was within his ostensible authority. In support of this submission he contended that the defenders, by allowing Mr Arkle the use of one of their vans with their name on it and possession of one of their business cards, even if unknown to them, had so acted as to bring Mr Arkle within the ostensible authority of the defenders. In furtherance of this submission he referred to the letter . . . from Mr Fare on behalf of the defenders in which he stated *inter alia*: 'We . . . confirm that site instructions were given to our men to use this plant.' The solicitor for the pursuers submitted that the terms of this letter although it referred only to . . . the hire of the first dumper must along with the other evidence prove that since Mr Arkle had hired the first dumper and the excavator at the same time either the area manager or the district supervisor had given site instructions for the hire not only of the first dumper but also of the excavator. . . . I am unable . . . to hold it proved that Mr Arkle was also given site instructions to hire the excavator by any person with authority or ostensible authority to act on behalf of the defenders. Accordingly the only question I have to decide is whether the possession of the defenders' van by Mr Arkle and also their business card conferred ostensible authority on Mr Arkle to contract for the hire of the excavator from the pursuers on behalf of the defenders. So far as relates to the possession of the business card, in the absence of evidence by the pursuers as to the defenders' knowledge thereof or as to why they ought to have known Mr Arkle possessed it, I consider that it can be disregarded. The only question that remains is the effect of the defenders allowing Mr Arkle to have possession of one of their vans when they knew that an innocent third party such as the pursuers would be aware that the defenders were sub-contractors to McAlpine for fencing on the site in Dundee and that Mr Arkle, in possession of one of their vans, was in charge of the only labour force erecting fencing on the said site for the defenders. I do not consider that such knowledge by the pursuers was sufficient to bring Mr Arkle within the ostensible authority of the defenders to hire plant on behalf of the defenders.

. . . The defenders ratified the unauthorised hire of the dumpers but did not ratify the unauthorised hire of the said excavator."

2. In *Dunbarton County Council* v. *George W. Sellars and Sons Ltd.*, 1973 S.L.T. (Sh. Ct.) 67, the question arose as to whether main contractors had acted as agents for the employer when engaging a sub-contractor.

S. Ltd. carried out painter work at Hartfield Secondary School, Dumbarton. The employer was Dunbarton County Council, and the principal contractor was Dougall and Co. Ltd., which went into liquidation. S. Ltd. contended that payment for the painter work should be direct to it, not to the liquidator of the principal contractor. One of the grounds for this contention was that in the making of the sub-contract the principal contractor had acted merely as an agent for a disclosed principal, namely the employer.

*Held* that agency could not be inferred from the terms of the contractual documents.

Sheriff M. Stone quoted from Hudson's *Building and Engineering Contracts* (10th ed.), p. 742: "Attempts have been made from time to time to argue that the main contractor or architect on the facts contracted as agent for the employer, and at one time this view appears to have prevailed in the courts, at least in relation to nominated or selected sub-contractors, but it is clear that only the most special and unusual facts, showing that the employer expressly or by his conduct authorised the main contractor or the architects so to contract, could justify such a finding, which is contrary to the sense of the usual main contract and the almost universal practice in the building industry."

Of the situation in the case before him the sheriff said (at p. 70): "The second proposition is that Sellars entered indirectly into the contract with the County, by concluding their agreement with Dougall who acted as agents for the County. . . . The second proposition, namely that Dougall acted merely as agents for the County is also untenable in my opinion. According to the whole tenor of the documents of contract, the County's role was that of employer with the right to nominate and approve the sub-contractor appointed by their principal contractor. . . . I have considered the terms of . . . the letter from the architects to Dougall . . . and Dougall's letter . . . to Sellars. Neither states that Dougall would act as agents of the County in accepting Sellars' tender. The terms of these letters, in my opinion, are clearly to be understood as referring to the County's right to approve and nominate the sub-contractor, and the architect's function in advising the County on the acceptance of tenders so that they could be officially so approved. I consider the suggestion that these letters mean that Dougall were merely agents of the County in the contract as an attempt to construe them in an artificial, strained and unreasonable way, when the true meaning is perfectly obvious. . . . In view of the clear and specific terms of the documents to the effect that Sellars were sub-contractors of Dougall, nominated and approved by the County, but having no contractual relationship with the County, this attempt to infer the contrary from scattered and minor provisions of these documents reduces the contract itself to meaninglessness and deprives it of operative effect. On the principle *ut res magis valeat* the construction which will make the contract valid is generally to be preferred, namely that it means what it says. Gloag on *Contract* — 2nd edition 1929 p. 402. In the argument as presented at the debate for Sellars, the submission was that Dougall were either 'mere agents,' as stated in their plea-in-law No. 2, with no responsibility for or interest in the painter work contract, or that they were, as the liquidator maintains, the principal contractors. . . . I find it surprising that in the construction of a long, complex, elaborate and detailed contract, involving a substantial sum of money, the first claimants suggest that the most vital questions of the relationship of the parties concerned to each other, be interpreted in a sense diametrically opposed to specific terms of the contract. If agency had been intended, surely it would have been written into the contract. Since this has not been done, I see no ground for reading it into the contract by implication, to the point of making it meaningless."

*Capacity*

**Tinnevelly Sugar Refining Co. Ltd.** v.
**Mirrlees, Watson, & Yaryan Co. Ltd.**
(1894) 21 R. 1009

On 11th July 1890, Darley & Butler, purporting to act on behalf of T. Ltd., which was registered on 29th July following, entered into a contract with M. Ltd. for the supply by M. Ltd. of certain machinery.

T. Ltd. raised an action of damages against M. Ltd. on the ground that the machinery supplied was defective and had caused great loss to T. Ltd.

*Held* that T. Ltd. had no title to sue M. Ltd., since Darley & Butler could not have acted as agents for T. Ltd. before it was in existence.

LORD PRESIDENT (J. P. B. ROBERTSON) (at p. 1013): "The contract, for breach of which this action was brought, was constituted by a tender and relative acceptance, dated respectively 26th Novmeber 1889 and 11th July 1890. The contract was for the supply of certain machinery and iron-work for a refinery. On the face of the documents the parties to the contract were the defenders on the one hand, and Messrs Darley & Butler . . . on the other hand.

"The pursuers of this action are the Tinnevelly Sugar Refining Company, Limited, with consent and concurrence of Messrs Darley & Butler for all right and interest they may have in the premises. The fact that Messrs Darley & Butler thus appear, not merely as consenting to the instance of the company, but as themselves pursuers, has no practical importance; for in this action of damages no averment is made that that firm has suffered damage. The action is therefore the action of the Tinnevelly Company Limited.

"Now, against this action the defenders' first plea is, 'No title to sue.' . . .

"The company was registered on 29th July 1890, and accordingly was not in existence at the date of the contract. It is therefore legally impossible that the contract can bind the company, unless the company since its registration, has in some way acquired the rights and submitted itself to the obligations of the contract. Accordingly, the defenders are in the right when they say that the question is, Do the pursuers set forth, on this record, anything done by the company itself which has this result? I have carefully examined the condescendence, and must answer this question in the negative. . . .

"They begin by saying that when Darley & Butler contracted with the defenders they were acting, and were known by the defenders to be acting, as agents for the Tinnevelly Company. This is the basis of the pursuers' case. It is in law an untenable position, for Darley & Butler could not be the agents of a non-existent company. I should infer from the record that the persons acting for the company had not realised this. Accordingly, it is quite consistent with the record to suppose that the persons acting for the company were unaware that if the company was to take the place of Darley & Butler it required, — that is to say, the shareholders or their executive required, — consciously to do so. In place of any such overt action on the part of the company things were allowed to rest on the original contract between Darley & Butler and the defenders, which was erroneously believed to bind the company. . . .

"Well, now, the law applicable to such a case seems to be tolerably clear. First of all, where there is no principal there can be no agent; there having been no Tinnevelly Company at the date of this contract, Darley & Butler were not agents of that company in entering into the contract. The next point is that, in order to bind the company to a contract not incumbent on it, it is necessary that the company should voluntarily so contract; and it is not equivalent to this if the company merely acts as if, contrary to the fact, the contract had from the beginning been obligatory on it. . . .

"I am for finding that the pursuers have not set forth on record any title in the Tinnevelly Sugar Refining Company, Limited, to sue."

## CHAPTER 2

# CONSTITUTION OF THE RELATIONSHIP

*Express appointment may be proved by parole evidence*

**Pickin v. Hawkes**
(1878) 5 R. 676

P. averred that in November 1876 he entered into an oral contract with H., whereby he was to act as sole agent for H. in Scotland from 1st January 1877 for three years, his remuneration to be £50 per annum and a commission of five per cent upon all sales of H.'s goods in Scotland.

In June 1877 H. intimated that P. was no longer in H.'s employment, and P. brought an action of damages for breach of contract.

H. argued that the contract, being a contract of service for a period of more than a year, could not be proved by parole.

Proof at large before answer was allowed.

LORD ORDINARY (CRAIGHILL) (at p. 677): "Service, undoubtedly, in a certain sense is involved, but agency is the fundamental characteristic. . . . To such a contract the rule which is observed in cases of master and servant has never hitherto been, and the Lord Ordinary thinks ought not now to be, applied. Limitations as to proof which have been fixed clearly and unambiguously must be observed, but new cases certainly are not to be brought within their operation."

NOTE

The Second Division recalled the Lord Ordinary's interlocutor, without delivering any opinions. The purpose of the recall was to allow a proof of the facts before the questions of law would be answered.

*Implied appointment*

**Barnetson v. Petersen Brothers**
(1902) 5 F. 86

The steamship "Rocklands" belonging to P. Brothers was chartered by them to Gans & Sell, who instructed B., a shipbroker in Methil, to do what brokerage was required on the vessel while in that port.

B., having made disbursements and rendered services accordingly, brought an action against P. Brothers for outlays and commission.

P. Brothers pleaded that they were not liable because B. had been employed by the charterers Gans & Sell.

*Held* that, as the master of the "Rocklands" had accepted B.'s services as shipbroker and as P. Brothers had got the benefit of these services, P. Brothers were directly liable to B. for his disbursements and services.

LORD TRAYNER (at p. 89): "I think this a very clear and simple case. The defenders' vessel, the 'Rocklands,' arrived at Methil in January 1900, there to load a cargo of coal. The services of a shipbroker were necessary, and these services were rendered by the pursuer. He did the ship's business at the Custom-House and elsewhere, and made all the necessary disbursements. He advanced money to the captain, paid the pilotage, towage, and dock dues, and the other sums enumerated in his account. That account amounts to £53, 3s. 6d., and is composed of payments made on account of the ship, and therefore on account of the defenders, to the extent of £44, 0s. 6d., the pursuer's fees and commission only amounting to the sum of £9, 3s. *Prima facie* the defenders are liable for the pursuer's account, as they took the benefit of the pursuer's services and are *lucrati* to the extent to which he made advances on ship's account. . . .

"The Sheriff-substitute proceeds upon the ground that there was no contract between the parties. But if the captain of the vessel put himself in the hands of the pursuer, and the defenders take the benefit of his doing so, there is contract enough to make them liable. They suffer no detriment thereby, because whatever broker had been so employed their liability would, as regards amount, have been exactly the same."

NOTES

1. The Second Division recalled the sheriff-substitute's interlocutor, against which B. was appealing.

2. The case gives an indication of the duties of a shipbroker.

3. Agency may also be implied by law, as well as from actings, *e.g.*, a partner is impliedly an agent for his firm (Partnership Act 1890, s. 5), and a director for his company.

4. In *Bank of Scotland* v. *McNeill*, 1977 S.L.T. (Sh. Ct.) 2, there were circumstances from which Sheriff Principal R. Reid held that agency could not be inferred.

Jean McNeill opened a current account with a bank. She did not tell the bank at the time that the account was to be operated "in conjunction with" her employer's account. Her salary was paid into the account. Substantial withdrawals were made from the account for obligations incurred on behalf of the employer. There was no evidence that the employer ever indicated to the bank an intention to be bound in liability for the account.

It was argued that the customer contracted with the bank to open and operate a current account as agent for her employer.

*Held* that (1) knowledge of the banker of the existence of an agency relationship and of the use of an account for agency purposes could not of itself change the *persona* of the customer and entitle the banker to look to the agent's principal for repayment of balances — the principal would require to have indicated an intention to be bound before he would incur that liability, and (2) an intention to be bound could not be inferred from the fact that the principal arranged for the account to be opened, or that he paid money into the account for agency purposes.

The Sheriff Principal (at p. 2): "It may happen that an agent uses a personal account for lodging money and making payments in transactions connected with his agency. Knowledge by the banker of the existence of the agency relationship and of the use of the account for agency purposes cannot of itself change the *persona* of the customer so as to entitle the banker to refuse to obey the agent's instructions as to the management of the account. Still less would such knowledge entitle him to look to the agent's principal for the repayment of debtor balances. The principal would require to have indicated an intention to be bound before he would incur that liability in the same way as an agent requires to indicate an intention to be bound along with a disclosed principal before the agent can incur liability on an account in his name on behalf of the principal (*cf.* Gloag on *Contract* (2nd ed.) 136)....

"In the present case, the current account was opened in the name of the defender. . . . She did not tell the bankers at the time the account was to be opened that it was to be operated 'in conjunction with' Daniels' account. . . . Her salary was paid into the account. It is true that certain other payments into the account were made by her employer and it is true that very substantial withdrawals were made from it for obligations incurred on behalf of her employer but these transactions could not make the account her employer's account in the sense that money in it — including her salary — belonged to her employer or, as she now contends, in the sense that her employer was liable to the bank for the debtor balance on it. . . .

"There is no evidence that Daniels ever indicated to the pursuers an intention to be bound. I do consider — as was argued — that such an intention can be inferred from the fact that he arranged for the account to be opened or that he paid money into the account to meet purchases the defender had made or that he gave the defender a valueless cheque made out simply to the 'Bank of Scotland' when she pressed him to pay an account she had paid for goods supplied to the house. These facts tend to show that the defender acted as agent for her employer in certain transactions but provide no ground for an inference that the account was opened and operated as an agency account."

5. There is an instance of an implied agency terminated by lapse of time and change of circumstances in *Ferguson and Lillie* v. *Stephen* (1864) 2 M. 804.

F. & L., tailors in Glasgow, supplied clothes to S. for himself and his two sons, Andrew and Samuel, from 1853 to 1857 when the family lived in Glasgow. Accounts were rendered to and paid by S.

In 1861, when S. had been residing for some years in Dundee and Andrew and Samuel (then 27 and 17 years of age respectively) were resident in Edinburgh, Andrew ordered from F. & L. a large quantity of goods, including 19 pairs of kid gloves, two frock coats, about three dozen shirts, four dozen pocket handkerchiefs and three and a half dozen stockings, at a total price of £53.3.9d., and Samuel placed a similar order amounting to £36.17/-. F. & L. sent the goods to Andrew and Samuel in Edinburgh.

*Held* that S. was not liable to pay for the goods.

Lord Justice-Clerk (Inglis) (at p. 807): "There is no reason to assume the same authority to supply the defender's sons with goods as when the father lived in Glasgow, and his sons lived in family with him. There was a material change. . . . Now what was it which took place in 1861? These two young gentlemen go to the pursuers, and each of them runs up a bill very unlike the previous ones which had been sent to and paid by their father. This one was extravagant and absurd in the highest degree. Mr Lillie is obliged to admit that the account is unlike previous ones. . . .

"What was the obvious course for a prudent man in the circumstances to take, where the goods were not ordinary furnishings? If he was not going to trust the young man himself, he should have made inquiry of the father; but he does nothing of the kind. . . .

"This was a new account, and a ridiculous one. Mr Lillie cannot say that it is a continuance of previous accounts. It has no resemblance. It is not a continuation of the others, even if there had been no interruption in point of time; but the interruption in point of time is all material, if you consider that the previous accounts were for necessaries which were sent home to their father's house, and that these accounts ceased when their father's house was no longer in Glasgow. When the account was renewed, the things were no longer sent to their father's house, but to Edinburgh, at a distance from their father's house.

"It is not possible to give effect to the plea of implied agency or mandate, or to say that the supplying of these things was authorised by the father; the dealings which he had authorised had been long before, were different in kind, and the goods were sent to his own house, not to a different place."

Lord Benholme (at p. 808): "The plea of implied mandate is based on the defender's previous practice. . . . But to sustain such a plea, it is essential that the circumstances should be the same or similar; for, if matters are altered as to the situation of the parties, the continuation of the previous implied mandate is necessarily excluded. In some circumstances notice may be necessary, in order that parties may not be deceived by a latent change of relations. . . . When a father has been in the habit of paying accounts sent in to him incurred by a son living in his house, so long as that state of circumstances continues, the tradesman may be entitled to rely on the father's credit; but when circumstances are entirely changed, and when, after an interval of years, the tradesman deals with that son as an independent party, and sends the goods ordered, not to the father's house, but to the son's separate residence, I think the tradesman is not entitled to rely on the father's responsibility and credit. In this case the extravagant character of the goods furnished ought, of itself, to have suggested doubts."

Lord Neaves (at p. 808): "Great stress was laid on the fact that the father had once paid his sons' accounts at this shop, and that no change was intimated. It may sometimes be necessary for a father or master to intimate that he will no longer pay accounts incurred by members of his family. But when there has been an overt change of circumstances no notice is necessary."

### *Ratification must be timeous*

**Goodall** v. **Bilsland**
1909 S.C. 1152

G., a wine and spirit merchant in Glasgow, applied to the licensing court for renewal of his public-house certificate.

Green and others authorised Kyle, a Glasgow solicitor, to lodge objections to the granting of that renewal at the licensing court.

The renewal was granted, and Kyle, without consulting his principals, lodged an appeal to the licensing appeal court. This court, consisting of Bilsland, Lord Provost of Glasgow, and others, sustained the appeal.

G. sought to reduce the deliverance of the licensing appeal court.

*Held* that (1) Kyle had had no authority to appeal to the licensing appeal court, (2) his actings could not be validated by homologation after the lapse of the period allowed for appeal and (3) the proceedings in the licensing appeal court were null and void.

LORD PRESIDENT (DUNEDIN) (at p. 1167): "The mandate . . . was in this form:—'To Robert Kyle, Esq., writer' . . . 'We hereby authorise you to sign and lodge on our behalf Objections to the granting of the Certificate for licence for a public-house applied for by Alexander Goodall for premises at 68 M'Alpine Street at the forthcoming Licensing Court of the City and Royal Burgh of Glasgow, and to appear on our behalf in support of said objections.'

"Accordingly, Mr Kyle did appear. . . . In all that, I think, he was entirely authorised by the terms of the mandate which I have just read. But the Licensing Court sat, and it granted the licence.

Whereupon, acting upon the idea (which I do not doubt was in good faith too) that this mandate which I have just read covered not only proceedings at the Licensing Court but also proceedings at the Appeal Court, Mr Kyle, at his own hand, put in, in name of one or more of these objectors, a note of appeal to the Appeal Court. . . . The Appeal Court reversed the determination of the Licensing Court and refused the licence, and it is for reduction of that proceeding that this action is brought.

"Now, the first question therefore that arises is — What is the true contruction of this mandate? I cannot say that I have had any difficulty in coming to the conclusion that the mandate must be construed according to its own terms, and that the Licensing Court is the Licensing Court, and not the Appeal Court. . . .

"This was a mandate which, upon its terms, limited Mr Kyle's authority — I will not say limited, but never gave Mr Kyle authority — to do more than appear at the Licensing Court, and . . . consequently, when he lodged an appeal in these parties' names, he did an entirely unauthorised act.

"Well, now, what is the result of that? I think the result is that there were in law no proceedings at all, because what the Act [Licensing (Scotland) Act 1903, s. 22] says is . . . 'it shall be lawful . . . to appeal . . . to the next Court of Appeal from such Licensing Court: Provided always that such appeal shall be lodged with the clerk to such Court of Appeal within ten days after such proceeding. . . .' Now, it is certain that within ten days of such proceeding there was no note of appeal lodged by the persons qualified. . . . The only thing that was done was that a note of appeal was lodged for them by an unauthorised person, Mr Kyle. . . .

"Now, it is said, and it was argued very strenuously, that although Mr Kyle had no authority when he lodged the appeal his proceedings were homologated afterwards. Now, it is first of all necessary to see exactly what homologation in this case means. Homologation in this case means that, after the whole thing was over and when this case of reduction was raised, then the parties in whose names the appeal was taken are asked, in the action of reduction, whether they approved of everything that Mr Kyle did, and they said, 'Oh, certainly we do.' Well, that is homologation of a very easy character. It is homologation — I am afraid it is not a very judicial expression, but it expresses it better than any other phrase — of 'the heads I win tails you lose' character, because it is homologation after you perfectly well know that the case has been decided in your favour. . . .

"It seems to me that the gentleman here who got his licence was entitled to hold that licence unless within the ten days a note of appeal was lodged by a person authorised to lodge that note of appeal; that no such person was here in this case; and that consequently the whole proceedings were *funditus* null and void."

LORD SALVESEN (at p. 1182): "It was further urged that, assuming the appeal was not authorised either by the written mandate or by any larger verbal mandate previously given, Mr Kyle's action in taking it might be subsequently ratified by the persons in whose names it was presented, and that in point of fact they did so ratify it. I do not doubt that if within the appealing days Mr Kyle had obtained the objectors' authority to proceed with the appeal — which he had lodged without authority — such ratification would have met the initial defect; but it is a totally different proposition that a ratification long after the time for appealing has expired will draw back to the date of the unauthorised act as in a question with third paries. We are not concerned here with questions as between principal and agent; because as between these parties it does not, so far as I see, matter how long after the unauthorised act the ratification was obtained; but where the element of a time limit and the interests of third parties enter into the question totally different considerations may apply.

"I hold that such a ratification could never draw back so as to validate the originally unauthorised act after the time fixed by the statute for appealing had expired."

## CHAPTER 3

# CATEGORIES OF AGENT

*Special agent distinguished from general agent*

**Morrison v. Statter, &c.**
(1885) 12 R. 1152

Calder was head shepherd on S.'s farm. Calder's duties included superintending other farm servants, but he did not buy and sell sheep without special instructions.

On one occasion Calder bought sheep from M. without instructions from S. M. brought an action against S. for the difference between the alleged contract price and the price obtained for the sheep at an auction.

*Held* that as Calder had had no particular authority and as there had been no general course of conduct by S. from which authority could have been inferred, S. was not liable to M.

LORD YOUNG (at p. 1154): "I think the law applicable to this case, and to all such cases, is clear enough; the difficulty is always about the facts to which the law is to be applied. Where you have a particular agent employed by a principal, to perform a particular piece of business for him, he must act within the instructions given for the particular occasion, and does not bind his principal if he acts otherwise. If you have a general agent, employed generally in his master's or his principal's affairs, or in a particular department, he is assumed to have all the authority which is necessary to enable him to serve his master as such general agent, or general agent in a particular department. . . . Now, here, Mr Murray [counsel for M.] says he is unable to prove special authority given by the principal to the alleged agent to make the contract which is now sued on. He therefore relies upon the general authority arising from the alleged agent's position, and his conduct in that position, to shew that that implies the principal's authority to make the purchase which is the foundation of this suit. . . .

"Apparently this is a sheep farm, and the alleged agent is a sort of head shepherd. It does appear that his master occasionally did instruct him to buy sheep. But it does not appear to me that anything is proved about his situation or position as head shepherd or manager, or in his previous conduct sanctioned by his master in the way of buying and selling sheep, which raised any implication of authority to make this purchase of sheep. If I had been of a different opinion, I should of course have arrived at another conclusion, and held that his position and conduct in the discharge of his duties in that position, as sanctioned by his master, implied authority to make such a purchase as that which in fact was here made. But I can find nothing to imply that. I think this man was just a head shepherd with some duty of superintendence or management of others in the defender's employment — a man who occasionally was sent by his master to buy sheep and cattle, with special instructions for the particular occasion. If he never meant him to buy sheep or cattle again, there is nothing to suggest to my mind that it would have been incumbent on the master or the principal to put the public on their guard by advertising that he had withdrawn that authority from him to attend markets and make purchases of sheep. The servant had no authority to make the purchase. He had no particular authority, and he had no situation, and there was no general course of conduct by the master from which authority could be implied."

*Factor who is a mercantile agent distinguished from factor who manages an estate*

**Macrae** v. **Leith**
1913 S.C. 901

L., who had acted as a factor on an estate, claimed a lien on leases and other estate documents as against a bondholder who had entered into possession of the estate.

*Held* that L. had no right of lien.

LORD PRESIDENT (DUNEDIN) (at p. 903): "This is a petition at the instance of Sir Colin Macrae, and it asks for an order upon the respondent, David Leith, to deliver to the petitioner the whole leases, writs, books, accounts, vouchers, and all other documents whatever, of or in connection with the estate of Thrumster, to which the petitioner, as heritable creditor in possession, has right, and which are in the possession or under the control of the said David Leith.

". . . Mr Leith . . . alleges that he is factor. . . .

"The respondent went on to contend that . . . he had a right of retention as factor. Now it seems very doubtful whether this gentleman is factor or not. That he has been acting as factor is pretty clear, but that he holds the position of factor is more than doubtful. I do not think it necessary to go into that question. I assume that he is factor. What right has he to resist the production of leases which he holds? The only person, according to the law of Scotland, who has got such a right against all and every other person is a law-agent, and he doubtless has that right even against the heritable creditor, although the heritable creditor's infeftment was dated long before the law-agent's account was incurred. That was settled a very long time ago by the case of the *Creditors of Hamilton of Provenhall* [(1781) Mor. 6253], and that case has been followed and regretted ever since, and in the various judgments . . . the learned Judges have always said that they cannot go back on the *Creditors of Provenhall* because it was settled so long ago, but that the doctrine is never to go one whit further, and certainly it has never been extended to anyone other than a law-agent. It was pled that the effect of the case of *Glendinning* v. *Hope & Company* [1911 S.C. (H.L.) 73], which was decided in the House of Lords about two years ago, was to extend that rule. I do not think that case has anything to do with it. That decision was based on the old doctrine that where there are contracts between A and B, A cannot call upon B to fulfil his part of either one or several contracts, while he, A, is refusing to fulfil his part of one or more of the contracts. In that case a stockbroker who refused to deliver a transfer which he had got was held to be entitled to refuse, because the client was himself refusing to pay under another stockbroking transaction. There is no contract whatever between this bondholder and the gentleman who calls himself factor. There is no question of mutual prestations between them, and therefore the case of *Glendinning* has no application."

LORD JOHNSTON (at p. 906): "I do not think that this gentleman is factor, although it is not necessary to decide that question. . . . But assuming that he is factor, it seems to me that the use of the term 'factor's lien' is misleading. There is a common enough use of the expression 'factor's lien,' but the use is, I think, confined to cases of mercantile agency, and has not been extended beyond that. It was because in mercantile agency goods are often bought and sold, shipped and received, advances made thereon, and responsibilities undertaken thereanent that the lien was given to mercantile agents over what could be turned into money, such as goods, claims, bills, and so on, and I do not think it has ever in practice been held that this factor's lien could or should extend to an estate manager, who is called in Scotland a factor, but who in England would be called a land-agent."

NOTE

For *Glendinning* v. *Hope & Co.*, see below.

*Stockbrokers*

**Glendinning** v. **Hope & Co.**
1911 S.C. (H.L.) 73

On 19th August 1909 G. instructed H. & Co., stockbrokers, Edinburgh, to purchase for him 100 shares in the Globe and Phoenix Gold Mining Co. Ltd. The shares were duly purchased, and G. remitted the price for them to H. & Co. on 26th August 1909.

On 1st September 1909 G. instructed H. & Co. to purchase a further 200 shares for him in the same company. G. became dissatisfied with the services of H. & Co., and arranged that another firm of stockbrokers should act for him in respect of this second purchase.

H. & Co. claimed that G. was indebted to them to the extent of £50.2/- in respect of the second purchase, and they declined to deliver to G. the transfer of the 100 shares already paid for.

G. brought an action for delivery of the transfer.

*Held* that H. & Co. were entitled to retain the transfer until payment for the subsequent transaction had been made.

LORD KINNEAR (at p. 78): "The next question is whether the appellants were entitled to retain the transfer of the first parcel of the Globe and Phoenix shares which was still in their hands until Mr Glendinning should pay his debt of £50, 2s. . . .

"It has been held by the learned Judges of the Second Division that the evidence adduced is insufficient to establish a custom amongst stockbrokers to retain a client's uncompleted transfer in security of a general balance. I venture to think, with great deference, that the evidence is sufficient. But the right claimed for the appellants does not, in my opinion, rest upon any local custom which requires to be proved by evidence in a particular case; it rests upon the common law rule and doctrine of retention which is part of the law of mutual contract. This is defined to be a right to resist a demand for the payment of money or the performance of an obligation until some counter obligation is paid or performed. . . . If the appellants' counter-claim against the respondent had arisen out of the same transaction as that which brought the transfer into their hands, I apprehend that there would have been no question at all as to their right to retain. The difficulty is that the respondent's debt arose out of a subsequent contract; and it is said that there is no authority for holding that the law of Scotland recognises a stockbroker's right of retention or lien for a general balance. It is true that there is no Scotch decision directly in point; but, if the question has arisen for the first time as regards a stockbroker, it must be determined by the settled principles which have been held to govern the general class of contracts to which that between a stockbroker and his client belongs. The principle which I take to be very well settled in the law of Scotland is that every agent who is required to undertake liabilities or make payments for his principal, and who in the course of his employment comes into possession of property belonging to his principal over which he has power of control and disposal, is entitled, in the first place, to be indemnified for the moneys he has expended or the loss he has incurred, and, in the second place, to retain such properties as come into his hands in his character of agent until his claim for indemnity has been satisfied.

"The most apt example of the principle is probably the case of mercantile factors and commission-agents. It is held both in Scotland and in England that for the balance which may arise on his general account the factor has a right of retention or lien over all the goods and effects of the principal which, coming into his hands in his character of factor, may be in his actual or civil possession at the time when the demand against him is made. This principle is said to have been established on grounds of justice and expediency; and the conditions upon which the right depends in the case of a mercantile factor are exactly those which govern the relation of a stockbroker and his client. The factor's general right to retention depends upon two considerations—first, that he is required to make payments or undertake liabilities for his principal; and secondly, that the goods and effects belonging to his principal come into his possession and control in the ordinary course of his employment. But that is exactly the position of the stockbroker who buys with a liability to pay the vendor and receives a transfer for delivery to his client.

"Mr Bell in treating of the subject remarks that the general lien or retention arises from the very nature of the contract of agency as a right resulting out of the *actio contraria* of the contract by which the principal engages to indemnify the agent. But that again is of the essence of the contract between the stockbroker and the client. . . . The liability was incurred, no doubt, in a different transaction, but it was one of a series of transactions in the course of which the stockbrokers were employed in the same capacity to act as agents for the same purposes for their customer; and their right at the close of the connection between them is to an adjustment of accounts, in which they are entitled to plead against the demand which has been made against them their counter right of retention until their demand upon their principal has been satisfied.

"I agree . . . that the English cases . . . cited, although they are not binding on the Court in Scotland, are sill valuable authorities in the appellants' favour."

LORD SHAW OF DUNFERMLINE (at p. 82): "Certain confusion has come into this case on account of allegations as to custom of trade. I am of opinion that Messrs Hope had a right of retention, and this not on account of custom of trade but on account of a principle in law."

NOTES

1. For comments on this case, see opinion of Lord President Dunedin in *Macrae* v. *Leith* (p. 19, above).

2. This case shows a stockbroker acting as a factor rather than as a broker in the usual sense of that term (a person who buys and sells commodities as an intermediary without having possession). On this, see also *Cunningham* v. *Lee* (p. 65, below) (1874) 2 R. 83, in which the agent was a law-agent who had bought shares in his own name for a client. Lord President Inglis said (at p. 87): "There was a great deal of argument upon the kind of relation which existed between Lee and Kirk. On one side it is maintained that he acted as a broker, and on the other that he acted as an agent. I do not think that a decision of this point is absolutely necessary to the settlement of the question before us. But the relation between them was undoubtedly that of principal and agent, and I should be inclined to say that Lee occupied the position of a factor rather than of a broker. Certain distinctions between the offices of broker and factor lead me to this conclusion. Thus a broker buys and sells, not in his own name, but in the name of his principal, whereas a factor buys in his own name. Again, a broker has no possession of the subject, no control over it, no power of disposal. The factor has such powers and a consequent lien over the subjects. In these respects Lee was rather a factor than a broker, and it is not necessary more precisely to determine the relation between the two. It is sufficient that Lee was agent."

## *Del credere agents*

NOTES

1. *Del credere* agents "are mercantile agents who for an extra commission undertake to indemnify the principal if the third party with whom they deal fails to pay what is due. Their liability is subsidiary only to that of the third party": David M. Walker, *Principles of Scottish Private Law* (2nd ed.), p. 707.

2. "An agent receiving a *del credere* commission is liable to his own principal for the solvency of the third parties with whom he deals"; *per* Lord Neaves (Ordinary) in *Millar* v. *Mitchell, &c.* (1860) 22 D. 833, at p. 848. For this case, see p. 113, below.

3. "A *del credere* commission is payable when an agent guarantees to his constituent the performance of the factorial contracts by the other contracting party": *per* Lord Curriehill *ibid.*, at p. 850.

4. In *Brydon* v. *Muir* (1869) 7 M. 536, there were circumstances in which B. stood to M. in the relationship of seller to purchaser, not in the relationship of principal to agent.

B., clothiers in Dunfermline, sent goods to M., underground manager of Wellwood Colliery. M. claimed that in selling these goods to workmen at the colliery he was acting as agent for B. and was entitled to deduct a commission from the invoice price. M. did not render any account of his dealings with the goods nor did he furnish the names of the customers.

*Held* that M. was not entitled to deduct the commission which would have been due to him had he been an agent in respect of these transactions.

Lord Neaves (at p. 537): "There are two contracts alternatively suggested — sale and agency. Assuming that the defender is right, and that he was an agent, he must either have been a *del credere* agent or an ordinary agent. If the former, he might not be bound to divulge the names of the purchasers, but he was bound to guarantee the price of the goods sold. If the latter, he was not necessarily bound to guarantee the payment, but he was bound to divulge the names of the purchasers. Here the defender, while pleading that he was an agent, denies that he guaranteed payment, and at the same time refuses to give the names of the buyers. I think he thereby places himself in the situation of a purchaser, and is liable for the price."

## Chapter 4

# AGENT'S IMPLIED AND OSTENSIBLE AUTHORITY

NOTE

A distinction is made between implied and ostensible authority.

Implied authority is authority which the agent *actually has*, though it has not been *expressly* conferred on him by the principal. It is contained, not expressly but by implication, in the *contract of agency between principal and agent*. In order to prove its extent reference will require to be made to evidence other than the express terms of the contract of agency — *e.g.* to usage of trade and to professional practice. The agent's implied authority will often be found to be the authority *usually* conferred on that category of agent to which the agent in question belongs.

Ostensible (also called "apparent") authority is authority which the agent *does not actually have*, but which is inferred (*i.e.* assumed by law to exist) through operation of the principle of personal bar by holding out (corresponding to "estoppel" in English law). It arises out of *representations made by the principal to the third party*, which justify the third party in believing that the agent has in fact authority to act for the principal in the particular transaction.

The distinction has been explained in English authorities (see *Bowstead on Agency* (14th ed.), pp. 1, 4, 29, 69-70, 71 and 236, and G. H. L. Fridman, *The Law of Agency* (4th ed.), pp. 43-44, 99-100 and 109-111, with cases there referred to), but has been sharply drawn only within the last twenty years or so.

In Scotland the distinction, as such, seems not to have received any significant judicial attention. In many Scottish cases, as in nineteenth century English cases, it is difficult, if not impossible, to disentangle the question whether the transaction is binding on the principal because he impliedly conferred the necessary authority on the agent (implied authority) from the queston whether the transaction is binding on the principal because he led the third party to believe that the agent had the necessary authority (ostensible authority).

Most of the cases in this chapter would appear to be more properly regarded as illustrations of implied authority than as illustrations of ostensible authority, but language such as "held out" (*Hayman* v. *American Cotton Oil Co.*), "justified in paying" (*Gemmell* v. *Annandale & Son Ltd.*), and "it was allowed to stand and no objection was taken" (*International Sponge Importers Ltd.* v. *Watt & Sons*) point to ostensible, rather than to implied, authority. The word "implied" has been used by Scottish judges on numerous occasions, and the word "ostensible" harldy ever (an exception is the sheriff in *Trojan Plant Hire Co. Ltd.* v. *Durafencing (Northern) Ltd.* — a comparatively recent case (see p. 5, above)).

*Ostensible authority not to be qualified by private arrangement between principal and agent*

**Hayman** v. **American Cotton Oil Co.**
(1907) 45 S.L.R. 207

A. & Co., an American firm of oil merchants, in newspaper advertisements and in letters to prospective customers, represented M'Nairn & Co., a Glasgow firm, as their exclusive agents for the sale of their cotton-seed oils in Scotland.

Ferguson, Shaw, & Sons, of Glasgow, bought 100 barrels of oil from M'Nairn & Co., and paid for them before delivery. M'Nairn & Co. then became bankrupt, and there were competing claims to the oil.

In an action of multiplepoinding, A. & Co. contended that M'Nairn & Co. had been merely buyers and distributors of their products, while Ferguson, Shaw, & Sons contended that M'Nairn & Co. had been acting as A. & Co.'s agents.

*Held* that A. & Co., having held out M'Nairn & Co. as their ordinary agents, were barred from maintaining that M'Nairn & Co. had been their agents only in the special and limited sense of being distributing agents.

LORD JUSTICE-CLERK (J. H. A. MACDONALD) (at p. 211): "The competition in this case relates to certain parcels of oil which were shipped from America to Glasgow by the American Cotton Oil Company, and which are in the hands of the Anchor Line of Steamers. It is clearly established by the evidence that some time previous to this despatch of goods to this country the American Oil Company had appointed the firm of M'Nairn & Company to be their exclusive agents for the sale of their oil. It is further conclusively proved that they held out M'Nairn & Company to proposing purchasers of their oil as being their sole agents, and that any business done must be through their agents. . . . They informed such proposing buyers that they were represented for the sale of their various brands by M'Nairn & Company, whom they in plain words called their 'agents' and expressed the desire to 'be favoured with your business through them,' stating that 'we cannot make offers except through our agents.'

"It seems to me plain the M'Nairn & Company were held out as being the American Company's agents in quite distinct terms, and without any qualification whatever. So far the case seems clear enough. In any ordinary sale M'Nairn & Company must be held to be selling for the American Cotton Oil Company by delegated authority, binding that company as if they themselves had directly made the contract of sale. In that view of the case it is unnecessary to consider any question as to whether as between themselves the company and M'Nairn & Company had some special arrangement whereby, although the latter were held out as agents, and only as agents, the position of M'Nairn & Company to the Oil Company was of a special nature, and did not put M'Nairn & Company in a position of ordinary agents. Of that the customers could know nothing, and certainly the claimants Ferguson, Shaw, & Company knew nothing.

"If, then, the sale which is in question here had been a sale in the ordinary course of business, in which the purchasers dealt with M'Nairn & Company under the accrediting of them by the Oil Company as their agents, the disposal of the case would have been easy. But the case is complicated by special circumstances. . . ."

NOTE

Other evidence showed that Ferguson, Shaw, & Sons had dealt with M'Nairn & Co. as principals, and accordingly their claim to the oil failed.

*Wife's praepositura: necessaries*

**Buie** v. **Lady Gordon, &c.**
(1827) 5 S. 464; (1831) 9 S. 923.

On 1st February 1824 Sir James Gordon of Letterfourie had written to B., a vintner in Fochabers, as follows — "I will not pay or be answerable for any accounts taken on with you from this date, without my written order for the same." He added that he was willing to pay the amount then due to B., namely £25.

Some years later B. brought an action against Sir James for £237.18.8d in respect of accounts covering the period from May 1821 to September 1825. The items in the accounts were mainly dinners, claret, port and other wines, with shrub, whisky and other spirits, which appeared to have been consumed by Lady Gordon and one of her sons in the inn kept by B. There were also charges for chaises, coach tickets, servants' victuals, *etc*.

*Held* (in 1827) that Sir James was not liable for any articles supplied by B. to Lady Gordon after 1st February 1824 except such as were "necessary for the maintenance of Lady Gordon and her family, according to her husband's rank and fortune."

The case was remitted to the Lord Ordinary for him to decide which items fell into that category.

The Lord Ordinary (Newton) found Sir James liable for all items, and Sir James appealed against this finding.

*Held* (in 1831) that the Lord Ordinary ought to have taken Sir James's embarrassed circumstances into consideration and had gone too far in finding him liable for the whole account. The Lord Ordinary was therefore required to remodel his finding.

*1827*

LORD PRESIDENT (HOPE) (at p. 466): "After the letter of the 1st of February 1824, the pursuer was not entitled, without the written authority of Sir James, to make any furnishings to Lady Gordon. Sir James was entitled to say to him, that he would not permit his wife to deal with *him*; and therefore I rather think, that after being so put upon his guard, he could not claim from Sir James even the expense of necessary furnishings. This is not like an inhibition; it is notification to an individual tradesman that he was not to furnish any goods whatsoever without written authority; whereas an inhibition interdicts all and sundry from furnishing any thing else than necessaries, which this letter could not do. Even, however, if he had a claim for necessaries, there seem to be very few articles of that description in the accounts. We have sustained a claim against the husband for funds advanced to enable a wife to go to Bath on account of her health; but here chaise after chaise appears to have been hired without any definite object."

LORD GILLIES (at p. 466): "I observe that there is £5 charged on one day for a dinner and wines to Lady Gordon and her son."

LORD CRAIGIE (at p. 466): "Sir James is clearly not liable for such articles as claret, port, shrub, &c., which should never have touched the lips of this lady at his expense; but I rather think that her separate fund may be attached for the debt."

LORD GILLIES (at p. 466): "Sir James admits his liability prior to 1st February 1824, and I apprehend that he must also be liable for those necessaries subsequently furnished, and that Lady Gordon must be liable *quoad ultra*."

LORD PRESIDENT (at p. 466): "On reconsideration, I rather think Sir James must be liable for necessaries even after the date of the letter; because, if the articles were such as he ought to have supplied, it is *jus tertii* to him from whom she got them."

*1831*

LORD ORDINARY (at p. 924): "It is averred that she had . . . access to a well-stocked cellar, of which she made liberal use. She denies all this. . . . As to the cellar, it is not credible, that if Lady Gordon had had free access to wine there, she would have ordered it to be sent from an inn. There is, no doubt, a large sum charged for chaise-hires; but as Lady Gordon appears to have had no carriage kept for her, and no means of visiting or travelling but in post-chaises, the Lord Ordinary cannot pronounce it unnecessary, considering her rank and station in society. The expense of entertainment at the inn seems also very large; but this seems to have been occasioned, not so much by Lady Gordon, as by other members of the family, for whom she cannot be held liable. The family might probably — and considering Sir James's embarrassments, perhaps, should — have been conducted with more economy; at same time the Lord Ordinary does not see sufficient ground either for throwing a part of the expense on her Ladyship, or for refusing the pursuer's claim for payment of it."

LORD PRESIDENT (HOPE) (at p. 924): "The husband of Lady Gordon is in very embarrassed circumstances. For her accommodation he gave up the use of Letterfourie house, and there her Ladyship is continually incurring fresh expense for chaise-hires; and a considerable consumption of claret and other wines takes place, conform to orders made by her. The Lord Ordinary thinks that her rank and station in society prevent him from adjudging these expenses to be unnecessary. But her husband's fortune must also be taken into account, and it was so by the terms of our former remit. Now Sir James appears to possess only about £80 per annum of free income, and her Ladyship has above £200 of pin-money; therefore I think the Lord Ordinary has gone too far in allowing this account against the husband; and instead of going over the items of the account here, I would propose that a new remit should be made to his Lordship, informing him generally of the view taken by the Court, and requiring him to remodel his interlocutor accordingly. I would observe, at the same time, that when I consider the relative incomes of the parties, I incline to hold her Ladyship's separate annuity as liable for her own individual maintenance."

NOTES

1. The *praepositura* may be terminated by express notice to suppliers, or

by letters of inhibition recorded in the register of inhibitions and adjudications.

2. The *praepositura* extends to other parties, *e.g.* a sister, daughter or housekeeper, who is *praeposita rebus domesticis* ("placed in charge of domestic matters") as a wife would normally be.

*Hamilton* v. *Forrester* (1825) 3 S. 572: H., a widower, retired to the sanctuary of Holyrood Abbey because of "embarrassed circumstances." His eldest, but minor, daughter, Jacobina, took charge of his house and in that capacity dealt with shopkeepers who furnished the family with necessaries.

F., a haberdasher, raised an action against Jacobina for payment of an account for haberdashery goods ordered by her, some of the articles having been for her personal use and others being for her younger sisters or the rest of the family.

*Held* that Jacobina was not liable.

(At p. 573): "The Judges were unanimously of the opinion, that Miss Hamilton being a minor, living in family with her father, and not having held herself out as major, could not possibly be liable for the account in question, which, as furnishings for Mr Hamilton's family, constituted him the proper debtor; and that even if Miss Hamilton's promise to pay were distinctly made out, (which their Lordships doubted,) still it was of the nature of a cautionary obligation for her father, by which she could not be bound."

### *Wife's praepositura: reliance on husband's credit*

**Arnot v. Stevenson**
(1698) Mor. 6017

S.'s wife bound her son as apprentice to A., an apothecary in Kirkcaldy, and paid part of the fee for his apprenticeship.

A. brought an action against S. for 100 merks, the balance of the fee not paid, and for damages on the ground that the son had run away from his apprenticeship after two years.

A. offered to prove by S.'s oath that, although S. had not bound his son as apprentice to A., yet S.'s wife, who had done so, was "*praeposita negotiis mariti*, which was sufficient to bind him to fulfil."

S. averred that "his wife did indeed buy and sell and take in the money, but he never gave her the power of binding; and particularly, he was dissatisfied with her putting his son apprentice to this pursuer."

It was alleged that, as the boy had stayed in the apprenticeship for two years without the father's objection, that "taciturnity" had to be regarded as "acquiescence and homologation of his wife's bargain."

*Held* that S. was not liable, since S.'s wife had not been acting as agent of her husband in relation to the apprenticeship.

"THE LORDS considered that it was not the husband but the wife who had paid that 100 merks; and that a man may be silent at the management and actings of an imperious wife, and yet must not be construed to approve of the same, else she may bring him into inconvenience enough; and therefore they found her praepositation *quoad* the binding her son apprentice not proved, and assoilzied the husband; seeing it was easy for the master to have entered into a written contract with the apprentice's father; and since he did not, *sibi imputet* that he has followed only the mother's faith, who should not dispose of their children's callings and educations without the father's consent."

*Family business: ostensible authority to receive payment and grant receipt*

**Gemmell v. Annandale & Son Ltd.**
(1899) 36 S.L.R. 658

G., a rag-merchant, brought an action against A. Ltd. for the price of rags supplied to A. Ltd.

A. Ltd. claimed that, when G. had been in prison for assaulting members of his family, the price had been paid to, and a receipt granted by, G.'s father as *praepositus negotiis*.

*Held* that in G.'s absence payment to G.'s father as *praepositus negotiis* had been good payment in a question between G. and A. Ltd.

LORD YOUNG (at p. 661): "The question which thus arises has nothing to do with whether the pursuer is solely interested in the business, or whether it is his father's, or whether other members of the family are interested in it. That is all a question among themselves. The question with the defenders is whether they were justified in paying this account to the father and taking his receipt, or whether they did something so irregular that they must pay the account again. . . .

"A crossed cheque was sent in the first place to pay this account. It was made out in name of James Gemmell junior. Then, on the representation of the father that James Gemmell junior was in prison, as he was, the defenders substituted for it a cheque payable to 'bearer.' There is no imputation on the defenders' good faith in doing so. They did so on the request of one of the Gemmells coming from the shop with which they had been accustomed to deal. The case was the same as if they had paid cash to the father in the shop and taken his receipt. It was not merely a bona fide payment, but the debtor was discharged. There is no doubt that for several years the father and his children other than the pursuer to a considerable extent carried on the business of the shop, and while the pursuer was in jail on this occasion they kept it open and took part in carrying on the business as they were wont to do when he was there, and I cannot countenance the proposition that a customer was not safe to pay an account to the father. I think we should find that the defence is sound, that as in a question between the pursuer and the defenders the account was paid and the receipt a good discharge."

LORD TRAYNER (at p. 661): "A cheque, it was admitted, was just the same as a payment in cash. If that be so, the defenders having paid cash for their purchase to the person in charge of the business, and received his receipt, are well discharged. . . . James Gemmell senior was *praepositus negotiis* during the pursuer's absence from the business, and payment to him was a good payment in a question between the owner of the business and the defenders."

*General agent has no implied authority to borrow money*

**Sinclair, Moorhead, & Co. v. Wallace & Co.**
(1880) 7 R. 874

S., M., & Co., produce merchants in Glasgow, had an important branch in Dundee. Low was general manager at the Dundee branch, but was not a partner in the firm.

Low borrowed money representing that it was for use in the firm's business. Later he absconded, leaving large deficiencies.

*Held* that the firm was not liable for the loan.

LORD YOUNG (at p. 877): "This is an important case. The facts on which it depends are very short, and are not in dispute. The complainers, Sinclair, Moorhead, & Company, are merchants in Glasgow, with a branch of their business in Dundee. The branch is of such importance that one-fourth of their whole business is transacted there. There is no partner in Dundee, but the business there was conducted by a person called Low as agent for the company, with all the general powers which an agent managing a mercantile business can have. He had power to buy and sell, accept bills, and open a bank account, — in short, general powers such as a general manager in his position is in use to have.

"In the end of 1879 Low applied to Mr Stewart, the Dundee partner of the respondents' business, for a loan of £150, saying that his principals required it for their business. . . . Had Low authority to borrow money in the name of his principals? That is a very important power, and when it is intended to be given it would be well that it should be given expressly, and within certain limits. I apprehend that such is the practice. No prudent money-lender would be likely to lend money to an agent without seeing his authority to borrow, and satisfying himself that the demand is within the prescribed limits. Here we have nothing of that sort. I know of no circumstances in the case which would lead me to suppose that Low had more than the general powers of a general agent, which do not include powers of borrowing on the credit of the principal.

"The Lord Ordinary, quoting from Lindley, says that an individual partner may borrow money on the credit of the firm. I agree that that is so, within limits, *i.e.*, if the business carried on is such as to require from its character loans to conduct it. But I am not of opinion, with the Lord Ordinary, that because this power can be implied in the case of a partner it therefore exists in the case of an agent. . . . A lender who trusts an agent in such matters without communicating with his principals is not hardly treated if he is compelled to go against the person whom he really trusted, viz., the agent.

"The agent here was defrauding his principals. . . . There was here no authority to borrow expressed, no authority to borrow implied, and if the lender has been deceived it was owing to his own misplaced reliance in this agent, who was really borrowing for his own benefit."

LORD GIFFORD (at p. 879): "It is a strong thing to say that a general agent for carrying on any business in a particular town is to be held to have power to borrow on the credit of his principals. It would require either that express authority to borrow money should have been granted, or that the agent's acts in borrowing should have been distinctly recognised and sanctioned by his principals. The trade in which he was employed was not one in which the borrowing of money was required or practised or in which such power is usually given to a local agent. A power to borrow, when given at all, is usually and indeed always given under limitations, and the amount restricted to a certain fixed sum. Here it is said that there was no limit at all. Low, the agent in the case before us, borrowed £150, but it might have been £1,500. I cannot see my way to hold that a general agent can bind his principal for borrowed money. . . . Low was not a partner of the complainers' firm. He was merely agent. The Lord Ordinary seems to think agents are in the same position as partners, but I do not think they are. I do not think an agent has the same powers as a partner. Many firms have agents in many different towns. Is each of these agents to be allowed to borrow on the credit of the firm, and that to any amount? I do not think there is anything in general agency to give an implied power of borrowing to the general agent. . . .

"If Low had no power to borrow, and Stewart lent money to him thinking he had such power, then he trusted him, and must look to him."

NOTE

Similarly, authority to open a bank account does not include authority to overdraw the account — *Royal Bank of Scotland* v. *Skinner*, 1931 S.L.T. 382 (O.H.).

S., a solicitor in Oban, opened a bank account for his client Mrs Cameron who was to be continuing the drapery business formerly conducted by her deceased husband. The account was headed "J. M. Skinner for Mrs Duncan Cameron."

After a few years the account fell gradually into debit, Mrs Cameron became bankrupt, and the bank raised an action against S. for payment of the outstanding principal sum and interest.

*Held* that S. was not liable.

Lord Mackay (Ordinary) (at p. 387): "This argument proceeds on an *esto*. *Esto* that the account was opened for Mrs Cameron as the principal it is said that the authority to open an account does not include authority to overdraw the account, that instructions to overdraw require to be specially proved, and clearly proved, and that in the absence of proof of any such instructions (*a*) the banker is disabled from suing the alleged principal, and (*b*) the agent makes himself personally responsible, on the double ratio that every agent is directly responsible who purports to contract without having in fact the necessary authority, and upon breach of warranty of his authority. . . . Now I do not doubt that, generally speaking, the doctrine is sound if, that is to say, the banker-customer relation is two-sided. The fact that a banker is willing to run an account in credit does not mean that he consents to make the loan involved by running it at a debit; and, similarly, the fact that a principal permits his agent to open an account with a credit does not involve that he is willing to let him draw upon it under his general agency so as to create indefinite debits. But when it is said that the mandate must be a written one and that in practice no bank would allow overdrafts without a written mandate directed to them and placed in their hands, then I hold that the law is not so, and that the alleged custom of banks is not proved. . . . A person who purports to contract as agent on behalf of an alleged principal is liable on an implied warranty of his authority *only* if the other party relied on the existence of the authority. . . . Now the bank do not, and could not, say that they so relied.

"A claim was lodged in name of the bank for this overdraft in Mrs Cameron's bankruptcy proceedings, and was not objected to by her or her trustee. It has been ranked upon and the corresponding dividend paid. How then could she, or any other, put forward the contention that as against her the debt was wholly without authority.

"In the result, applying the law, simple enough as I think it is, to the facts, it is very easy to hold that the bank which sets out to establish personal liability for the balance of this overdraft against Mr Skinner has failed to sustain the *onus*. I think, however, it fair to go further and say that in my opinion as a jury Mr Skinner has satisfied me that in the important interview he made the important facts sufficiently clear to Mr Jack's apprehension, so that he could not reasonably think Mr Skinner acted as other than an agent for a widow executrix who was going to run a business, itself well known to the banker, and the account as part of that business, equally as agent."

### *Commercial traveller's ostensible authority to receive payment*

**International Sponge Importers Ltd. v. Watt & Sons**
1911 S.C. (H.L.) 57

Cohen, a commercial traveller for a sponge importing company, was in the habit of selling to saddlers parcels of sponges which he was allowed to carry with him and hand over to purchasers. He had no authority to receive payment except by crossed cheques in favour of the company.

Occasionally W. & Sons, saddlers in Edinburgh, had paid for sponges by cheque in favour of Cohen, and the company knew of this but did not object.

On one occasion W. & Sons paid £120 in cash to Cohen.

Cohen was shown to have been acting dishonestly, and the company sought to recover the irregular payments from W. & Sons.

*Held* that W. & Sons were not liable, since, in the circumstances, they had had no reason to believe that Cohen was not entitled to receive payment by those methods.

LORD CHANCELLOR (LOREBURN) (at p. 63): "It is a peculiar case. The Sponge Company employed an agent named Cohen, who proved to be a rogue. His authority was to carry round with him parcels of sponges, to sell them and fix the price, to deliver them, and to receive cheques in payment. He had dealt with Messrs Watt for a considerable time, and generally — nearly always in fact — Messrs Watt paid for the sponges they bought by crossed cheque payable to Cohen's principals. In 1904, however, if not earlier, Cohen commenced a system of fraud. He sold and delivered sponges to Messrs Watt as before, but on four occasions he induced them to pay at once, either by open cheque payable to Cohen or by coin and notes, and then embezzled the money. The International Sponge Company now say that these four transactions were beyond Cohen's authority, and this action relates to three of the transactions. . . .

"What determines me, though not without doubt, in upholding these payments in the present case is this. The good faith and integrity of Messrs Watt are undisputed and indisputable. Cohen occupied a position of fuller authority than is usual. The only limit of his actual authority was as to the kind of cheque he might receive. And, finally, it is clear that on one occasion, a year or so before the last transactions, Messrs Watt had paid by open cheque payable to Cohen, and, though the attention of the Sponge Company was drawn to the sale and a question arose about it between them and Messrs Watt, yet it was allowed to stand and no objection was taken.

"In the same way, the later transactions passed at the time without complaint or objection, and it was only after Cohen's dishonesty had been discovered that, on investigation of his frauds, the responsible managers of the pursuers' business found that their traveller had sold and delivered these sponges and received payment for them himself."

LORD SHAW OF DUNFERMLINE (at p. 70): "The case . . . is of importance to the mercantile community, and especially, as one can easily figure, in the practice of business as between wholesale and retail traders. . . .

"The retail customer, visited by the well-known representative of a wholesale firm, does not, in my opinion, make an unreasonable or improper or careless supposition when he assumes that, if such an agent or traveller holds the double position of, first, being actually charged with the custody of goods and the delivery of these, and, secondly, being trusted by his employers to collect moneys due upon account, the same agent or representative is empowered to make even better terms for his employers by taking cash — rather than postponed terms of payment — for the goods handed over. . . .

"In short, I do not doubt that not only did Messrs Watt & Sons in good faith believe, but they were warranted in believing, that the trusted agent of the appellants had power to take the best terms for goods delivered, — that is to say, cash, or its equivalent, namely, a cheque in his favour which could be cashed on the spot."

NOTE
*Cf. Gemmell* v. *Annandale & Son Ltd.* (p. 30, above).

*Salesman's implied authority to take orders*

**Barry, Ostlere, & Shepherd Ltd. v. Edinburgh Cork Importing Co.**
1909 S.C. 1113

B. Ltd., manufacturers of floorcloth and linoleum, negotiated with Lawrie, the manager or salesman of cork merchants, for the supply of cork shavings to B. Ltd.

Delivery was not made, the price of cork shavings had risen, and B. Ltd. brought an action of damages for breach of contract against the cork merchants.

The cork merchants claimed that they had not intended Lawrie to make a final bargain.

*Held* that a contract had been formed.

LORD PEARSON (at p. 1117): "The pursuers are manufacturers of floorcloth and linoleum in Kirkcaldy, and in the course of their business they have occasion to use large quantities of cork shavings. They claim that on 29th January 1907 they purchased from the defenders, who are cork merchants and importers in Leith, 300 tons of cork shavings . . . to be delivered at Kirkcaldy . . . during 1907. . . . No deliveries were made by the defenders, and prices having risen, the pursuers bring this action of damages for breach of contract. . . .

"The pursuers' case is that the contract was made at an interview between the representatives of the parties, which took place at Kirkcaldy on 29th January. They say that the terms of the contract were in the first instance settled verbally; that before the close of the interview they were reduced to writing by the pursuers' representative in the document No. 56 of process and that this document was then and there delivered to the defenders' representative, who took it away with him and handed it to the defenders, his principals, in Leith. . . .

"The main question in the case is whether the interview of 29th January resulted in a completed contract. . . . It is . . . a question . . . as to the agent's authority to bind his principal. . . . In a question with the pursuers, that is, with the other party to the negotiations, it is not a relevant answer to say that the defenders did not intend their agent to make a final bargain, or that they did not understand that he had done so. That depends on the position of the agent.

"Now it does appear to me that upon the facts of this case the pursuers were warranted in assuming that Mr Lawrie had authority to conclude the bargain. He is described . . . by the defenders themselves as 'the defenders' manager.' He describes himself as their 'salesman.' I hold that he was in such a position as to be within the rule stated by Professor Bell (*Comms.* iii. 1, 3, vol. 2, p. 515): 'In general, it appears that a riding or travelling agent has not only authority to receive payment for his principal of the moneys due to him, but to take orders by which the principal shall be bound as much as if he himself had accepted and bound the contract' — (see the case of *Milne* v. *Harris, James, & Company* ((1803) Mor. 8493) there referred to). Nor was there here in the surrounding circumstances anything to put the pursuers on their inquiry as to the extent of Mr Lawrie's authority. . . . In this particular the present case stands distinguished from the case of *The North of Scotland Banking Company* v. *Behn, Möller, & Company* ((1881) 8 R. 423), to which we were referred; for there the agent's authority to sign bills per procuration of the firm had not only been recalled, but the bank knew that it had been recalled, and yet they discounted bills signed by the agent. The case was decided on the footing that the circumstances were such as to give rise to grave suspicion of the agent's honesty, and to throw upon the pursuers the duty of making inquiry. There is nothing corresponding to that in the present case."

LORD M'LAREN (at p. 1120): "I have very little doubt that thousands of sales in this country are effected by manufacturers and wholesale dealers by means not materially different from the circumstances of the present case."

NOTES

1. *Milne* v. *Harris, James, & Company*: In 1800 M., merchant in Edinburgh, gave an order to Callendar, the rider or travelling agent of H. & Co., merchants in London, for certain goods, which were duly transmitted. There was considerable delay in payment to H. & Co.

In 1801 Callendar came again as a travelling agent to Edinburgh, and received an order from M. for a quantity of tea, which he transmitted with his other orders to H. & Co.

H. & Co. immediately wrote to M. informing him that his mode of payment had been so unsatisfactory on the former occasion that they did not wish to resume the correspondence and therefore that he should not expect the tea which he had commissioned.

M. wrote to H. & Co. insisting upon the execution of the order, and subsequently brought an action against H. & Co. for damages on account of their refusal to execute the order.

*Held* that the bargain between M. and Callendar, agent or rider for H. & Co., was valid and ought to have been implemented by H. & Co., and that, as H. & Co. had failed to deliver the tea, they were liable to M. in damages.

"Although there was great difference of opinion upon the Bench with respect to the circumstances of this case, it seemed to be the decided opinion of the Court, that the nature of commercial dealings required it to be held as a general rule, that a rider or travelling agent, who receives an order, comes under an obligation for the merchant by whom he is accredited. But several of the Judges held, that this general rule might be departed from, if sufficient cause be shown for the refusal; and that in this case the conduct of the pursuer in the former transaction was enough to justify the defenders from declining to enter into any farther correspondence."

2. With regard to the question which arose in the other case referred to by Lord Pearson, see now Bills of Exchange Act 1882, s. 25: "A signature by procuration operates as notice that the agent has but a limited authority to sign, and the principal is only bound by such signature if the agent in so signing was acting within the actual limits of his authority."

*Partner's statutory authority after dissolution of firm*

**Dickson v. The National Bank of Scotland Ltd.**
1917 S.C. (H.L.) 50; 1916 S.C. 589

A sum of £155 forming part of a trust-estate was deposited with a bank on terms that it was to be repayable on the signature of A, B, & C, a legal firm who were the law-agents to the trust. At the date of the deposit-receipt the partners of A, B, & C were A, B, and C.

A, B, & C was subsequently dissolved, and some years later B endorsed the deposit-receipt with the firm name, and uplifted and embezzled the money.

D. and others, beneficiaries under the trust, brought an action against the bank for payment of the £155.

*Held* that, as, by s. 38 of the Partnership Act 1890, B had had authority to uplift the money, the bank had been justified in paying it over to him. The action was therefore *dismissed* as irrelevant.

LORD CHANCELLOR (FINLAY) (at p. 52): "Section 38 of the

Partnership Act 1890 really embodied the old law relating to partnership derived originally from the Roman law, and it is this — that for certain purposes a partnership continues notwithstanding dissolution. . . .

"Now section 38 is this:—'After the dissolution of a partnership the authority of each partner to bind the firm, and the other rights and obligations of the partners, continue notwithstanding the dissolution so far as may be necessary to wind up the affairs of the partnership, and to complete transactions begun but unfinished at the time of the dissolution, but not otherwise.' In my opinion that section applies. This really in my judgment was a transaction begun but not finished. The firm had undertaken the duties referred to in that receipt and the transaction was not completed until the money was somehow or other disposed of. That being so, any member of the firm of A, B, & C, which was dissolved in 1896, had, after the dissolution, power to append the signature of that firm for the purpose of uplifting that money, and the Bank were, in my opinion, justified in paying upon that signature. It is to no purpose to aver that Mr B, when he applied for the money to the Bank, applied for it, not in order that he might hand it over to the true owners, but in order that it might be converted to his own purposes, as we are informed it afterwards was. With all that the Bank had nothing to do. They had contracted with the executors to pay on the order of the firm, but no one contends that this was a forgery. The only question is, was it authorised. In my opinion the Inner House was right in holding that section 38 applied, and therefore that the Bank were discharged by that payment."

LORD JUSTICE-CLERK (SCOTT DICKSON) (whose opinion was approved of in the House of Lords by Lords Dunedin, Shaw of Dunfermline, Parker of Waddington and Wrenbury) (at p. 594): "Section 38, like a great many other sections of the Partnership Act, simply expresses and declares what was then the state of the law, and the previous authorities, both English and Scottish, are in harmony with the provision of the statute. It is noticeable that the statute does not say that the partnership is to continue. What it does say is that the authority of the partner to bind the firm and the other rights and obligations of the partners are to continue — notwithstanding the dissolution — limited only by this, that what is done must be necessary, first, to wind up the affairs of the partnership, or, second, to complete transactions begun but unfinished at the time of the dissolution.

"In this case what Mr B did in adhibiting the signature of the firm of A, B, & C to this receipt could be justified either on the ground that it was necessary to wind up the affairs of the partnership, or on the ground that it was necessary to complete a transaction begun but unfinished at the time of the dissolution. On the face of the document the defenders knew nothing more than this, that they received a sum of £155, which they were told was derived from Robertson's executors. . . . The obligation they undertook was that . . . they would pay it . . . on the signature of A, B, & C. . . .

"What happened was that the money was not asked for . . . until some time in 1904, before which date the firm of A, B, & C had been dissolved. I think the effect of the statute was that the partners of A, B, & C still remained after dissolution invested with authority entitling them to use the firm's signature, and that the partnership continued for anything that was required to wind up its affairs or to complete any transaction begun and not then finished. But the affairs of the partnership could not be properly wound up without getting the money in this deposit-receipt paid over to the parties entitled to it; nor do I think the transaction which was begun by the depositing of the money in the bank on 7th August 1890 could be held as completed until the deposit was uplifted and paid to the parties entitled to it.

"I think Mr B was quite within his legal rights in using the signature of the firm so as to enable him to go to the Bank with the endorsed receipt and demand the money. On the other hand, I think the defenders were entitled to say that if the documents bore the signature of the firm on whose signature they agreed to pay the money — and it was not said to be a forged signature — then they were bound to pay the money to the person who presented the receipt. I think the Bank were not only within their right, but discharged their duty, when, on presentation of the consignation receipt endorsed as it was, they paid the money.

"It is said that Mr B failed to hand over the money to those entitled to it. That may be; but that failure occurred after the Bank had discharged their duty, and accordingly there is no liability on the Bank."

*Shipmaster has no implied authority to make unnecessary deviation*

**Strickland and Others v. Neilson and MacIntosh**
(1869) 7 M. 400

N. & M. were owners of the ship "Tornado." Merchants in Liverpool chartered the ship from N. & M. for a voyage to carry passengers and cargo from Liverpool to two ports in New Zealand — Auckland and Wellington. The charterers' agents at Auckland were S. & Co.

After the arrival of the "Tornado" at Auckland, the master arranged with S. & Co. that the ship should not proceed to Wellington and that passengers and cargo for that port should go by other vessles. S. & Co. furnished the money necessary for this purpose, and the master drew bills of exchange in their favour on N. & M.

N. & M. refused to accept the bills, and S. & Co. brought an action for their disbursements against N. & M.

*Held* that as the deviation had not been necessary for the safety of the ship it had not been within the master's authority, and that N. & M. were therefore not liable for the expense incurred by S. & Co.

LORD BARCAPLE (at p. 403): "The ports chosen, before the vessel sailed from Liverpool, were Auckland and Wellington; but when the ship reached the former port, where the pursuers, Strickland and Company, were agents of the charterers, the pursuers say that the crew, having become dissatisfied with the captain, refused to proceed to Wellington. From the evidence it appears that a new crew could easily have been obtained, so that difficulty could readily have been overcome. It was arranged, however, between the captain and Strickland and Company, that the 'Tornado' should not proceed to Wellington at all, but that the passengers and cargo should be forwarded by other vessels. Strickland and Company undertook to forward them, and did so. The first matter we have now to deal with is their claim for the sums disbursed by them for this purpose. The defenders resist the claim, on the ground that the expense was not a necessary one for which the captain had authority to bind them as the owners of the vessel. If the disbursements were necessary for the ship, the owners would undoubtedly be liable in the obligation undertaken by the captain in their name. . . .

"The question for our consideration is, therefore, was the captain justified in making this deviation from the charter-party? . . .

"Was he entitled to do so to the effect of binding the owners of the vessel? . . . It is well settled law that, except in special cases, the captain alone has power to act for the owners as to the disposal of the ship, and that, in order to authorise him in deviating from the voyage agreed on in the charter-party, there must be a case of necessity. A prospect of advantage will not justify such a proceeding. There must be an overruling necessity, arising either from it being impossible to carry out the original voyage, or from the certainty of great loss accruing to the owners in the event of the voyage being persisted in.

"Now, what are the circumstances in this case? Has any necessity, in this sense, been proved to justify the deviation? I think not. The witnesses all say that there was nothing to prevent the 'Tornado' proceeding to Wellington; and certainly no new difficulty in connection with the voyage had arisen since the charter-party had been entered into. In this state of matters, therefore, no resulting gain being pleaded in support of the claim — the captain having had no special powers conferred upon him — and no necessity having been proved to justify the deviation which occasioned the outlay, I think we cannot do otherwise than . . . reject this claim against the owners for the expense of transhipment of the passengers and cargo."

*Architect's implied authority to employ surveyor*

**Black v. Cornelius**
(1879) 6 R. 581

C. engaged Deas as his architect in connection with certain houses and shops which C. was about to erect on a site in Edinburgh.

Deas had the plans measured by B., a surveyor.

The buildings were not proceeded with, and B. claimed fees from C.

C. resisted payment on the ground that he had not employed B., and further, that he had made an express agreement with Deas, by which Deas's fee was to include the surveyor's work.

*Held* that C. was liable to pay B.

LORD ORMIDALE (at p. 582): "I can find no trustworthy evidence that Deas was not employed as any other architect. I have no doubt that an architect employed in the ordinary way has authority to employ a surveyor, and that the surveyor, if not otherwise paid, has a good claim against the person who employs the architect."

LORD GIFFORD (at p. 582): "I concur. I think that the architect is a general agent of his employer for all purposes necessary for carrying out the works."

NOTE

This case was distinguished in *Knox & Robb* v. *The Scottish Garden Suburb Co. Ltd.*, 1913 S.C. 872.

K. & R., measurers in Glasgow, brought an action against a building company for payment of an account of £121.8.2d for measuring plans, altering schedules, and preparing estimates for houses which the company was proposing to erect in connection with a proposed Government torpedo factory at Greenock.

K. & R. averred that they had been instructed by Salmon, the official architect of the company.

*Held* that there was no custom of trade which gave Salmon in these circumstances an implied authority to engage the services of K. & R. to the effect of making the company liable for K. & R.'s charges.

Lord Mackenzie (at p. 873): "I find it impossible to formulate what the custom of trade is under which the defenders are supposed to be liable. It is intelligible that where a private individual or a company has employed an architect and definitely settled plans with him, and he is instructed to proceed with the work, the architect may then proceed to employ a measurer in accordance with the custom of trade. . . . The present case, however, is different. At the time Mr Salmon instructed the measurer the position of matters was still inchoate, although certain plans had been apparently adjusted with the Admiralty."

Lord President (Dunedin) (at p. 873): "I wish to say most distinctly that the proposition which is laid down by the Sheriff-substitute in his note, that, by the custom of trade, the official architect of a company proposing to build has implied authority to engage the assistance of a measurer is not, in my opinion, good law, and is certainly not borne out by the case which he quotes — the case of *Black* v. *Cornelius*. I have no doubt whatever that when an architect is employed, plans have been approved of, and he is instructed to go on with the building, that he has a right, with no further order, to employ a measurer, without whom the whole matter cannot be gone on with or proper schedules for contractors given out. That was all that was decided in *Black* v. *Cornelius*. But the idea that, because a man has the position of official architect, he has a free hand to employ measurers when he likes is perfectly out of the question."

(On other grounds the company was held liable to pay the account.)

### *Implied authority of solicitor: appeal to higher court*

**Stephen v. Skinner**
(1863) 2 M. 287

The estates of Morison, a merchant in Stornoway, had been sequestrated. Stephen claimed to be ranked for a loan of £41, but the trustee rejected the claim.

Stephen instructed Munro & Ross, writers in Stornoway, to appeal to the sheriff court against the trustee's deliverance. This appeal was successful. The trustee in the sequestration then appealed to the Court of Session, and Munro & Ross instructed Skinner, S.S.C., Edinburgh, to protect Stephen's interests in the appeal. The

Court of Session sustained the appeal and found Stephen liable in expenses.

*Held* that Stephen, not having authorised or subsequently approved of Munro & Ross's actings in connection with the Court of Session proceedings, was not liable for the expenses incurred in these proceedings.

LORD PRESIDENT (M'NEILL) (at p. 290): "In January 1857 Messrs Munro and Ross raised an action against the suspender for their account, including the account for opposing the appeal in the Court of Session, and it is the decree in absence in that action (which has been assigned to Mr Skinner) that is now under suspension, and the suspender says he is not liable for the Court of Session account. He admits that he is liable for the expense of the proceedings before the Sheriff. He says he gave no authority to go to the Court of Session. . . . It does not appear that he gave any antecedent authority to Messrs Munro and Ross to appear for him in the Court of Session. . . . The question then is, whether, irrespective of antecedent authority, Messrs Munro and Ross were warranted in employing the charger to oppose the appeal in the Court of Session. I am of the opinion that they were not. The mandate of a Sheriff-court practitioner does not entitle him to follow a case to the Court of Session, any more than the mandate of a Court of Session practitioner warrants him to go to the House of Lords. But then, if the suspender had got notice, he might have homologated what had been done. Intelligence that the appeal had been presented reached Stornoway on 1st June, and there is no attempt to give notice till the 25th, by which time he was absent from the country. Then, again, the question was raised, whether, during the absence of the suspender, it was the right or duty of Messrs Munro and Ross to protect his interests. In the first place, it is to be remarked that these gentlemen were not the general agents of the suspender; and, in the next place, it cannot be here pleaded that they were acting for an absent party, because the statement of the charger on the record is that Munro and Ross did not know that the suspender was absent. They, therefore, took up the matter at their own risk, and I am of the opinion that the suspender is not liable in payment of their account."

LORD DEAS (at p. 290): "So far as appears, the suspender was in Stornoway on 1st June, and for three weeks thereafter. If so, it was the duty of Messrs Munro and Ross to have intimated to him the fact that an appeal had been presented. This was not done. Had Mr Stephen been informed, it is very probable that he would have declined to support the judgment, because it does not follow that he was willing to have incurred the risk of a litigation in the Supreme Court for the chance of a dividend on a claim of £40. It is not necessary that we decide anything as to the power of the agent of an absent party to defend in the Supreme Court a judgment he has obtained in the Sheriff-court. No such question arises."

NOTES

1. *Cf. Goodall* v. *Bilsland* (p. 14, above).

2. In *Robertson, &c.* v. *Foulds* (1860) 22 D. 714, F., the client of Glasgow solicitors, was held liable to Parliamentary solicitors in London who had been instructed by the Glasgow solicitors to conduct a House of Lords' appeal in F.'s name. The Glasgow solicitors had acted without consulting F., but F., on having been made aware of the proceedings, was held to have ratified his solicitors' actings.

Lord Curriehill (at p. 717): "There is no evidence . . . that any mandate existed before the proceedings commenced. But ratification, after he knew them to be in progress, is equivalent to mandate."

3. In *Urquhart* v. *Grigor* (1857) 19 D. 853 (an unsuccessful action of damages brought by "an old woman of humble rank" against her solicitor on the ground of his alleged negligence in the conduct of a litigation), Lord Justice-Clerk Hope said (at p. 855): "Whatever opinion I might form on the facts of this case, I could not adopt the doctrine of the Sheriff-depute, that an agent stopping short in a cause, and not going on to proof, so that the case is at once decided against his client, without previous communication to that client, shall not be liable in damages, unless he acted collusively or fraudulently. In many cases the partial abandonment of the cause without communication with the client, may at once be a ground of liability, although the agent *bona fide* believed that the case was hopeless. Having accepted the employment, communication with the client before the case is thrown up is in most circumstances a positive duty, especially when that client lives at the distance only of a few miles. But a great deal may depend on the nature of the case, the instructions received, and the character and conduct of the client. . . .

"It cannot be maintained that an agent is bound to appeal every interlocutor, or to communicate with a client in regard to every interlocutor in the cause. On that subject the agent must have large discretion."

4. In *Thoms* v. *Bain* (1888) 15 R. 613, a mandatary appointed by parties who were abroad "to prosecute and follow forth" an action of damages for slander instituted by them was held to have no implied authority to settle the action.

Lord President (Inglis) (at p. 614): "It is contended that this mandate implied an authority to settle as well as to prosecute and follow forth the case. But it appears to me that it is no part of the office of an ordinary mandatary to give up a client's case. No one could contend that he was entitled to abandon it. But if he were entitled to settle it, he might do so on such terms as would virtually amount to abandonment. No doubt a mandatary might be fortunate enough to effect a good settlement for the mandant, but such a settlement, in order to be effectual, must be adopted by the mandant. . . .

"I am of opinion that the agreement made by the mandatary in this case was not binding on his constituent, and that the pursuers are quite entitled to prosecute their case notwithstanding that arrangement."

5. In *Black* v. *Laidlaw* (1844) 6 D. 1254, a solicitor was held to have had no implied authority to enter into a reference to arbitration on behalf of his clients, with the result that his clients were entitled to proceed with an action.

### *Implied authority of solicitor: repayment of loan*

**Peden v. Graham**
(1907) 15 S.L.T. 143 (O.H.)

P., a miner, obtained a loan of £100 through a solicitor, Aitken. P. paid interest on the loan, and also two repayments of £20 each of the capital, to Aitken.

Aitken embezzled the £40, and subsequently became bankrupt and mentally deranged.

*Held* that the loss fell on P., as Aitken had had no authority to receive repayment of the capital.

LORD SALVESEN (ORDINARY) (at p. 143): "The question in this case is on which of the two innocent parties the loss of the £40 must fall. . . . Unless Aitken is proved to have had authority to receive the payments on behalf of his principal, the loss must fall upon the complainer, for it was he who enabled the law agent to commit the fraud by placing the money in his hands, without ascertaining whether it ever reached his creditor. The case of *Withington* v. *Tate* [1869] L.R. 4 Ch. App. 288, is a distinct authority to this effect; and although it is an English decision, I apprehend that there is no distinction between the law of England and Scotland in this matter."

NOTE

*Cf. Bowie's Trustees* v. *Watson*, 1913 S.C. 326.

Trustees in the course of administering their trust lent £500 to Goudie and received in security of the loan a bond and disposition in security over Goudie's house at Bridge of Weir. Bowie, a solicitor in Paisley, was agent for both parties in the transaction, and as agent for the trustees retained the bond.

Some years later Goudie sold the property to Mrs Watson for £650, and on receiving this sum Bowie gave to Mrs Watson a disposition of the property, a forged discharge of the bond and the bond itself.

On Bowie's death it was found that he had embezzled the sum in the bond, and the trustees brought an action against Mrs Watson for delivery of the bond.

*Held* that the trustees were entitled to delivery of the bond since Bowie had had no authority to discharge it.

Lord President (Dunedin) (at p. 329): "Mrs Watson wished that the property should be conveyed to her clear of encumbrances, and arranged with Bowie that that should be done. Accordingly, having paid a full price, she was handed a disposition of the property, and at the same time was handed the bond over the property, and also a discharge of the bond. After Bowie's death it was discovered that the discharge of the bond was a forgery, but that Bowie had lulled the pursuers into security by going on paying the interest to them as if nothing had happened.

"The pursuers now bring this action, first of all, for reduction of the discharge as a forgery, and, secondly, for delivery of the *corpus* of the bond. Mrs Watson admits the forgery, and therefore has no defence, admittedly, to the reductive conclusions; but she seeks to retain the *corpus* of the bond until she is paid the sum of money which she parted with in respect of it.

". . . The forgery being admitted, the discharge goes for nothing, and *prima facie* therefore the bond belongs to the persons who are designated as creditors in the bond. Now, what right can Mrs Watson have to retain it? She must in some way connect herself with it by some form of title flowing from the pursuers. But that is just what she cannot do. It seems to me that to succeed she would have to establish this proposition, that the mere leaving of a bond and disposition in security with your agent is equivalent to a mandate to that agent to deal with it. That is a perfectly impossible proposition. . . .

"Accordingly — although I think it is a very hard case for this lady — it seems clear that the pursuers, who were in no way to blame, are entitled to possession of their bond."

Lord Mackenzie (at p. 330): "The bond is now in the hands of the purchaser of the property over which it was granted, she having obtained it from Bowie, the seller's agent, who, as the agent of the creditors, had custody of the bond. That agent was the forger, and the question is — Which of two innocent parties is to suffer by his forgery?

". . . I quite admit that if Bowie had in some way been clothed with authority to deal with the bond in the way of receiving payment and granting a discharge — if he had got that authority from the creditors, then, even if he had fraudulently discharged it, it might have been that the creditors who were his clients would have had to suffer, and not the innocent buyer who provided the money to enable the bond to be discharged. But there is nothing of that kind here; there is no suggestion that there was any authority, either written or verbal, given by the creditors to their agent Bowie to become a party in any way to the transaction that was carried out."

*Agent's implied authority to employ solicitor depends on circumstances*

**J. M. & J. H. Robertson v. Beatson, M'Leod, & Co. Ltd.**
1908 S.C. 921

B. Ltd. employed Fulton, C.A., Glasgow, to carry through an amalgamation of B. Ltd. with another company, and paid him £200 to cover his charges, expenses and outlays.

Without informing B. Ltd., Fulton employed a firm of law-agents to prepare a certain deed.

On Fulton's failing to pay the law-agents' account, they brought an action against B. Ltd. for payment.

*Held* that, as Fulton had had no authority to employ the law-agents, B. Ltd. was not liable.

LORD PRESIDENT (DUNEDIN) (at p. 926): "The decision of the case will depend upon whether there was or was not employment. It had its origin in the fact that Beatson, M'Leod, & Company, Limited, wished to effect an amalgamation with a firm called Taylor & Company, and in order to bring about this amalgamation they employed a person of the name of Fulton, who professed himself skilled in those things. The amalgamation was brought about, and in the course of dealing with it Fulton, who did not think himself equal to drawing one of the deeds which was necessary, went to the present pursuers, Messrs Robertson, writers, Glasgow, and there is no question that Messrs Robertson executed the work in perfect good faith, and with perfect ability and skill; the question is on whose credit did they do it? . . .

"The Lord Ordinary has found the defenders liable although he agrees that Fulton had long ago been paid, because he considered that he had the power to do such things as were necessary for his agency. As regards that general proposition there is no doubt; but I do not think that the business of arranging an amalgamation of companies or company promoting is so well defined that it necessarily carries with it a right to involve the principal's credit with a law-agent. I think that such a business must be on very much more regularly known lines to admit of any such general proposition. The sort of class of case where right to employ a law-agent could be necessarily understood is well illustrated by one of those cases which is in the books, where it was held that a person who told an Edinburgh agent to prosecute an appeal before the House of Lords must be presumed to know that the Edinburgh agent could only do it by employing a Parliamentary solicitor; and even although the client had never any direct relations with the Parliamentary solicitor he must pay the Parliamentary solicitor's bill. That I quite understand, because there is only one way of doing that; but when you come to arrange about amalgamations of companies, there are many firms of accountants who do such work who would carry through the whole transaction themselves. There are many persons . . . who have been before your Lordships in Court who are capable of conducting large amalgamations, and who would never think of employing a law-agent. To say that the defenders were to take the measure of Mr Fulton and to see . . . that that gentleman was not very clever — and that they must necessarily have said to themselves, 'we are giving him authority to pledge our credit with any law-agent to whom he chooses to go,' is a proposition which I cannot bring myself to face."

## CHAPTER 5

# DUTIES OF AGENT TO PRINCIPAL

*Express instructions: agent liable for value of lost goods*

**Gilmour v. Clark**
(1853) 15 D. 478

G., merchants in Edinburgh, instructed C., a carter there, to cart a bale of goods to Leith to be put on board "The Earl of Zetland" bound for Orkney.

C.'s servant put the goods on board "The Magnet" instead, and that ship was lost.

*Held* that C. was liable to G. for the value of the goods.

LORD PRESIDENT (M'NEILL) (at p. 479): "The next inquiry is, whether he acted according to his instructions, or violated his instructions. First, What were his instructions on that point? The proof is, that he was told to put the goods on board 'The Earl of Zetland.' He did not do so, but put the bale on board 'The Magnet.'

"The next point in the case is, Did the pursuers acquiesce in this violation of their instructions? I see no evidence of this, nor do I see any evidence that they were aware of such violation.

". . . There were here express instructions to an agent to send the goods by a particular vessel. . . . If a party receive express instructions, as in this case, to send a parcel by a particular ship, he takes the risk upon himself if he violates these instructions, and sends by another vessel."

NOTES

1. Express instructions are not necessarily detailed instructions. For instance, in *Fearn* v. *Gordon & Craig* (1893) 20 R. 352, a law-agent employed to prepare a conveyance of heritable property in his client's favour was held to have failed in his duty to his client if he did not make a search for incumbrances.

Lord President (J. P. B. Robertson) (at p. 356): "The facts are comparatively simple. The pursuer, an innkeeper at Brechin, buys hotel premises for £1,375, and employs the defenders to 'make up his titles,' or to 'prepare a conveyance.' . . . The defenders made no search of the records, and thus failed to discover the existence of a bond for £300 which burdened the property. The practical result is that the pursuer has to pay, not £1,375, but £1,675.

". . . In the ordinary case if a law-agent is asked to prepare the deeds necessary to complete a contract of sale of heritage, he is bound to have a search made, or to have specific instructions that it should not be made. That law was very clearly laid down, and the tone of the discussion shewed that the rule was well settled in the conduct of business.

". . . The instructions here were to take the steps necessary for giving the pursuer for £1,375 a house free of burdens. . . .

"We must proceed on the well-settled general rule that the agent must either make a search or get special instructions to dispense with a search."

Lord Adam (at p. 357): "There is no doubt that when an agent is employed by a purchaser to make up a title, there is involved a duty either to make a search or to communicate with his client and explain the nature and objects of such a search, and obtain from him a dispensation. As to this general duty there is no dispute."

Lord M'Laren (at p. 357): "The main defence is that the solicitors were only employed to prepare a conveyance and had no duty to advise as to incumbrances.

"A law-agent is not an artificer to carry out mechanically the instructions of his client. He is a legal adviser as well as an executant. The client, in general, is no more capable of telling his lawyer how to proceed in the business for which he is employed than a patient is able to tell his physician or surgeon how to operate.

"Accordingly, when a purchaser employs a conveyancer, he is not expected to tell the solicitor what deeds he is to prepare, and what inquiries regarding previous transactions are necessary. It is for the solicitor to tell him what is necessary to be done to make up a title to the property."

2. In *Batchelor* v. *Pattison and Mackersy* (1876) 3 R. 914, an action of damages raised by a client against his counsel and solicitor for alleged misconduct in an action in which the client was interested, the solicitor was held not to be answerable to the client for what he had done in obedience to directions of counsel and contrary to the client's instructions.

Lord President (Inglis) (at p. 918): "The general rule may fairly be stated to be that the agent must follow the instructions of his client.

"But the general rule is subject to several qualifications. . . . Above all in importance, as affecting the present question, is the undoubted special rule that when the conduct of a cause is in the hands of counsel, the agent is bound to act according to his directions, and will not be answerable to his client for what he does *bona fide* in obedience to such directions. . . .

"The conduct of the case was in the hands of Mr Pattison, who was entitled to decide what was to be done in regard to the whole of these matters. He did decide, and instructed Mr Mackersy to act according to his advice and direction. Mr Pattison himself is not answerable for the exercise of his own judgment in these matters; and Mr Mackersy, as agent, is not answerable because he acted under the instructions of Mr Pattison."

3. On the presumption *delegatus non potest delegare* ("an agent cannot delegate"), see *Black* v. *Cornelius* (p. 42, above), *Knox & Robb* v. *The Scottish Garden Suburb Co. Ltd.* (p. 42, above), and *J. M. & J. H. Robertson*

v. *Beatson, M'Leod, & Co. Ltd.* (p. 48, above).

*Express instructions: agent not entitled to commission after breach*

**Graham & Co. v. The United Turkey Red Co. Ltd.**
1922 S.C. 533

A contract entered into in February 1914 between G. & Co. as agents and U. Ltd. as principal prohibited G. & Co. from selling cotton goods supplied by parties other than U. Ltd.

From 10th July 1916 G. & Co. regularly sold goods in contravention of that term.

In November 1917 G. & Co. brought an action of accounting against U. Ltd. for the whole period of the agency.

*Held* that G. & Co. were entitled to an accounting only for the period prior to 10th July 1916.

LORD ORMIDALE (at p. 548): "It is clear enough on the proof that the pursuers did for a considerable time act in strict compliance with the terms of the agreement of 1914, rendering valuable services to the defenders. . . . It is clearly proved that in and after July [1916] they were engaged in transactions in material breach of the agreement, a flagrant instance of which is their agreement and transaction with Elia Torres. . . . They failed to confine their activities as agents solely to the defenders' productions. They handled and offered for sale cotton goods which were not the production of the defenders. They also engaged in transactions in such goods as ordinary merchants. In the end it was not disputed by their counsel that they were in material breach of both the agreements. . . .

"In such a position of affairs it is impossible to give effect to the contention of the pursuers that they are entitled to claim an accounting for the commissions alleged to be due under the contracts which they themselves have broken, leaving the defenders to seek a remedy by way of an action for damages. . . . A person who has broken a contract cannot sue upon it. . . .

"The pursuers are entitled to the agreed on commission prior to the date when they breached the agreement and commenced to act improperly, and thereafter not. Having ceased to perform the stipulated services in terms of their contract they forfeited the right to call for commissions — the reward stipulated in the contract for these services — the one being the direct counterpart of the other. It is obvious that the defenders may have been seriously prejudiced by the wholly indefensible actings of the pursuers. I cannot agree with the Lord Ordinary that the pursuers in any view were entitled to a *quantum meruit* and that the *quantum* would be found to be just what is sued for as commission. If the defenders were benefited at all by the services of the pursuers after July 1916, the question would be not *quantum meruit* the pursuers, but *quantum lucrati* the defenders, and the burden of proof would be on the pursuers.

". . . The accounting must be restricted to the period commencing on 26th February 1914, and terminating at July 1916."

LORD HUNTER (at p. 554): "The real question that arises in this case is whether the pursuers, from the date when it is established that they were in breach of their agency obligations, are entitled to make a claim for commission under the contract. . . . In my opinion . . . it is impossible to treat the clause as to remuneration as separable from, and independent of, the agents' obligation as to not selling the goods of rival traders. I do not think it can be said that, if they had reserved to themselves liberty to act for competitors in trade of the defenders, they would necessarily have received the commission stipulated in the contract. . . . From July 1916 the pursuers appear to me to have been continuously acting in breach of obligations to the defenders that affected their claim to commission, and during that period they are therefore not entitled to found upon the contract as giving them a claim to remuneration, whatever may be their claim independent thereof."

NOTE

For a case where there was no similar express term, see *Lothian* v. *Jenolite Ltd.* (p. 69, below).

*Skill and care: agent liable for damage caused by negligence*

**Stiven v. Watson**
(1874) 1 R. 412

S., a merchant in Dundee, purchased from Annan & Co., Pitscottie Mills, Fife, a quantity of yarn. Annan & Co. failed to deliver all that had been purchased, and S. threatened to take legal proceedings to compel delivery.

W., a mutual friend, proposed an arrangement, which was agreed to, by which Annan & Co. were to forward a quantity of tow belonging to them and then lying at Dundee to Dairsie station and to grant a delivery-order for it in favour of W. Annan & Co. handed to S. a delivery-order addressed to the station-master, Dairsie, requesting him to deliver the tow to W. S. posted this delivery-order to W.

W. did not intimate the delivery-order to the station-master. The tow arrived at Dairsie station and was removed by Annan & Co., who became bankrupt a few days later.

S. never received delivery of the balance of the yarn, and he brought an action of damages against W.

*Held* (1) that W. was liable for the damage caused by his failing to intimate the delivery-order; and (2) that W.'s plea that no damage had been suffered because the transaction would have been reducible under the Bankruptcy Act 1696 could not be sustained since there was no certainty that the retention of the tow would not have compelled Annan & Co. to deliver the yarn.

Lord Benholme (at p. 416): "It is true that if the tow had been delivered to Watson to be retained for the pursuer's benefit the Act 1696 might afterwards have come into operation, and the tow might have been recovered by the trustee for the bankrupts' creditors. But Stiven might have hoped and expected that the deposit and detention of the tow might stimulate and perhaps oblige the Annans to perform their contract by delivering the yarns which he had bought and paid for. Plainly the debtor had purchased the tow for the purposes of his manufacture, and he might have been glad to relieve it from pledge by delivering the spindles.

"The only answer to a claim of damage for the defender's failure to perform his contract would have been that there was absolutely no chance of the pursuer benefiting by the performance of the obligation which the defender undertook."

Lord Neaves (at p. 416): "The intention was that Watson (at his own suggestion) should become the agent or mandatary of Stiven. That relation once constituted, a duty arose, and Watson was liable in damages if he failed to perform it, which it is clear that he did. We are now asked on that footing to hold that the agent or servant may turn round and say — 'It would have done you no good if I had performed my duty.' I should have great difficulty in any case in sustaining that defence. It is not a plea to be favoured, and I doubt whether it is relevant, unless at least it is demonstrated that the performance of the duty could under no circumstances have been of use to the person for whose benefit it was undertaken. An agent is not allowed to dispute the title of his principal to call him to account. I think that he should as little be allowed to maintain, except at least on the clearest grounds, that the principal could have derived no benefit from the execution of the thing stipulated for by him and undertaken by the agent. Both parties expected substantial benefit from what was arranged, and I think the defender cannot be allowed to set up supposed rights or possibilities on other parties to defeat that contemplated course."

LORD JUSTICE-CLERK (MONCREIFF) (at p. 416): "There are two questions in the case (1) whether there was negligence on the part of the defender. I think there can be no doubt that there was. Although he came forward as a friend, it was a serious obligation which he undertook, and he was bound to execute it with reasonable care. I cannot think that he did so. There could be no reason or excuse for his not informing the station-master that he held this order, and requiring him to act on it. (2) A somewhat novel plea is urged to the effect that even if the defender had intimated the order Stiven would have been none the better, as he could not have made use of the security, because it was granted within sixty days of bankruptcy, and might therefore have been set aside by the trustee on Annan's estate. I have no doubt that it was a security, and perhaps it might have been challenged with success. But the defender to make his plea plausible must be able to say that it would have been reduced. But how can we tell? The effect of the possession of this tow by the creditor might have been the delivery of the overdue yarns, in which case the other creditors would have had nothing to say."

NOTES

1. This case was taken as an authority for the decision of *Alexander Turnbull & Co. Ltd.* v. *Cruickshank & Fairweather* (1905) 7 F. 791.

T. Ltd. brought an action of damages against C. & F., chartered patent agents, Glasgow, for loss sustained through the lapse of two patents. T. Ltd. alleged that C. & F. had failed in their duty to intimate to T. Ltd. that renewal fees had become payable to the Patent Office.

C. & F. pleaded that there was no loss because the patents were invalid. *Held* that that defence was irrelevant.

2. There is an instance of failure to exercise reasonable care in *Copland* v. *Brogan* (p. 2, above).

*Skill and care: solicitor*

**Free Church of Scotland v. MacKnight's Trustees**
1916 S.C. 349

The Income-Tax Act 1842 provided that allowances should be made in respect of income tax on trust funds "applied for charitable purposes." In the English case of *Income-Tax Commissioners* v. *Pemsel* [1891] A.C. 531, the House of Lords, disapproving of the Scots case of *Baird's Trustees* v. *Lord Advocate* (1888) 15 R. 682, held that "charitable purposes" in that context included "religious purposes."

The Free Church of Scotland sought to make trustees and their law-agents liable for sums which had been paid during certain years as income tax and which had not been recovered from the Inland Revenue because of ignorance, as the Church alleged, of the House of Lords' decision.

*Held* that neither the trustees nor their law-agents were liable.

LORD PRESIDENT (STRATHCLYDE) (at p. 354): "The complaint that is made against the defenders is that they negligently failed to recover from the Inland Revenue certain sums of income-tax upon an application of revenue, made by them in terms of the trust-deed, for the support and maintenance of a religious mission at Bathgate. . .

"Now, I consider first the case set out on the record against the testamentary trustees. . . . The question is . . . whether or no the testamentary trustees were guilty of negligence in not claiming the repayment.

"Now, I think it is a sufficient defence for the testamentary trustees as testamentary trustees to say that they employed reputable law-agents and factors to manage the business of the trust. . . . I think there was no responsibility on the part of the law-agents and factors for negligence for failing to recover this income-tax.

". . . Did they know or ought they to have known that they were entitled to claim repayment?

"Now, in order to decide that question in favour of the pursuers, I should have desiderated on this record a clear and distinct averment to the effect that it was well known in the profession, during the period over which these payments were made, that 'charitable' meant not, as ordinary men in Scotland would believe it to mean, 'charitable' merely, but 'religious'; and that, according to the common practice and common knowledge amongst professional men, claims were regularly made on the Inland Revenue authorities for repayment of income-tax upon allowances paid out, as this was, for a religious purpose. There is no such averment on this record, and the law-agents and factors frankly say — one of them, that his attention was never directed to the question, and the other (who appears to have bestowed anxious care upon the trust), that, while he was quite aware of the statute and quite aware of the Scottish law on the subject, he had no knowledge whatever of the English decision. I cannot hold that he was guilty of any negligence because of that ignorance, in the absence of any averment to the effect that it was common knowledge in the profession at the time.

"This case seems to me to stand in marked contrast to the case of *Frame* and the case of *Simpson* which were cited to us, where, in the former, a law-agent made a flagrant error in libelling the wrong section of the statute, and where, in the latter case, he was guilty, if the averments of the pursuer were true, of gross negligence in not knowing the provisions of the Public Authorities Protection Act. But in this case, aided by the ordinary light of reason, he could not by any possibility have known that there was the right to recover these payments.

"Accordingly I hold, in the absence of any averment such as I have suggested, that there was no ground for holding the factors and law-agents responsible."

NOTES

1. The case of *Frame* was *Frame* v. *Campbell* (1836) 14 S. 914, affd. *sub nom. Hart* v. *Frame* (1839) M'L. & R. 595; 9 E.R. 218.

F. & Co., calico-printers, employed C., writer in Johnstone, to prepare petitions at their instance to the justices of the peace for Renfrewshire against two of their apprentices for having deserted their work and for other misconduct.

C. prepared and presented petitions, but referred to the third, instead of to the first, section of the relevant Act.

The apprentices were convicted and imprisoned, but later liberated by the Court of Justiciary because the wrong section had been founded on. They then sued F. & Co. for damages and expenses.

*Held* that C. was liable to relieve F. & Co. of that liability.

Lord Justice-Clerk (Boyle) (at p. 921): "I think, then, that the agent is liable on the principle of the responsibility of professional persons for skill. Had this been a very nice point, as to which the agent had gone wrong, . . . I might have held him not liable; but the case is otherwise, when the statute is so clear, and he chooses rashly to found on a wrong section: this not being a question of nice construction, on which it was difficult to have light thrown."

Lord Meadowbank (at p. 921): "The question is, whether his proceeding on the third section of the statute inferred such *culpa lata* or extreme negligence as to make him liable? Looking to the statute alone, and even to the marginal reference, which directed him right, no one, holding himself out as a practitioner could reasonably doubt as to the proper clause, and I cannot acquit him of such negligence."

Lord Chancellor (Cottenham) (at p. 614): "Professional men, possessed of a reasonable portion of information and skill, according to the duties they undertake to perform, and exercising what they so possess with reasonable care and diligence in the affairs of their employers, certainly ought not to be liable for errors in judgment, whether in matters of law or of discretion. Every case, therefore, must depend upon its own peculiar circumstances; and when an injury has been sustained, which could not have arisen except from the want of such reasonable information and skill, or the absence of such reasonable skill and diligence, the law holds the attorney liable. In undertaking the client's business he undertakes for the existence and employment of these qualities, and receives the price of them.

"Such is the principle of the law of England, and that of Scotland does not vary from it. I think this case clearly within the principle. . . . There was clearly a want of that reasonable degree of information, skill, care, and diligence which is required to protect professional men from the liability to indemnify their employers against the consequences of any error they may commit.

"It is much to be regretted that the appellants did not see their liability, and discharge the obligations they had incurred, when that might have been done at the small expense of the two sums of £25, which the apprentices have received."

2. The case of *Simpson* was *Simpson* v. *Kidstons, Watson, Turnbull & Co.*, 1913, 1 S.L.T. 74 (O.H.).

Spittal had been injured by an electric car belonging to Glasgow Corporation, and instructed K. & Co., writers, Glasgow, to raise an action of damages. K. & Co. delayed doing so until the action was barred by the Public Authorities Protection Act 1893.

Spittal became bankrupt, and Simpson, the trustee in the sequestration, brought an action of damages against K. & Co. for the loss sustained by Spittal through the fault and negligence of K. & Co.

*Held* that K. & Co. had failed in their duty to Spittal.

Lord Skerrington (Ordinary) (at p. 74): "This is an action for damages for professional negligence alleged to have been committed by the defenders, who are a firm of writers in Glasgow, when employed by a Mr Spittal to raise an action at his instance against the Corporation of Glasgow. The pursuer is the trustee on the estates of Mr Spittal, . . . and he maintains that this claim of damages is now vested in him. . . .

"The defenders' counsel strenuously contested the relevancy of the averments of professional negligence contained in Cond. 5, but in my view they were undoubtedly relevant. I can give no countenance to the suggestion that a solicitor who was instructed in the year 1902 to raise an action of damages against a municipal corporation would have performed his duty to his client if he omitted to read and consider the Public Authorities Protection

Act 1893. . . . I should not say that a lawyer was incompetent or had committed a breach of duty merely because he misconstrued a badly-drawn statute. The real question is whether a lawyer has performed his whole duty when he has read a statute and formed an honest opinion of its meaning according to his own lights. Plainly not. If he is a counsel his duty is to consider the authorities, both Scottish and English, when instructed to advise upon an imperial statute. A solicitor would be in the same position if he undertook to advise his client upon a legal question; but he would be entitled to say that such work was not in his line, and that counsel should be instructed. If the client demurred to the expense, the solicitor would discharge his duty by explaining that unless the action was raised within six months there would be a serious risk of its being dismissed. The client could then judge for himself whether to accept this risk or not. There is direct authority for the view that a solicitor must 'mak siccar' and must not expose his client to unnecessary risks (*Frame* v. *Campbell* . . .)."

*Accounting: unexplained deficiency*

**Tyler v. Logan**
(1904) 7 F. 123

T., a shoe factor, Leicester, owned a number of branch establishments for the sale of boots. He appointed L. as manager of one of his branch shops in Dundee. Boots marked with the selling prices were sent from T.'s stores to Dundee as required, and receipts for the goods so received were signed by L.

At a stock-taking conducted by an agent on behalf of T. there was a deficiency of £62.1.9d, and T. brought an action against L. for payment of that sum.

There was no evidence of dishonesty or negligence on L.'s part, but no explanation of the deficiency.

*Held* that T. was entitled to payment.

LORD JUSTICE-CLERK (J. H. A. MACDONALD) (at p. 126): "The appellant was employed as the manager of an establishment in which there were a large number of goods for sale, and it was part of his duties to take the management and care of these goods. The history of the case is, that when goods were sent to this establishment they were all duly labelled, with classes and prices mentioned, and invoices were presented and signed for all the goods that were sent. These invoices were signed by the appellant on the footing that the goods mentioned in the invoices and the goods received corresponded — it cannot be taken off his hands that they did not. If he did not see, when he passed the invoices, that the goods invoiced corresponded with the goods received, he was not fulfilling his duties as a manager. For a considerable time the stock showed a proper balance, there may have been some slight errors, but there was a reasonable balance in the circumstances. Then, on this particular occasion, when the appellant was about to be promoted to another establishment under the same employer, the general manager came to examine the stock, and his examination disclosed a shortage of more than £60. That shortage has never been accounted for. It is suggested that there may have been theft. That might account for the loss of a few pairs of boots, but as a general explanation of the deficiency it is quite out of the question. In these circumstances I think . . . that the appellant, as manager, is responsible for the loss. In so deciding I express no opinion whatever against his honesty. I think there is no evidence of dishonesty, but that he is responsible I have no doubt."

NOTE

The case of *Brown* v. *Inland Revenue*, 1964 S.C. (H.L.) 180 (aff. 1963 S.C. 331), clearly established that where a solicitor receives interest from depositing or otherwise using sums drawn out of his clients' account the interest does not belong to him but to his clients. The decision in the case was to the effect that the solicitor in question could not obtain earned income relief on the interest.

Lord Guest (at p. 195): "It is not disputed that the interest received or allowed in each case is on clients' money entrusted to the appellant in his capacity as solicitor or man of business. The interest on this capital is therefore *prima facie* money to which the client is entitled. A solicitor is not entitled, without the client's consent, to make profit out of his client's money. Accordingly, unless there is some agreement between the solicitor and his client entitling the solicitor to retain the interest, this belongs to the client. . . . There would have . . . to be very clear and explicit evidence from which any such agreement could be implied, having regard to the duty imposed on a solicitor to account to the client for any money acquired in the utilisation of his client's funds.

"It was also suggested that such an agreement could be implied from a general custom of the profession. The evidence falls far short of any such custom."

*Relief*

**Milne v. Ritchie, &c.**
(1882) 10 R. 365

A house was being built for Davison and Paterson. M., an architect acting for them, had authority, limited to £1,465.17/-, to enter into a contract for the mason-work.

M. accepted an offer from R., a builder, to execute the mason-work for £1,646.17/-.

R. raised an action against Davison and Paterson for payment of £1,646.17/-, and was successful.

Davison and Paterson then raised an action of relief against M., and were successful.

(Subsequently M. brought an action against R. for reduction of the acceptance of the offer, alleging that he had been induced to sign it through fraudulent misrepresentations of R.

*Held* that M. had a title to sue.)

LORD YOUNG (at p. 366): "After the building had been erected the builder raised an action against the architect's employers for the alleged contract price — that is, the price according to the contract which the present pursuer made between his clients and the builder. His clients said that they never authorised him to agree to that price, and that it was not binding on them. They said, 'We authorised him to agree for another sum, not this one'; and they thereupon raise an action of relief against the architect, saying, 'You made this contract without our authority, and so you are liable for the amount in excess of our instructions, and must relieve us of this action.' And in that action they have got decree in absence, ordaining him to relieve them of the action on the contract which he, unauthorised by them, had made with the builder, but for which the Lord Ordinary ultimately found them liable as in a question with the builder. . . .

". . . Now, the pursuer here is between two fires. He is liable to the builder if, without being induced by fraud, he made a contract in excess of his authority. But if he bound his principals to a contract which he was not authorised to make, he is under liability to them, as they have shewn by the action of relief which they brought, and by decree in that action which they obtained."

LORD CRAIGHILL (at p. 367): "The pursuer supposed that the contract was that Ritchie should do the mason work of the buildings for £1,465, while Ritchie says it was for £1,646, and that is the sum in the offer and also in the acceptance. The buildings were put up, and then comes the action by Ritchie against Davison and Paterson, to which the defence is that the contract sued on was made without their authority, Milne having been limited by them to a particular sum. They then raise an action of relief against Milne, saying, — 'This is your fault, and you must relieve us of this action,' and then, this second action having been raised against the architect, and decree in absence obtained against him, comes the present reduction at his instance."

*Fiduciary position: must not purchase principal's property for himself*

**M'Pherson's Trustees v. Watt**
(1877) 5 R. (H.L.) 9

W., an advocate in Aberdeen, bought for his brother, Dr W. of Darlington, four houses in Aberdeen from M'P.'s trustees.

W. was also the law-agent for the trustees.

Before the contract had been made, W. had arranged with his brother, without the knowledge of the trustees, to take over two of the houses himself on paying one-half of the price.

*Held* that, because W. had not disclosed to the trustees the fact that he was purchasing partly for himself, the transaction was invalid on account of W.'s confidential relationship to the trustees.

LORD O'HAGAN (at p. 17): "On the law of the case there has been no real controversy, either in Scotland or at your Lordships' bar. An attorney is not affected by the absolute disability to purchase which attaches to a trustee, but for manifest reasons if he becomes the buyer of his client's property he does so at his peril. He must be prepared to shew that he has acted with the most complete faithfulness and fairness; that his advice has been free from all taint of self-interest; that he has not misrepresented anything or concealed anything; that he has given an adequate price, and that his client has had the advantage of the best professional assistance which, if he had been engaged in a transaction with a third party, he could possibly have afforded; and although all these conditions have been fulfilled, though there has been the fullest information, the most disinterested counsel, and the fairest price, if the purchase be made covertly in the name of another without communication of the fact to the vendor, the law condemns and invalidates it utterly. There must be *uberrima fides* between the attorney and the client, and no conflict of duty and interest can be allowed to exist."

LORD BLACKBURN (at p. 20): "Mr John Watt junior is an Aberdeen advocate, that is the same thing as what would be called in other parts of Scotland a writer, and is almost though not quite identical with what we should call in England an attorney or solicitor; as such he not only pursued the branch of the profession which relates to the conducting of law-suits, but also acted as a conveyancer, and what used in old times to be called a 'money scrivener' in making and procuring loans, and he also acted to some extent as a broker in the purchase and sale of estates. All those branches of the profession are pursued by writers in Scotland, and by attorneys and solicitors in England, and they all necessarily involve this, that the writer or attorney must stand towards his client in a position in which there has been, or rather in which there is, confidence more or less reposed in the attorney by his client. . . .

"I think the law both in England and Scotland is that in such cases we do not inquire whether it was a good bargain or a bad bargain before we set it aside. The mere fact that the agent was in circumstances which made it his duty to give his client advice puts him in such a position that, being the purchaser himself, he cannot give disinterested advice — his own interests coming in contact with his client's, that mere fact authorises the client to set aside the contract, if he chooses so to do. . . .

"Every attorney dealing at all for himself will certainly be wise and prudent, if it is not known to the vendor that he is dealing for himself, to disclose that fact to any persons who may be his clients; it will save him the risk of having his contract set aside; but further than that I do not, as at present advised, think it is shewn that there was anything morally wrong in the conduct of Mr John Watt junior, and Dr Watt is free from blame altogether, as far as I can perceive, except so far as he was aware that his brother was very likely to make the contract with people who might trust him — certainly not further than that. Then came the question, notwithstanding that, is the contract to be set aside in the case of Dr Watt as well as in the case of John Watt junior? My Lords, I have come to the conclusion . . . that the contract is one entire contract for all the four houses as a lump thing, and if we were to say that one part of it should be set aside and the other part enforced we should really be making two contracts of it. . . . The appeal must be allowed *in toto*.

NOTES

1. The House of Lords reversed the judgment of the First Division (*diss.*

Lord Shand) — *Watt* v. *M'Pherson's Trustees et e contra* (1877) 4 R. 601. The First Division had held that it had not been proved that W. had acted as law-agent for the trustees in the sale of the property.

Lord President (Inglis) said (at p. 609): "As to the law applicable to such a case, there is very little doubt. It is not unlawful for a law-agent to purchase from a client. But he must do so openly and without disguise, and even then he is under the necessity of shewing that the bargain was fair, the price adequate, and all the conditions of the transaction such as a law-agent would have advised his client to agree to in the ordinary course of business. If he fails in this he is liable to have the transaction set aside. There is another rule equally well established. If a law-agent puts forward some person to buy for him then the sale is bad, without proving any inadequacy of the price or other objectionable condition. It is a piece of deception which an agent is not entitled to practise, and which is in the eye of the law a fraud.

". . . The case . . . turns entirely on the question of fact, whether John Watt junior was or was not the agent of the sellers.

"I have come without difficulty to the conclusion that the character of agency is in no way established."

Lord Shand (at p. 617): "As to the law on the subject there is no difficulty. The Lord Ordinary states it quite correctly when he says, — 'It may be conceded to the pursuer that a purchase by an agent is not illegal in the sense in which a purchase of trust property by a trustee is illegal. But it is a transaction which the law regards, and rightly regards, with jealousy, and, in order to justify such a purchase when challenged, an agent who has bought the property of his client — at all events when he has been employed to sell that property — must come into Court with clean hands, and must shew that his client was acting with full information upon every material matter, and that the price was adequate.' He must shew that he has 'given the same disinterested advice that he naturally would have given if the contract had been made with another party.' That is so when the agent is openly and avowedly transacting for himself. If, however, an agent conceals the fact that he is himself the purchaser, and purchases in the name of another, the purchase is illegal and bad. . . .

"I am of opinion that as Mr Watt was *de facto* purchasing for himself the sale is in law invalid."

2. The fiduciary relationship between client and solicitor was commented on further in *Brown* v. *Inland Revenue* (p. 60, above).

Lord Upjohn said (at 1964 S.C. (H.L.) 197): "One of the most settled principles of the law of Scotland, as of the law of England, is that a person who is in a fiduciary relationship to another may not make a profit out of his trust, and the contrary was not argued. A professional adviser, whether he be solicitor, factor, stockbroker or surveyor, is of course in a fiduciary relationship to his client, and if and when he is entrusted with his client's money, he can make no profit out of it. He may make proper charges to his clients for the professional services he renders to them, including, no doubt, the investment of their money, but he cannot, without his clients' agreement, make indirect charges by way of retaining interest on the investment of his clients' money. . . . But the client may agree to allow his adviser to retain such interest, provided that the true legal position is explained to him, and he fully understands it. Such an agreement may be expressed, or may be implied from the course of dealing between the client and his adviser, but can, in my view, only be implied where, at all events, it can be shown that the client knew of his rights and by his course of conduct agreed or assented to their waiver and to the substitution of this practice."

### *Fiduciary position: agent not entitled to recover hypothetical loss on purchase of principal's stocks and shares for himself*

**Cunningham v. Lee**
(1874) 2 R. 83

Kirk instructed L., an S.S.C., to buy certain shares for him. L. did so, but Kirk failed to pay the price on the settling day. L. carried the shares over in his own name, and sometime later sold them without loss.

Kirk became bankrupt, and L. lodged a claim with C., the trustee in the sequestration, for the difference between the price at which the shares had been bought for Kirk and the market price on the settling day.

L.'s claim was disallowed, on the ground that L. had not been entitled to appropriate the shares to himself.

LORD PRESIDENT (INGLIS) (at p. 86): "Mr Lee, who is a solicitor in Edinburgh, seems to have done a good deal in the way of Stock Exchange business. In 1873 he was empowered by Kirk to carry through a transaction on his behalf, and out of that transaction the present claim has arisen. The particular shares or stocks in question were bought by Lee for Kirk on 29th October 1873. . . .

"Lee bought for Kirk these stocks for settlement on the 14th November following. . . .

"Kirk had conceived the intention, or what Lee understood to be the intention, not to take delivery of the shares on the settling day, the 14th of November, but to carry over till next settling day, and so Lee desired to have written instructions to do so. Kirk, however, took no notice of Lee's request. In this he acted very unreasonably, and placed Lee in a position of considerable embarrassment. The question is, what in these circumstances Lee did, and what he ought to have done? There was a great deal of argument upon the kind of relation which existed between Lee and Kirk. . . . The relation between them was undoubtedly that of principal and agent, and I should be inclined to say that Lee occupied the position of a factor rather than of a broker. . . . It is sufficient that Lee was agent.

"Now . . . Lee was left without instructions. He says that he sold on 12th November. . . .

"What he actually did was in effect to take the shares and the speculation himself, and to claim the loss as upon a sale on settling day. This was not a sale, but a speculation on his own account, in the hope that the shares would rise before another settling day. . . . The result is, that instead of selling the stocks, Lee took them himself, and from that time the shares in the broker's books stood in his name as owner. Was he entitled to do this?

"In circumstances of this sort, when a principal will not advance funds or give instructions, either a broker or a factor is entitled to sell, to take the price he receives in order to cover his loss, and to charge his principal for any balance which may remain. But, instead of selling, is the agent, be he broker or factor, entitled to appropriate the subjects to himself? That, also, is very well settled. No agent can buy the property of his principal in any case, except when he is specially authorised to do so. But here there was no authority or consent. Lee obviously took the course which he did in the belief he was entitled to do so. He seems to have acted in perfect good faith, and with great forbearance towards Kirk. But still, upon the question whether he was entitled to do what he did, I am of opinion that he was not. His actings were quite against the settled rule of law.

"On that ground Lee's claim falls to be rejected, and it is a matter of indifference what became of the shares after he took them. For he cannot say that £1,600 are due to him on the sale of shares which he did not sell, but retained. It is, however, satisfactory to know that the loss which he sustained was ultimately very small or nothing at all."

LORD DEAS (at p. 88): "What he did was to carry over the shares in his own name, and sell them afterwards at a profit which he proposes to keep, and at the same time to charge his client with a sum equal to the loss which would have been incurred if the shares had been sold on the settling day. I am clearly of opinion that Mr Lee is not entitled to do that."

LORD ARDMILLAN (at p. 89): "I do not doubt that Lee, on Kirk's failure to remit the funds, was entitled to dispose of the stock in the market. He was entitled to sell the stock to another. . . . But there was no sale to a third party. In point of fact, Mr Lee became himself the purchaser of the stock, and after a stock-jobbing procedure, called carrying over, had been completed in regard to this stock and other stocks held by Lee, a sale ultimately took place, I think, in December, the result of which was not a loss, but a gain to Mr Lee of about £400. The claim now made is for the loss which would have resulted from an actual sale on the 12th or 13th of November, the price of that time having been low. The sum claimed is £1,623,5s.

"In any view of the case I could not sustain this claim. At the close of the whole transaction there was no loss. Mr Lee is not seeking reimbursement of a loss; but, having ultimately been a gainer, he is suing for payment of a sum which would have been lost if the transaction had terminated by sale on Kirk's failure to remit funds on the 12th or 13th of November. That Lee was the purchaser of the shares at that time, and the holder of the shares after that time, is clear, and he having so purchased and so held the shares, I am disposed to agree with the Lord Ordinary in thinking that he is not entitled to demand from Kirk, or his estate, the sum here claimed, which is a theoretical or hypothetical loss as on 12th November. He cannot recover the loss which he avoided, and at the same time keep the gain which he made.

"But separately, and on a broader ground, I fully concur with your Lordship in opinion that Mr Lee being agent for Kirk, — agent in this speculative transaction, — could not lawfully purchase for himself the stock which he sold as agent for Kirk. He represented Kirk, and as Kirk's agent he sold to himself the stock which he held for Kirk. . . . I am clearly of opinion that he was not entitled so to act as to transfer the shares to himself. It is well settled, both in England and in Scotland, that an agent cannot purchase what he is employed to sell, nor sell what he is employed to purchase. If directed and empowered to sell for his client, he cannot be himself the purchaser. If directed and empowered to purchase for his client he cannot purchase from himself. . . .

"Such a proceeding by an agent, whether stockbroker or not, was, in my opinion, illegal. It necessarily involved the purchase by himself from his client, — or rather by himself as an individual from himself as an agent, — a purchase which terminated in a resulting gain to himself. Such a transaction is, in my view, contrary to law.

"On this separate ground, even more clearly than on the ground stated by the Lord Ordinary, I am of opinion that Mr Lee's claim has been rightly rejected.

"When I say that Mr Lee's conduct in this transaction was illegal, I do not mean to impute or suggest any fraud or intentional unfairness on his part."

*Fiduciary position: no secret profit allowed*

**Ronaldson, &c. v. Drummond & Reid**
(1881) 8 R. 956

Hill, W.S., acting for Gray's trustees, engaged Dowell, an auctioneer, to sell furniture.

Dowell paid to Hill a portion of the commission charged by him, describing the sum as a "donation" directly out of his own pocket.

*Held* that Hill was bound to credit Gray's trustees with that amount.

LORD JUSTICE-CLERK (MONCREIFF): (at p. 957): "My opinion is that the system of commissions, as they are called, being a mode by which law-agents wish to make, or are to make, more than they would be really entitled to, and to make it at the expense and without the knowledge either of their clients or of their client's opponents, is not a creditable system, and one which, so far as I am concerned, I shall always discountenance and discourage. It is a system that goes a great deal too far both in high and low transactions; and, in this case, I think, the attempt to charge the unsuccessful party more than was actually paid to Mr Dowell for the work he did cannot be countenanced. I think the objection . . . is well founded, and that the commission should be given credit for in settling the profit and loss."

LORD YOUNG (at p. 957): "I assume that Mr Dowell was properly paid with the money which he received, and not that he gave back as a charity or an act of kindness to Mr Hill, or any other, a portion of his own proper payment. He gives discount upon receiving payment of his account, and I assume, as I have stated, that he is well and rightly paid with what he actually receives. If Mr Hill charges against his clients, and consequently his clients against their adversaries in this litigation, more than he paid, he charges so much in excess of what he is entitled to. He is remunerated for his services according to the established rules and scale of remuneration, and the law does not permit him to receive more as in a question with his clients; nor consequently will it permit their adversaries in this litigation to be charged with more. If he pockets this, he is pocketing so much more than he is entitled to for his professional services."

LORD CRAIGHILL (at p. 958): "I think a practice like that which has been brought under notice is one which is discreditable to the agents, and certainly injurious to the client. At the time when the money was said to have been received, and the account paid to Dowell, Mr Hill acted for and represented his clients, Gray's trustees, and he was bound at once to carry to their credit the sum he received.

"On the whole matter, I am of opinion that the practice — if there is a practice, which I must assume, after what has been said — is a most reprehensible one; and as this is, so far as I recollect, the first occasion on which this matter has been brought up for judicial determination, so I hope it will be the last."

*Fiduciary position: agent's interests in conflict with those of principal*

**Lothian v. Jenolite Ltd.**
1969 S.C. 111

J. Ltd., an English company, entered into an agreement with L., whereby L. was to sell certain of J. Ltd.'s products in Scotland and receive a commission on sales. The contract was to last for four years from July 1964, but in November 1965 J. Ltd. terminated it.

L. brought an action of damages for breach of contract against J. Ltd.

In defence J. Ltd. averred that L. had without their consent bought and resold products supplied by a competitor of theirs and had instructed his staff to sell these products in place of J. Ltd.'s products, and was therefore in material breach of contract.

*Held* that it was not an implied condition of L.'s contract with J. Ltd. that L. should not, without J. Ltd.'s consent, sell a competitor's products.

LORD MILLIGAN (at p. 117): "In this action the pursuer and respondent, who trades under the name of L. W. Lothian and Company, concludes for damages against the defenders and reclaimers on the ground that the defenders wrongfully terminated a contract which he had entered into with them, in virtue of which he was granted a commission in respect of sales by him in Scotland of certain chemicals marketed by the defenders. The defenders, while admitting the existence of the contract, maintain, *inter alia*, that, as the pursuer was in breach of certain material conditions of the contract and in any event had been guilty of gross misconduct, they were entitled to terminate the contract and that accordingly no damages are due. . . .

"As finally adjusted the contract was to run 'for a term of four years from 1st July 1964 to 30th June 1968.' . . . On 24th November 1965 the defenders wrote a letter to the pursuer stating that it had come to their notice that he was 'actively selling a competitor's material and products.' They went on to say in said letter that this was 'contrary to our arrangement whereby you were appointed sole distributor for Jenolite products in Scotland.' . . .

"The pursuer denies that he was in breach of any implied condition in the contract and avers, *inter alia*, that, *esto* he was in breach of any such condition, the breach was not in the circumstances so material as to justify the defenders in rescinding the contract. . . .

"It was submitted on behalf of the defenders that the contract between the pursuer and themselves was a contract of agency, and that in every contract of agency in which the sale of goods was involved there fell to be included the implied conditions upon which the defenders were founding. There were, it was conceded, no special features in this contract. In any event, even if certain of the actings of the pursuer of which the defenders complain were permissible, his action in giving instructions to his sales staff to sell his own products, where possible, in place of those of the defenders could not on any view be justified. Counsel conceded that there was no reported case in which it was decided that there was in every contract of agency an implied condition that the agent would not compete with his principal even when acting outside the sphere of his contract with his principal. . . .

"The proposition which the defenders invite us to affirm is that in all agency cases there is an implied condition that the agent will not without the permission of his principal act, even in an outside matter, in such a way as to bring his interests into conflict with those of his principal. There is admittedly no case in which such a proposition has been affirmed, and the proposition is a sweeping one which, if it is sound, would undoubtedly affect a very large number of cases where an agent acts for two or more principals. There would normally be no objection to such a condition or term being expressly included in a contract of agency . . . but it is a very different matter to imply such a condition when it does not appear expressly in the contract. It is, moreover, more difficult to imply a condition in a written contract than it is in a verbal contract. . . .

"The introduction of the condition would . . . make the contract a different contract altogether, and moreover it was a condition to which the parties could readily have given expression if that were their intention. (See, for example, *Graham & Co.* v. *United Turkey Red Co.*)

"The many authorities quoted by the defenders establish that, while actually performing his principal's business, an agent is not entitled to take advantage of his position and make a profit for himself, but, as I have said, no authority was quoted for the much wider proposition for which the defenders now contend, namely, that there is in every contract of agency an implied condition that an agent will never without the permission of his principal 'even in an outside matter' act in such a way as to bring his interests into conflict with those of his principal.

"The circumstances in which a condition may be implied are, particularly where the contract has been reduced to writing, rightly very limited, and I am satisfied that they have not been shown to exist in the present case. If the defenders had wanted to restrict the activities of the pursuer, they could have asked him to agree to their proposed restriction. Not having done so, they cannot now seek to rectify the position by attempting to discover an implied condition."

LORD WALKER (at p. 124): "The defenders had not stipulated that the pursuer should be their full-time agent, or that he should sell their goods exclusively, or that his freedom to carry on his own business should be restricted in their interests. Mr Bennett, as senior counsel for the defenders, conceded that he could find no case which affirmed the proposition that the existence of the agency was in itself sufficient to impose a restraint on the pursuer's freedom to trade. He maintained, however, that as a pure question of principle applicable in the case of any agency, and as part of the legal relationship of a fiduciary nature, such a restraint was necessarily implied.

". . . What Mr Bennett was founding on, if I followed him correctly, was the rule that the agent must act with a single eye to the interests of his principal. But that rule is, I think, limited to what the agent does in the course of his agency. Here what he did as agent and what he did as an individual were quite separate from one another. . . . If the defenders intended to impose a restriction on the pursuer's freedom to trade, they should have contracted with him to that effect."

NOTE

For *Graham & Co.* v. *The United Turkey Red Co. Ltd.*, see p. 52, above.

*Fiduciary position: confidentiality*

### Liverpool Victoria Legal Friendly Society v. Houston
(1900) 3 F. 42

H. had been an agent of a friendly society for about four years, during which time he had had the opportunity of seeing lists of persons insured with the society.

After having been dismissed by the society, H. offered lists of such persons to officials of a rival society.

*Held* that the lists contained confidential information acquired by H. in the course of his agency and that he was not entitled to make use of them to the detriment of his former principal. H. was also held liable in damages for the loss of business which the society had sustained as a result of having its members canvassed by the agents of the rival society.

LORD JUSTICE-CLERK (J. H. A. MACDONALD) (at p. 46): "The defender in this case, who was formerly sub-agent of the pursuers' society, having while in their employment the means of seeing the lists of persons insured with the pursuers, the allegation is that he copied these lists, and after ceasing to be in their employment made use of these lists in aid of the canvassing of another friendly society to obtain the transfer of their insurers to the other company, he getting a commission on the effecting of the insurances. . . . I am satisfied on the evidence that the defender did make copies of the lists, and did so with a view to put them to his own uses. Only one of these copies of lists has been recovered. . . . The Lord Ordinary has expressed his opinion that the evidence of the defender on this and cognate matters is not trustworthy, and a perusal of the evidence leads one to agree in that view. I think it is established that the defender gave the use of this list to the agent of another society, intending it to be used in the interests of that society, and necessarily against the interests of the pursuers' society. I agree with the Lord Ordinary that this was illegal. This list has been recovered by the pursuers, and therefore no order in regard to it is required. But it is a question whether they are not entitled to protection from other similar lists being used by the defender. It is clear on the evidence that the defender admitted to numerous witnesses that he had such lists. This he now denies, but the Lord Ordinary would not believe him, and therefore granted interdict. On the question of damages, the Lord Ordinary has awarded only £5, and I would not propose to interfere with his decision."

LORD ORDINARY (PEARSON) (at p. 47): "Where a servant acquires confidential information in the course of his service, the law implies a contract that the information shall not then or afterwards be ultroneously disclosed to a third party. To constitute a breach of this contract, it is not necessary that the confidential information should be published to the world, nor that the information is communicated gratuitously. It is enough that the information so acquired is supplied to a third person without any just or legitimate occasion for supplying it."

## CHAPTER 6

# RIGHTS OF AGENT AGAINST PRINCIPAL

*Remuneration: quantum meruit*

**Kennedy v. Glass**
(1890) 17 R. 1085

G. was a dealer in old building material and old machinery.

K., an architect, had on several occasions introduced G. to persons who had old material for sale, and for this K. had been paid a commission by G.

In 1883 K. introduced G. to Kerr, the managing clerk of the Glebe Sugar Refining Company in Greenock, with a view to a proposed sale of machinery and plant by the company. Negotiations were protracted.

In 1888 G. entered into a contract with the company for the purchase of the machinery and plant at the price of £7,250. G. subsequently failed to carry out the contract.

K. claimed that there had been an oral arrangement between himself and G. by which he was to receive £250 commission. G. contended that he had only arranged to give K. £50 if anything came of the transaction. There was evidence to show that throughout the negotiations K. had acted as G.'s representative and had taken a great deal of trouble in promoting the transaction.

*Held* that although K. was not a professional broker he was entitled to £50 commission, *i.e.*, to commission on a *quantum meruit* basis.

LORD PRESIDENT (INGLIS) (at p. 1086): "The defender is a person who is in the way of buying old material, and is anxious, accordingly, to be put in the way of such transactions, and is indebted to anyone who can put him in the way of such transactions, and that is precisely what the pursuer here did. . . .

"Throughout the negotiations the pursuer acted as the representative of the defender, and took a great deal of trouble in promoting the transaction. . . . The precise facts summed up amount to this: The pursuer introduced the defender to the Glebe Sugar Refining Company, and did all he could to promote the transaction between the parties, and spent a considerable time in the discharge of this duty.

"The question, in these circumstances, is whether the pursuer is entitled to commission.

"The only difficulty in the matter is that the pursuer is not a professional broker. If he had been, the remuneration payable to him would have depended very much upon the custom of trade. But he is not in that position though he was acting as broker, *i.e.*, performing the functions of a broker. Now, if he was placed in the same position as a broker, I am not prepared to say that, because he is not by trade a broker, he has no right to charge a commission, particularly as he is in the habit of acting in that capacity and had previously so acted for the defender.

"If that be so, the only point left is the rate of his remuneration. The price agreed upon for the old material by the letter of 6th October 1888 was £7,250. The commission claimed is £50, which is under one per cent on the purchase money, and I do not think that it is possible to say that that is an unreasonable amount."

LORD ADAM (at p. 1087) "The question arises whether the pursuer is entitled to a sum as *quantum meruit*. . . .

"The difficulty I have felt in the case is that the pursuer is not a recognised broker. If he had been, we should have known what rules were to be applied, and among other rules there would have been this, that if the contract was completed between purchaser and seller it would be no matter to the broker whether or not the purchaser could pay the price. The difficulty is whether we can apply these rules to the relations between the parties here. All that we know is that the pursuer was in the habit of giving information to the defender, who is a purchaser of old iron and such materials. What, in these circumstances, are the rules we should apply? The defender says that he agreed only to pay commission if the transaction turned out profitable. The difficulty is that it is not a probable contract, and it is not to be presumed that a party would agree to do work for nothing, and in the absence of clear proof it is difficult to arrive at that result. On the other hand, it is a known principle that if one man uses another for the purpose and with the effect of doing business, the ordinary rule is that the person employed is entitled to some remuneration. In the case of the professional broker, the amount is fixed by usage of trade or otherwise. We have no usage to guide us here, and the question being whether £50 is too large a remuneration for the pursuer's services to the defender, I have come to the conclusion that it is not."

NOTES

1. *Manson* v. *Baillie* (1855) 2 Macq. 80 is authority for the proposition that the employment of a professional person implies an undertaking to remunerate him but the inference may be rebutted by circumstances.

In that case M., an S.S.C. who was one of six trustees, was held not entitled to the remuneration which he claimed.

Lord Chancellor (Cranworth) (at p. 86): "Certainly, I think the Appellant, the Pursuer, has a right to this observation in his favour, that, when you employ a professional person, *prima facie*, you employ him for reward, as it is called, upon the understanding that he shall be paid for his services. The question here is, whether the circumstances are such as to rebut the presumption."

(The House decided that the circumstances were such as to rebut the presumption.)

2. In *Graham & Co.* v. *The United Turkey Red Co. Ltd.* (p. 52, above), opinions were expressed that for a period subsequent to a breach of the contract of agency, the agent's claim for remuneration would be a claim, not for *quantum meruit* the agent, but for *quantum lucratus* the principal.

*Remuneration: contract to pay commission not proved*

## Moss v. Cunliffe & Dunlop
(1875) 2 R. 657

M., a commission merchant in Liverpool, introduced C. & D., shipbuilders, Port-Glasgow, to Beckmann of London, who was contemplating the purchase of a small steamer for the price of £13,850.

Beckmann was actively concerned in the promotion of a company for the establishment and maintenance of a line of large ocean steamers between European ports and Brazilian ports. This company purchased a steamer from C. & D. for £31,000.

M. sued C. & D. for 2½ per cent commission on the price of that steamer.

*Held* that M. had failed to prove any contract between himself and C. & D. for payment of the commission sued for, or to show that the order was the direct result of his intervention, and consequently that he was not entitled to commission.

LORD NEAVES (at p. 661): "The custom at the foundation of the pursuer's case is not unknown to the law. Any custom which is reasonable ought to be enforced, provided it is clearly proved, and provided the facts of the case support the application of the custom.

"The custom is stated in very general terms, viz., that a broker who introduces a shipbuilder to a purchaser is entitled to commission on the first business done. . . .

"It is not proved that the Rio Grande Company wanted the steamer first mentioned. Beckmann, who was looking after the interests of the Rio Grande Company certainly, but also after his own, wanted a steamer, not of the proper class for the company's ocean trade, but a smaller steamer. . . .

"The first thing that brings the defenders into contact with Beckmann was the smaller steamer. The pursuer gives the defenders an introduction to Beckmann, who, in order to satisfy himself of their efficiency, sends down Le Couteur to Port-Glasgow, and Le Couteur forms a favourable opinion of the defenders as shipbuilders. Nothing more is said about the smaller steamer. The defenders are employed to execute an order for a large steamer for the company. . .

"I do not think that . . . the party who gave the order was identical with the party to whom the builder was introduced. I have great doubts whether any custom is proved which will cover the real facts. The smaller steamer was not necessarily for the Rio Grande Company, but for a speculation that might be quite independent.

"There seems a great difference between a general and a special introduction. A broker acts for both parties, and acts according as he has been appointed. If general business is wanted on both sides, the broker is entitled to commission on the first transaction. But a recommendation of a shipbuilder to build a small steamer is not necessarily a recommendation to build a large steamer. If the parties . . . drop the business for which they have been introduced and take up a much larger transaction, I see no evidence of a custom that the broker shall still get a commission on the first piece of business that may be brought about, however large, and after an interval however long. The broker there is not the *causa causans* but only the *causa causae causantis*.

"The fact that the persons who gave the employment were not the same as the person to whom the introduction was given is a special difficulty in the way of the pursuer proving that he has done the work for which he claims payment."

LORD ORMIDALE (at p. 663): "Cunliffe, one of the defenders, went to London, and got into communication with Beckmann. And it was he, and not Moss, who introduced Cunliffe to the Rio Grande Company, from whom an order was obtained for a large or ocean steamer.

"Such are briefly the circumstances in which the question arises, whether Moss, the pursuer, has established his present claim for commission against the defenders on the cost of the large or ocean steamer just referred to. I concur with Lord Neaves in being unable to find any sufficient evidence to support such a claim on the part of the pursuer.

"In the first place, there is not sufficient evidence that Moss gave the defenders any general, or, indeed, any introduction at all, to the Rio Grande Company. Looking at the correspondence I find nothing but a special introduction having reference to a special object, viz., a small, or river steamer; and that introduction was not to the Rio Grande Company, but to certain subordinate parties. . . . Moss may have had a good claim against the defenders in reference to the small steamer, if an order had been obtained for it; and he may still have such a claim for anything that appears to the contrary. In the second place, it is not proved that the Rio Grande Company was identical with the persons who required the smaller steamer, and if so, this raises an additional bar to the pursuer prevailing in his present claim. If a broker give a shipbuilder an introduction to A, for the purpose of obtaining an order for the construction of a small, or river steamer, and the shipbuilder, in the course of his negotiation with that purpose, comes into contact with a third party, who gives him an order for a large or ocean steamer, I cannot hold that this would give the broker a claim for commission against the shipbuilder on the latter transaction, merely because it may be said that in a certain loose sense it arose indirectly from, or in consequence of, the introduction which had been given to a different party, and in reference to a different kind of transaction.

"In short . . . it appears to me that there are wanting in the present case the elements of employment and service necessary to support the pursuer's claim."

LORD GIFFORD (at p. 664): "I have arrived at the same conclusion. The action is brought by a commission-agent or broker, in order to recover his commission. Commission is the remuneration to which a broker is entitled under the contract of agency. There must always be a contract of agency to warrant the charge of commission. If there is no agency — no 'commissioner' appointed — there is no room for 'commission.' In general, commission is due to the agent as recompense or payment for his skill, trouble, and responsibility. . . . When parties make a distinct contract for an introduction or recommendation, and where the introduction or recommendation is stipulated and agreed to be paid for — then, if the contract is fair and reasonable, it will receive effect. But there must be such a contract before the agent is entitled to remuneration, and the law will look somewhat narrowly to see that it is fair and reasonable, especially when the commission is really added to the price, and charged against the purchaser, who did not employ the broker, and was not a party to the contract of agency. . . . I read the bargain as an agreement that if the defenders should be employed to build the river steamer which was wanted then they should pay the pursuer, in consideration of his introduction and influence, 2½ per cent on the price. But the pursuer maintains that his introduction was not special for any particular order, but general, and that a general introduction implies by custom of trade or by express stipulation a commission of 2½ per cent upon the first order which may be obtained, and the pursuer's claim is for a commission upon the first order, whatever that may be, and however different in its nature it may be from the river steamer which was originally contemplated.

"I do not think that this contention is well founded, and I am not satisfied that any such custom of trade has been proved. There may no doubt sometimes be such a bargain, but I think it must always be specially alleged and proved, and there is no such bargain proved in the present case. I think the pursuer has failed to shew that the defenders agreed to pay him commission on the large ocean steamer which they built for the Rio Grande Company.

"The first defence is that the larger steamer was not ordered by the same parties who were prepared to order the river steamer. I think this defence has been made good. . . . It may be that some of the parties interested in the Rio Grande Company were also interested in the river steamer, but there was no identity between the concerns.

"In the next place, there was a material and essential difference between the things ordered. Suppose that instead of a large steamer, a very small vessel had been ordered, or it may be a mere boat, would Moss have been contented with commission on that, as being the first order? If the introduction was general, he would have been obliged to be contented with the first order, however small.

"Still further, it was indirectly and not directly from Moss that Cunliffe and Dunlop got the order for the larger steamer. . . . It would be a strong thing to hold that because a broker introduces parties for one contract, that will entitle him to commission on another contract, not even between the same parties, but indirectly brought about, in consequence of the parties being brought together and introducing a third party, with whom new transactions arise. . . . It was Captain Le Couteur, and not the pursuer at all, who was the means of the defenders being employed by the Rio Grande Company to build the ocean steamer now in question, and I cannot hold that

Moss was the *causa causans* of the order, or that he is entitled to any commission thereon.

"Upon the whole, I am of opinion that the pursuer is not entitled to prevail, (1) because it was a special contract for which alone he was agent, and (2) because he was only the indirect and not the direct cause of the order in question."

NOTE

Of this case, Lord Shaw of Dunfermline said in *A. R. Brett & Co. Ltd.* v. *Bow's Emporium Ltd.*, 1928 S.C. (H.L.) 19, at p. 20: "On very special facts, it was held that the order to build a ship was not the direct result of a certain shipbroker's intervention. I would only say of that case that, if it went further than its own special facts, it was a very doubtful decision. . . . I leave the case with the observation that, if it ever comes to be cited as illustrating this branch of the law of agency, it will have to be very carefully considered."

### *Remuneration: payment excluded by proof of contrary custom*

**Leo Dinesmann & Co. v. Mair & Co.**
1912, 1 S.L.T. 217 (O.H.)

D. & Co., commission agents in Koenigsberg, Prussia, brought an action for payment of £1,084.14.2d. against M. & Co., fish curers, Lerwick. This sum was made up of (1) advances made by D. & Co. to M. & Co. which had not been repaid, (2) disbursements made by D. & Co., and (3) interest. In particular D. & Co. averred that on three dates in June 1910 they had advanced to M. & Co. £350, £375, and £225 against three consignments of herrings sent to them by M. & Co.

M. & Co. averred in answer that the payments had been made and the expenses and charges had been defrayed on the footing that the pursuers were to rely entirely for repayment on the proceeds of sale, that being in conformity with the usual and customary course of dealing between commission agents in Koenigsberg and Scottish fish curers.

Parties were allowed a proof of their averments.

LORD HUNTER (ORDINARY) (at p. 218): "The defenders aver that the pursuers are employed as agents upon the footing, *inter alia*, that in making advances against consignments of herrings they rely for repayment on the proceeds of the sale of the goods, but that the defenders are not personally liable to the pursuers therefor. That is certainly not a condition ordinarily found in the contract of agency; but the defenders allege that it is in conformity with the usual and customary course of dealing which exists between commission agents in Koenigsberg and Scotch fish curers; and that this custom of trade was known to, and relied upon by, both parties as governing the contract of agency between them. . . . I was not referred to any Scots case; but as I do not think such a contract is unlawful or that it is against Scots legal principle that it should be inferred from an established custom of trade, I do not see my way to exclude enquiry."

*Remuneration: whether agent has earned it: shipbroker*

**Walker, Donald, & Co. v. Birrell, Stenhouse, & Co.**
(1883) 11 R. 369

W., D., & Co. were shipbrokers in Glasgow, and one part of their business consisted in introducing persons wishing to purchase ships or have them built to persons who could supply the ships on either of these footings. B., S., & Co. were shipbuilders in Dumbarton.

W., D., & Co. introduced Macbeth & Gray, ship-chandlers, Glasgow, to B., S., & Co., and negotiations followed for the building of two steamers, one for W., D., & Co. and one for Macbeth & Gray. These negotiations did not result in a contract.

About a month later, a contract was concluded between Macbeth & Gray and B., S., & Co. for the building of a steamship at the price of £21,500.

W., D., & Co. sued B., S., & Co. for 2½ per cent commission on the price, founding on a custom of trade, which they alleged existed on the Clyde, that "the broker or middleman who introduces a purchaser to a shipbuilder, and thereby aids the latter to procure an order, is entitled to receive from the shipbuilder a commission on the contract price of the vessel." They further alleged that the percentage was a fair and reasonable charge, and the rate usually recognised in the absence of a special agreement.

B., S., & Co. answered that commission in such cases was a matter for stipulation, and that the ship ultimately contracted for was an entirely different one, with which the pursuers had nothing to do.

*Held* that W., D., & Co. were entitled to commission at 1 per cent.

LORD PRESIDENT (INGLIS) (at p. 373): "Sometime afterwards Macbeth renewed negotiations with the defenders for building such a vessel as was proposed before. It is said that the vessel which was actually built was different, but I think the differences were immaterial. The vessel in both cases was a screw steamer, the only difference between the one originally proposed and the one actually built being that the latter was somewhat larger and dearer, the difference in price being £21,500 as against £20,750. That truly was a renewal of the negotiations as far as Macbeth was concerned, which ended in business between the parties.

"In these circumstances, it is contended that the brokers are entitled to a commission, on the ground that they were the persons who introduced the customer to the defenders, and that according to the usage of trade that gives them a right to claim commission. I am of opinion . . . that this claim is well founded, and on this ground, because I think the custom of trade has been clearly proved, and notwithstanding the fact that there has not been actual employment beforehand by the shipbuilder of the broker, yet if the broker brings a customer to a shipbuilder, and the shipbuilder accepts the employment, that entitles the broker to a commission. That statement of facts would be exactly applicable to the circumstances of the present case were it not for this, that the first negotiations had been broken off and then renewed. But that circumstance does not affect the broker's right to commission, for commission is due in consequence of the transaction, as if it had taken effect after the first negotiation. It is quite true that the first negotiation was of a peculiar kind, and if it had been brought to a conclusion it would have been on the footing that all claims for commission were to be waived or abandoned. But the proposal of the shipbuilder was not accepted, and it certainly cannot be assumed that such a proposal was renewed and assented to as regards the later negotiations."

LORD SHAND (at p. 374): "Two points are clear in this case: 1st, That the purchasers of the vessel were introduced by the pursuers, as brokers, to the shipbuilders; and 2nd, that the result was that the vessel for which this price has been charged was ordered. In the ordinary case it would appear that commission would in these circumstances be due to the broker.

"There has been a proof of the practice of the trade led in this case, and we well know from other cases, both here and in England, that the practice is that when the services of a broker are accepted, and business results, a commission is due. Therefore, unless there is something here to take off the effect of the custom, the pursuers are entitled to commission. There are specialties in this case, which have been advanced in argument, and are worthy of serious consideration, to the effect that brokerage is not due. I am of opinion that these circumstances are not sufficient to amount to a waiver by the brokers of their claim. . . .

"The question is whether the waiver by the broker ran on, and is to be held as applicable to the second transaction. I think not. . . . I think the waiver by the broker only applied to the negotiations at the two first meetings, when he was to get an advantage in respect of which he waived his right to commission. But there was nothing of this kind in the subsequent dealings. Then the builder took the benefit of the introduction, business resulted, and therefore giving effect to the custom of trade, which has been proved, the builder is liable for the broker's commission."

NOTES

1. The sheriff-substitute (Guthrie) said (at p. 370): "I do not think it doubtful that there is a custom on the Clyde, and, indeed, throughout the United Kingdom, to the effect alleged; but there is no uniform custom as to the amount of commission. . . . The evidence shews that the rate of commission is generally from 1 to 2 per cent, rarely 2½, and if there is any usage about 2½ per cent, it is that shipbrokers generally aim at it (naturally enough), not that they generally get it, in the absence of special agreement. In the present case, I think that commission is due; but, in the circumstances . . ., I think 1 per cent a reasonable rate."

The rate of commission was not made the subject of argument in the Inner House, and the judges there did not deal with that question.

2. In *White* v. *Munro, &c.* (1876) 3 R. 1011, a shipbroker was held not entitled to commission because, although he had introduced seller and purchaser, the sale which was ultimately effected did not result from anything done by him.

Lord Ormidale (at p. 1019): "I think the question in dispute is well raised in the first letter which the pursuer wrote to Messrs Mories, Munro, and Company. He there says that Messrs Matheson and Company of London are desirous of purchasing a spar-deck steamer, and that he has named the 'Europe' to them as likely to suit; and concludes — 'In the event of business, which I trust will result, please reserve my commission.'

"The custom applicable to such matters is that where a broker introduces a person who has a vessel to sell to one who is desirous to buy, and the introduction results in the purchase of the vessel, the broker is entitled to commission. The pursuer states the question fairly enough in the letter which I have referred to. When he speaks in that letter of the business which he trusts will result he can only mean business resulting from his introduction. That, again, raises the question of fact, whether the sale of the ship in question, the 'Europe,' resulted from the pursuer's introduction. . . .

"The pursuer's connection with the matter must, I think, be held to have terminated in October, and the subsequent negotiations in the spring of 1874 were by other parties altogether and entirely independent of him. . . . I cannot therefore hold that White's introduction in 1873 led to the sale of the vessel, or that White had anything to do with the sale which ultimately took place in 1874. . . .

3. Likewise, in *Jacobs & Co.* v. *Archibald M'Millan & Son Ltd.* (1894) 21 R. 623, shipbrokers were held not entitled to commission.

Lord Young (at p. 629): "The commission is not due to those who recommend a shipbuilder and whose recommendation is acted upon. The commission is due in law, sense, and according to the custom of trade, to the broker through whom a contract is effected. There may be a dozen brokers recommending the same shipbuilders as being likely to build a desirable vessel at a low price, but it does not follow that all these are entitled to commission. Only the one who effects the contract is entitled to it. Now, M'Millan & Son were of opinion that this contract in October was not effected by or through the instrumentality of the pursuers, from whom they had heard nothing, — with whom they had had no communication whatever since they applied for the quotation, the receipt of which they had never acknowledged in the month of August preceding. I think that that was a just conclusion on their part, and that they were entitled accordingly to give a commission which I assume to be due, — but I have not to determine that, — to Galbraith, Pembroke, & Company, through whom the contract was effected, and who had also applied for and received a similar quotation in the month of August preceding."

Lord Trayner (at p. 629): "From that date, 17th October, until the 25th October, when the contract was concluded, Galbraith, Pembroke, & Company busy themselves in the matter of the contract, and ultimately bring the parties together, and get the contract completed. In these circumstances I think it clear that the contract which was executed by M'Millan & Son was brought about through the agency of Galbraith, Pembroke, & Company, and through no other intermediary, and they are therefore . . . entitled to the commission; and that Jacobs & Company are not entitled to any commission, in respect they had no direct influence in bringing about the contract."

4. See also *Moss* v. *Cunliffe & Dunlop* (p. 76, above).

*Remuneration: whether agent has earned it: solicitor*

### Menzies, Bruce-Low, & Thomson v. M'Lennan
### (1895) 22 R. 299

A firm of brewers wrote to their law-agent: "We are willing, on your obtaining for us the price arranged for brewery, to pay you a commission of 1½ per cent, but on the distinct understanding that . . . in the event of there being no sale you are to have no account against us."

The law-agent found a purchaser, and the contract of sale was completed, but the purchaser failed to pay the price.

*Held* that the law-agent had acquired right to the commission on the completion of the contract of sale.

LORD PRESIDENT (J. P. B. ROBERTSON) (at p. 304): "This is an action to recover commission on the sale of a brewery, and the question upon which the pursuers of the action claim our judgment is whether, upon the admitted facts on record, the commission has not been earned.

"The agreement to pay commission is set forth in the defenders' letter. . . .

"Now, the pursuer found a purchaser in the person of a certain Mr Beal, and he presented to the defenders, in writing, the terms upon which Mr Beal was prepared to contract, and was proffered as purchaser. Mr Alexander M'Lennan, one of the three partners of the defenders' firm, perused the agreement, and wrote to the pursuer authorising him to sign a minute of agreement for sale of the brewery to Mr Beal, on the understanding that the price to be paid was £32,000 for everything except stock in trade and book debts. . . . The other two partners of the firm subsequently added to the letter, and signed the following docquet:—'We homologate the above letter. We also homologate the arrangement made by our senior as to commission to be paid to you on the sale.'

"Thus authorised, the pursuer proceeded to execute the minute of agreement, as did Mr Beal. The pursuer's case now is that upon this being done his commission was earned, and, in my opinion, he is right.

"The sequel of the story is this: The defenders and Mr Beal entered into a new agreement, which superseded that executed by the pursuer and Mr Beal. Under this new agreement Mr Beal deposited a part of the price. After this had been done difficulties arose with Mr Beal; the purchase was not proceeded with; and, in the end, the defenders obtained no more than the deposit, their right to which had to be asserted by law. Of course they kept the brewery.

"Now, in answer to the pursuer's demand for his commission, the defenders say two things, — first, that, on a true construction of their agreement with the pursuer, commission was not to be paid unless and until the purchase-money was in their pockets; and second, that even assuming that the commission was to be earned on the completion of a binding contract of sale, the minute executed by the pursuer and Mr Beal was not such a contract.

"1. What, then, is the sound construction of the letter of 29th May 1889? The letter says that the pursuer is to have his commission 'on your obtaining for us the price arranged for brewery,' and 'in the event of there being no sale you are to have no account against us.'

". . . Now, as soon as there was a contract between buyer and seller, there was most certainly a sale; and this being accomplished the pursuer's relation to the transaction came to an end. He had no duty to carry the matter further, and could not claim to manage for the defenders the carrying out of the transfer. *Prima facie* (I am stating not a proposition of law but of ordinary observation), a commission on a sale (whether of goods or anything else) would seem to be earned when a *bona fide* bargain is made; and it is only in special agreements, such as the agreement for a *del credere* commission, that the agent's remuneration depends on the bargain being duly implemented. Now, in the agreement before us I see nothing to shew that the event contemplated is the implement and not the execution of a contract of sale. The words 'obtaining the price' are explained by the fact that it was a particular sum which had been arranged. 'Getting' would seem to be a very close equivalent for 'obtaining,' and if the bargain with a commission-agent, or anyone else, were that he was to have 1½ per cent on getting certain specified prices for goods he would be a good deal surprised if he were refused his commission on the ground that, subsequent to the sale, the purchaser had failed to pay.

"2. The other ground upon which the defenders rely is that, in the minute of agreement executed by the pursuer and Mr Beal, there was a clause providing that Beal should make certain deposits, and that in the event of his failing before a particular date to pay the purchase-money, then the moneys deposited should be forfeited. The defenders say that this clause reduces the agreement from being a contract of purchase and sale to being a contract either to pay the purchase-money and get the brewery, or to forfeit the deposit and not get the brewery, whichever the purchaser preferred. In this, I think, the defenders are wrong. I do not think that the purchaser had any such option, and I consider that the sellers could have enforced the obligation to pay the purchase-money on tender of a disposition. In the agreement signed by the pursuer and Mr Beal there was not, as there was in the agreement which superseded it, a provision that the forfeiture of the deposited moneys should be in full satisfaction of all causes of action; and, without such a contractual exclusion, I think that an action for implement would have lain.

"There is, however, a separate and conclusive answer. When the pursuer presented Mr Beal to the defenders, he presented, at the same time, Mr Beal's terms; the minute of agreement was considered and approved by the defenders themselves; and, with direct relation to those terms, the two partners said to the pursuer, in their docquet, 'We also homologate the arrangements made by our senior as to commission to be paid to you on the sale.' After this it is, in my opinion, impossible for the defenders to maintain that the bargain with Mr Beal was not a sale."

LORD M'LAREN (at p. 306): "It is . . . consistent with the ordinary use of language that the expression 'obtaining for us the price arranged' should mean obtaining for us a contract of sale at the price arranged. When it is considered that the business of a commission-agent is to procure a contract of sale, and not necessarily to enforce the performance of the contract, and when it is further considered that according to ordinary usage a commission is earned when the contract is made, unless a *del credere* commission be specially undertaken, I agree with the Lord President that the construction which is consistent with the nature of the employment is the true construction, and that Mr Menzies' right to a commission was not made conditional on the purchaser's performance of his contract."

*Remuneration: whether agent has earned it: estate agent*

**Walker, Fraser, & Steele v. Fraser's Trustees**
1910 S.C. 222

F., the owner of the estate of Balfunning in Stirlingshire, employed W. & Co., estate agents, to sell it at a minimum price of £38,000.

In 1903 Scott applied to W. & Co. for information regarding the estate of Dalnair, and in reply W. & Co. sent particulars also of a few other estates including Balfunning. Negotiations were then broken off for a time.

In 1906 Scott applied to W. & Co. for particulars of Balfunning, and was urged by them to make an offer for it, but did not do so.

In October 1907 Scott advertised in the *Glasgow Herald* for property of the general description which he desired, and the following month received from F. a letter about Balfunning. Negotiations followed which resulted in a sale of that property to Scott at £31,000.

W. & Co. sued F. for £310 commission.

*Held* that, as W. & Co.'s exertions had to a material degree contributed to the sale to Scott, W. & Co. were entitled to the commission.

LORD DUNDAS (at p. 228): "In this case the pursuers, a well-known firm of property agents in Glasgow, sued the now deceased John Fraser, sometime proprietor of the estate of Balfunning in Stirlingshire, for £310, being commission at the rate of 1 per cent on the purchase price of that estate, which he sold to a Mr Scott in the end of the year 1907. Mr Fraser's testamentary trustees were, on 10th June 1909, duly sisted in his room and place; but, for the sake of convenience, I shall throughout allude to him as 'the defender.' There was no dispute at our bar as to the percentage claimed, if commission is payable; but the defender pleads that no commission is due, because the estate was not sold through the pursuers' 'intervention,' and that they did not render him 'any services in connection with the sale.' . . .

"Shortly put, I think the test is whether or not the ultimate sale of Balfunning was brought about, or materially contributed to, by actings of the pursuers, as authorised agents of the defender. Actual introduction of the purchaser to the seller is not a necessary element in a case of this sort; it is enough if the agents introduce the purchaser to the estate, and by their efforts contribute in a substantial degree to the sale. A careful consideration of the evidence leads me to hold that the pursuers have sufficiently complied with the test indicated. . . .

"It was through the pursuers that Mr Scott first really got into touch with this estate, and got full information and particulars about it; and that they did not effect an actual introduction between him and the defender was only due to the facts that Mr Scott did not permit them to disclose his name in any way, and that he did not choose, at the pursuers' invitation, to submit an offer. It seems to me that the facts of this case bring it well within the region in which property agents have been found entitled to a commission upon a resulting sale. I think the fair inference to be drawn by the Court, viewing the matter as a jury, from the evidence, is that the pursuers' exertions, as duly authorised agents in the matter for the defender, did to a sufficient extent contribute to the ultimate purchase of the estate by Mr Scott. We should therefore, in my judgment, give decree for the pursuers."

NOTES

1. *Cf. Gibb* v. *Bennett* (1906) 14 S.L.T. 64 (O.H.).

B. for health reasons was contemplating selling his public-house in Glasgow, but had not yet conclusively resolved to do so when G., a commission agent whom he had known personally and in business for a number of years, suggested to him that the time was then opportune to part with the public-house. B. authorised G. to get him a purchaser at £1,500, and undertook to pay him a commission of £50 in the event of his doing so.

G. soon brought on the scene a genuine intending purchaser of means, in the person of M'Cabe. Terms were adjusted, but no binding contract was made. M'Cabe found other premises which suited him better and acquired them instead.

Wallace's firm were spirit merchants with whom M'Cabe dealt, and because of M'Cabe's negotiations with B. Wallace was made aware that B. was seeking, and was now without, a purchaser for his public-house. It occurred to Wallace that the premises would suit another of his customers, and he at once took steps which resulted in Kernan buying the premises for £1,650. The meeting at which this bargain was made was attended by G. and M'Cabe as well as by B., Wallace, and Kernan.

G. brought an action against B. for £50 commission on the sale to Kernan.

*Held* that G. was entitled to the commission.

Lord Johnston (Ordinary) (at p. 66): "Was or was not, then, the sale of defender's business to Kernan a remote consequence, or was it obtained by or through the pursuer's agency? This class of question must always be one of circumstances, on which different minds may form different impressions, but I have come to the conclusion that the ultimate transaction in the present case was not a remote consequence, but was brought about by or through pursuer's agency in a sufficiently direct manner to entitle him to his commission. . . .

"The pursuer was, in my opinion, the primary or originating influence which brought about the sale, though the actual sale was not effected by him, and, accordingly, I think that he is entitled to his commission. That commission was not to be a percentage, or a *quantum meruit*, but a definite slump sum, and I shall therefore decern in his favour, as concluded for, with expenses."

2. Lord Dundas's judgment in this case was adopted by Lord Shaw of Dunfermline in *A. R. Brett & Co. Ltd.* v. *Bow's Emporium Ltd.*, 1928 S.C. (H.L.) 19.

A company carrying on business as "agents for the sale of businesses" brought an action against Bow's Emporium Ltd. for a sum representing commission which it alleged was due to it by Bow's Emporium Ltd. in connection with the purchase by Bow's Emporium Ltd. of a business in Glasgow. Bow's Emporium Ltd. denied that any commission had been earned.

*Held* by the Lord Ordinary (Morison), the First Division (*diss.* Lord Blackburn) and the House of Lords that commission had been earned.

Lord Shaw of Dunfermline (at p. 19): "The appellants' counsel seemed to maintain that no commission was due because there was not an 'introduction' of the two parties, seller and buyer, to each other. Such transactions may be conducted and concluded without any introduction, in that sense, whatsoever. Introduction is not a *vox signata*; all that is meant is that the agent shall have been the means of bringing a willing seller and a willing buyer into relations with each other in regard to a business transaction, and that a business transaction results. . . .

[After expressing doubt about the decision in *Moss* v. *Cunliffe & Dunlop* (p. 80, above)] "In Scotland, later decisions appear to me to have come exactly into line with the acknowledged law of England. I refer to *Walker, Donald, & Co.* v. *Birrell* and to *Kennedy* v. *Glass* — and in particular, to the judgment of Lord Adam in the latter case (at p. 1087), in which the common sense of the matter is put as a principle of law:—'It is a known principle that if one man uses another for the purpose and with the effect of doing business, the ordinary rule is that the person employed is entitled to some remuneration.' This was a case in which remuneration was granted to an agent who was not a professional broker. I desire, however, with your Lordships' leave, to adopt the judgment of Lord Dundas in *Walker, Fraser, & Steele* v. *Fraser's Trustees*. 'Shortly put,' says Lord Dundas, 'I think the test is whether or not . . . substantial degree to the sale.' . . .

"In my view the sum of the matter is as follows:—(1) When it is proved — and it must, of course, be proved — that parties to a transaction are brought together, not necessarily personally but in the relation of buyer and seller, through the agency of an intermediary employed for the purpose, the law simply is that, if a transaction ensues, the intermediary is entitled to his reward as such agent; (2) nor is he disentitled thereto because delays have occurred, unless the continuity between the original relation brought about by the agent and the ultimate transaction has been, not merely dislocated or postponed, but broken; and (3) finally, the introduction by one of the parties to a transaction of another agent or go-between does not deprive the original agent of his legal rights, and he cannot thus be defeated therein."

3. *Dudley Brothers & Co.* v. *Barnet*, 1937 S.C. 632, was an action of damages for breach of contract brought by an English firm of estate agents against B., a draper carrying on business in Edinburgh and other centres.

B. wished to vacate a shop in Sunderland, which had been let to him. He wrote to the estate agents stating the terms on which he was prepared to assign the lease. The estate agents stated the amount of their commission "in the event of business resulting through our efforts," and B. agreed to pay that commission.

The estate agents arranged that Hurst & Sandler Ltd. should take an assignment of the lease, and this offer was "accepted subject to contract."

When the estate agents requested B. to forward a copy of the lease to Hurst & Sandler Ltd.'s solicitors, however, B. intimated that he had received and had accepted an offer from another firm.

*Held* that an agreement had been concluded between the estate agents and B. whereby the estate agents were entitled to commission on finding a person who was willing to complete a formal contract; that it was an implied term of that agreement that B. should not prevent the estate agents from earning their commission; and that, as B. had made completion of the contract impossible, the estate agents were entitled to damages, the measure of which was the commission which they would have earned if the contract had been completed.

Lord Justice-Clerk (Aitchison) (at p. 638): "Treating the question as purely one of construction of the contract between the pursuers and the defender I think . . . that 'business resulting' just means finding a customer who was able and willing and ready to take on the terms authorised by the defender, and did not mean in the event of a sale going through to completion. In the latter sense business did not result, but that was due to the refusal of the defender to carry events to completion, and was not due to any failure of the pursuers to perform their employment, which in fact they had performed as agents of the defender.

"There is a dearth of authority in Scotland upon this topic, but some guidance is afforded by decisions in England, and particularly by the judgment of the Court of Appeal in *Trollope & Sons* v. *Martyn Brothers* ([1934] 2 K.B. 436). In that case the plaintiffs, who were estate agents, were instructed by the defendants to find a purchaser for certain property, subject to contract. It was a term of the arrangement that the defendants should pay the usual scale commission 'in the event of the sale materialising.' The plaintiffs found a purchaser who was ready and willing and able to buy the property, but the defendants declined to complete the contract. It was held by the Court of Appeal . . . that, as the defendants had without just cause refused to complete, they were liable to the plaintiffs in damages, the proper measure of which in the circumstances was the amount of commission the plaintiffs would have earned had the transaction been completed. . . .

"The case . . . falls directly within the principle of *Trollope's* case. I respectfully think, in agreement with the majority of the Court of Appeal, that the principle enunciated is sound in this class of contract, and that it is in conformity with the principles of our own law. But it is sufficient in the present case that the lease which was the subject of sale is an English lease, and that the contract fell to be completed in England according to English law and practice. The present case is in a sense *a fortiori* of *Trollope*, because the judgment in *Trollope* proceeded on the view that the agreement was to pay commission on a completed sale. In this case I think the contract may be read as meaning — on finding a willing purchaser on the terms authorised by the employer. But, even reading 'business resulting' in a more stringent sense, the case is still within the principle which was affirmed in *Trollope*."

Lord Wark (at p. 643): "I have no doubt that the principles of law enunciated by the majority of the Court of Appeal in the case of *Trollope* are also principles of the law of Scotland. I, therefore, think that the pursuers are entitled to damages; and that the measure of damages is the whole commission stipulated for in the contract."

*Trollope's* case was overruled by the House of Lords in *Luxor (Eastbourne) Ltd.* v. *Cooper* [1941] A.C. 108, a circumstance which casts doubt on the authority of *Dudley Brothers & Co.* v. *Barnet.*

*Reimbursement of outlays*

**Knight & Co. v. Stott**
(1892) 19 R. 959

K. & Co., commission-agents of Glasgow, brought an action against

Captain S. of Dumfries, averring that at Carlisle races Captain S. had instructed them to make bets on certain horses, that they had paid out for him £190.10/- on unsuccessful bets and had received £20 in respect of the only successful one. K. & Co. sued for the difference of £170.10/-.

Captain S. pleaded that the alleged transactions, being *sponsiones ludicrae*, were null and void.

*Held* that this plea was ill founded.

LORD PRESIDENT (J. P. B. ROBERTSON) (at p. 962): "We have to deal with the question whether the action is not open to the objection that its subject-matter is *sponsio ludicra.* I think this plea is ill founded.

"The pursuers seek reimbursement of moneys expended by them on the instructions of the defender. They say that on his instructions they engaged to pay, and did pay, certain sums to certain persons in the event which happened, of certain horses not winning at Carlisle Races. They do not ask us to try the question which horse won in the races in question; the plea would then have application."

NOTE

*Cf. Auchie & Co.* v. *Burns* (1822) 1 S. 538.

In 1814, B. consigned a parcel of Alover shawls, invoiced from 90/- to 78/- per dozen, to Dollar, Auchie and Company, at Jamaica, a branch of A. & Co.

"A great part remained unsold for five years, of which notice was regularly given, and instructions requested as to the disposal of them; but no answer was returned."

In 1819, A. & Co. wrote to B., claiming a balance of £115.2.6d as due to them and promising to give B. an order on Dollar, Auchie and Company to deliver the goods still in their hands. No answer was made, and A. & Co. then sold the shawls at 19/9½ per dozen, and raised an action against B. for the balance still due.

*Held* that A. & Co. had been entitled, "for their own indemnification," to dispose of the goods at whatever sum they would bring, and that, since the goods had been kept for so long unsaleable in Jamaica, the price at which they were sold, so far below the invoice price, afforded no presumption of improper conduct on the part of A. & Co.

*Reimbursement of expenses properly incurred*

**Drummond v. Cairns**
(1852) 14 D. 611

D. instructed C., a stockbroker in Glasgow, to purchase 100 shares of the East India Railway Company. The price was 20/6d per share, and the settling day was 28th May.

C. duly intimated the transaction to D., but when the settling day arrived D. was not prepared to pay the price.

On 10th June C. sold the shares at 9/4d each.

*Held* that D. was liable to reimburse C. for the difference between the two prices.

LORD CUNINGHAME (at p. 614): "This is the clearest case possible, whether it is viewed as between broker and broker, according to the rules of the Stock Exchange, or at common law, as between merchant and merchant."

LORD IVORY (at p. 614): "The defender employed the pursuer to purchase certain shares for him. He knew the settling day, and it was announced to him; and he knew that if the shares were not paid for on that day, his broker would be answerable. The broker's safety depends upon the rapidity of the transaction, and if the principal does not come forward at the proper time, the broker has been over and over again authorised by the decisions of the Courts, both in this country and in England, to make the best of the transaction by selling out against the principal. That is the proved usage of the Stock Exchange; and in a climate so variable, it would be ruinous to any person in his position, if he had to abide a litigation as to his right to dispose of shares purchased by him. The broker is not bound to make advances for his constituent, and he is therefore entitled to sell at the risk of the party dealing with him. That is the whole extent to which I carry the principle. As to buyer and seller, or in transactions regarding heritage, the principle has no application.

"If a commission agent advances money on goods, and cannot sell within the limits specified, he may sell the property placed in his hands, unless the advance is paid, without applying to the Judges Ordinary. Universal usage allows him to protect himself in that way, under the implied condition that he does not sell below the market price. The position of a broker is infinitely more favourable than that of an ordinary commercial agent."

NOTE

Expenses incurred by an agent in defending himself, even successfully, against charges of unlawful transactions in the course of the agency are not recoverable from the principal: *Tomlinson* v. *Liquidators of Scottish Amalgamated Silks Ltd.*, 1935 S.C. (H.L.) 1; 1934 S.C. 85.

The articles of S. Ltd. provided for the indemnification of any director against all costs, losses and expenses which he might incur by reason of any act done by him as director.

S. Ltd. went into voluntary liquidation, and T., who had been a promoter and director, was tried for alleged fraud, the charges being that he had issued a fraudulent prospectus and had fraudulently misapplied funds of the company.

T. was acquitted, and thereupon lodged a claim in the liquidation for the expenses, amounting to £11,524.13.2d, incurred by him in his defence.

The liquidators rejected T.'s claim, and T. appealed to the court.

*Held* that T. was not entitled to his expenses either under the indemnity clause in the articles or at common law, since expenses incurred in defending himself against an allegation that he did something, which he did not in fact do and which it was not his duty to do, were not expenses incurred by him as a director or as an agent of the company in the discharge of his duties.

Lord Tomlin (at p. 6): "Here the allegation against the agent was that he had done something which he did not in fact do, and which it would have been against his duty to have done; and the question really is, upon the construction of the article, whether the expenses incurred by him by reason of an allegation that he did something which he did not do, and which it was not his duty to do, are expenses incurred by him by reason of an act done by him as a director in discharge of his duty. Upon the true construction of that article I am unable to see how that can possibly be maintained. In my view the expenses incurred by reason of the allegations made against the deceased, being allegations of matters which would have been a breach of his duty and which were held to be disproved or non-proven, are not expenses incurred by him by reason of an act done by him as a director in the discharge of his duties.

"If the case does not fall, as I think it should not fall, within the language of article 160 of the articles of association, it is difficult to see upon what principle it can possibly be brought within the common law rule. My conclusion is that this appeal fails."

Lord President (Clyde) (at p. 88): "The claim is founded on the indemnity clause (article 160) in the company's articles of association. . . . Alternatively, the claim is presented under the general right of an agent at common law to be indemnified by the principal against expenses and losses incurred in the discharge of the agency. . . .

"I am unable to read article 160 . . . as conferring on a director any indemnity so high as this. . . . It clearly covers any expense incurred for the purpose of carrying out the duty of the director, as such. Expense of that kind is a proximate consequence of the execution of the duty. But I do not think the article can be fairly read so as to include a consequence so remote as the incurring of expense in successfully resisting a public prosecution brought against the director personally on the ground of fraud alleged to have been committed by him on the public, or on the ground that he had misappropriated the shareholders' money, notwithstanding that the acts done by him were done in his capacity as a director.

"The same distinction between proximate and remote losses or expenses applies in the sphere of principal and agent — which is the alternative category within which the claimant seeks to bring himself. . . . No doubt . . . it is a question of fact and circumstance whether a defence against proceedings, civil or criminal, is the proximate, or the remote, consequence of the execution of an agent's mandate. But I cannot find in the facts of the present case any circumstances . . . which could bring the public prosecution against the claimant within the description of a proximate consequence of the execution of his duties as agent of the company."

Lord Sands (at p. 90): "The appellant relies upon two arguments in support of his claim — (1) common law, and (2) the indemnity clause in the articles of the company. I take common law first. An agent or a servant is, apart from any special stipulation, entitled to be indemnified by his principal or employer for all expense which he may incur in lawfully carrying out the duties entrusted to him. But he has no claim for indemnity against casual personal misfortunes which may overtake him in doing so. Injury by accident affords an illustration. . . . At common law there is no liability. . . . I am accordingly of opinion that the claim at common law fails.

"The appellant founds also and specially upon an indemnity in article 160. . . . In my view the expense of defence against a criminal prosecution is too remote to fall under this indemnity. . . . A criminal prosecution appears to me to be of the nature of a misfortune which must rest where it lights."

*Relief from liability incurred to third parties in proper execution of agency*

**Stevenson v. Duncan**
(1842) 5 D. 167

D. instructed stockbrokers to sell 20 shares of the London, Leith, Edinburgh, and Glasgow Shipping Company on his behalf. D. did not in fact hold such shares.

The stockbrokers purported to sell the shares to Cullen.

In an action brought by Cullen against the stockbrokers, Cullen was found entitled to £83 damages. The stockbrokers raised an action of relief against D.

*Held* that D. was bound to relieve them.

LORD MACKENZIE (at p. 169): "They [D.'s agents] employed the Stevensons to sell the stock, and the Stevensons sold it to Cullen. But they could not make good the conveyance in respect that the title to the stock was not in Duncan. Cullen brings his action of damages against the Stevensons, and they bring their action of relief. That claim of relief was good from the beginning. . . . Suppose I employ a dealer to sell a horse to a third party, and he does so. The purchaser claims implement of the bargain; it ultimately turns out that I am not the owner of the horse, and on that account the dealer cannot implement the bargain, and is found liable in damages. Can there be a doubt that I would be bound to relieve him? But the present is just a parallel case. The Stevensons were found liable in damages solely for acting on the defender's instructions."

NOTES

1. *Cf. Mackenzie* v. *Blakeney* (1879) 6 R. 1329.

B., a draper in Dundee, employed M., stockbroker there, to sell on the London Stock Exchange some Australian bank shares, the certificates for which B. exhibited to M. but did not leave in M.'s hands. The shares stood on the "Colonial register," whereas, as B. knew, it was only shares standing on the "London register" that could be sold on the London Stock Exchange.

M. had merely glanced at the certificates to see the number of shares represented. An inspection of the certificates would have shown that the shares were on the Colonial register, but M. did not become aware that the shares were on the Colonial register until the sale had been effected.

In accordance with the rules of the Stock Exchange, M. had to buy in, after the price had risen, London registered shares for delivery to the purchaser.

M. then sued B. for the difference in price and for his commission.

*Held* that M. was entitled to recover from B.

Lord Gifford (at p. 1333): "The question is one between stockbroker and employer; it is a claim by the broker to be relieved of liability incurred by fulfilling his instructions. It is an action of the class termed *actio contraria mandati* in the civil law. The question is, Did the defender authorise and instruct the pursuer to write the letters which he wrote to his London correspondents, ordering the sale of these shares? If he did, he is bound to relieve the pursuer of the obligation which he came under. I think that the pursuer was authorised to write these letters. True, if he had been very cautious he might have taken copies of the certificates and forwarded them to London, but I do not think that the defender can complain of the pursuer not having taken this precaution. The defender knew the difficulty and did not disclose it; why, it is impossible to say. The fault of the stockbroker in not sending copies of the certificates was, if fault at all, *culpa levissima*, whereas the defender's omission to disclose what he knew was *culpa lata*, and I think that in these circumstances the pursuer is entitled to throw the loss on the defender."

2. *Glassford &c.* v. *Brown &c.* (1830) 9 S. 105 was a case in which an agent had undertaken personal liability to the third party, and was held entitled to full relief in respect of that liability against his principals.

Mr and Mrs Morrison, described as "persons in an inferior condition," unexpectedly succeeded, at a somewhat advanced period of life, to a fortune of about £20,000 on the death of a son who had returned from India.

For correspondence and for the management of their financial affairs the

Morrisons obtained the assistance of B., a farmer in their neighbourhood.

B. arranged to invest £10,000 of the Morrisons' money by lending it on heritable security to G.

At first the Morrisons agreed to this loan, but later, after the terms had been settled and the deeds had been prepared, they became convinced that the sum lent would be totally lost and they refused to complete the transaction.

B. in a letter of explanation and apology to those who had been acting for G. stated: "At all events, I shall see you paid the expense incurred."

*Held* that G. was entitled to decree for the expenses against B., and that B. was entitled to full relief against the Morrisons.

Lord Glenlee (at p. 109): "What Brown founds on is — not that he had a direct mandate or authority to lend this money; but what he says is, I was in that general situation or management of your affairs that warranted my proposing you lend it; and you knew what I was about, and you never expressly prohibited me from proceeding. He goes on proposing a particular measure, and they do not stop him, but allow him to go on, reserving to themselves to determine if they shall ultimately complete it. It is plain they should be liable for any loss sustained by him."

Lord Cringletie (at p. 109): "This appears to me the simplest case possible, though the parties have managed to make it abominably complicated. Mr and Mrs Morrison admit communications with Brown on the subject of the loan, but they say they never gave direct authority to make it; and when the deeds are prepared, and the expense incurred, they are rendered useless by the refusal to lend. Brown gives a direct obligation to pay the expenses incurred; and what had Glassford to do, but to raise his action on that document? He, however, brings an action against him and Mr and Mrs Morrison, conjointly and severally; and she says she gave no authority, though it is clear she authorized him to commence the transaction. It is also clear Brown acted *factorio nomine*; and, but for his letter, Glassford could only have brought this action against Mrs Morrison; and if he insists on decree against her, I think he should have it. As to the question of relief, I have no doubt the interlocutor is right. There is sufficient confessed to establish that the Morrisons authorized Brown to act; and though they did not give an express mandate to lend the money, they gave him reason to believe that it would be advanced, and allowed him to carry on the negotiation on that footing; and therefore I am for adhering."

Lord Meadowbank (at p. 110): "There certainly can be no difficulty in finding Mrs Morrison liable in relief."

3. In *Robinson, &c.* v. *Middleton* (1859) 21 D. 1089, an agent who had not acted properly in the execution of his agency was held not entitled to relief.

M., a wood-merchant in Strathmiglo, engaged R., an agent in London, to effect a sale of wood.

R. sold the wood to Perry, who was acting for a firm in Melbourne, Australia. Perry arranged with R. that he (Perry) should incur no liability. This arrangement was not communicated to M.

The price took the form of a bill of exchange drawn by Perry upon the

Melbourne firm. The bill was discounted in London, and the proceeds were paid to M.

When the cargo reached Melbourne, the drawees were insolvent, and the bank which had discounted the bill sold the cargo.

The proceeds were insufficient to cover the bill, and R. paid the balance, £1,043.4.7d, to the bank.

R. then brought an action against M. for that amount.

*Held* that as R. had, without M.'s knowledge or consent, transacted with Perry so as to release him from his liability as drawer of the bill, R. was not entitled to recover from M.

Lord President (M'Neill) (at p. 1097): "It appears to me that this transaction is not the one that the pursuers intimated to the defender that they had made on his behoof. They did not give him payment in the way that they had told him they would do. They have not given him that available bill on which he was entitled to rely, in respect of having parted with his cargo. I do not go into the question of liability of an agent for a foreign purchaser, on whose purchase for behoof of the foreign house the proprietor of the goods has parted with his property, but who has not put his name on the bill drawn for the price. But when he has so put his name on the bill, and nothing special is communicated to the owner of the goods in regard to it, the owner of the goods is entitled to rely on that credit. The agent is bound to disclose at the time of the transaction what the position of matters truly is; and if he states merely that he has sold the goods on receiving an order by A B, the purchaser, on C D, that necessarily implies the liability of A B."

Lord Deas (at p. 1098): "We are dealing with the case on the footing of its being admitted that the pursuers expressly agreed with Francis Perry that he was not to incur liability by putting his name on that bill. . . . When Perry put his name on the bill, and the proceeds were remitted to the defender, the latter was entitled to rely that, whatever might have been Perry's liability otherwise, this was put beyond question by his signature and indorsation of the bill. If the pursuers, by a private compact with Perry, released him from liability, they must themselves be answerable. That they did release Perry they admit; and it is upon this footing, coupled with the absence of all pretence, that the defender either knew or approved of what they had thus done, that our judgment, as I understand it, now proceeds."

### *Retention and lien: factor*

**Sibbald v. Gibson**
(1852) 15 D. 217

S., corn factor, Leith, employed Gibson & Clark, corn merchants in Glasgow, for several transactions during the years 1850-1.

In December 1850 S. instructed Gibson & Clark to purchase for him a large quantity of Irish oats. The oats were placed in store by Gibson & Clark, and subsequently sold in small parcels by S., Gibson

& Clark forwarding them to different parts of the country according to S.'s orders. There was disagreement as to the rate of commission due to Gibson & Clark in respect of these transactions, Gibson & Clark claiming four per cent and S. maintaining that it should not be more than one and a half per cent.

In September 1851 S. forwarded to Gibson & Clark a quantity of beans, his property, for sale. The rate of commission in respect of the beans was agreed as three per cent. Having sold the beans, Gibson & Clark transmitted £72.16/- as the net proceeds to S. Their account showed that in doing so they had taken credit for £56.4.3d as three per cent commission on the oats.

S. refused to allow this charge, and brought an action against Gibson & Clark for the balance of the price of the beans.

*Held* that Gibson & Clark were entitled to retain their commission on the oats from the proceeds of sale of the beans.

LORD JUSTICE-CLERK (HOPE) (at p. 220): "The point raised by this reclaiming note is of very great general importance, and it is very material that the judgment should be placed on a clear, as well as a sound ground.

"The plea of the defenders is founded on an alleged right of retention, and that right of retention is said to arise out of their employment by the pursuer as factors for him in the purchase and sale of goods. It is not a right of retention founded on general grounds, but is said to be that which is competent to a factor as to goods or money coming into his possession in his character of factor. . . . I have expressed my great regret, that while we have in our law certain very broad and general principles applicable to retention, parties, and sometimes judicial opinions, have resorted to English law, and attempted to import rules and distinctions derived, or said to be derived (for we can have no certainty as to such deduction), from their law of lien, which in many important particulars, arising out of differences between the laws of the two countries as to the contracts of sale and location, has little analogy to our law of retention.

"Retention is a most valuable principle in the law of Scotland, and is of plain and easy application, and most useful and equitable in operation.

"The principle is well explained by Erskine. . . .

"In his *Principles*, Bell has an important passage, which is of importance in reference to this case. . . . That the debt is illiquid, therefore, is in itself no answer to the plea of a right of retention. . . .

"Then, if the right of retention arises out of transactions falling

H

under a certain employment, or relation in which the parties, or one of them, stand to each other, the character of such employment, while it renders in certain circumstances the right of retention absolute, may yet regulate and limit the extent of retention, and the exact circumstances in which it is competent. Between two merchants engaged in general mercantile dealings with each other, in which claims arise *hinc inde*, the right is as general as their dealings. If, again, one is employed as factor, and his alleged right or counter claim, for which he claims retention, arises out of that character, he must be able to shew that the monies over which he claims the right, *come into his hands in that character*, and he shall not be allowed to bring forward a claim, arising out of such employment, against goods, or the price thereof, coming accidentally into his hands in another way, or without previous consent of his principal — at least that is the general rule. . . . Mr Bell . . . in . . . sect. 1448 . . . says expressly, that the factor's right of retention applies distinctly to a claim for commission. . . .

"When a balance, no matter, as Mr Bell says, from what cause, remains due to the factor, though, in full reliance on the consigner, he may have remitted the whole price of his last sales, the right of retention for that balance attaches to all goods, or monies from the sale of goods, coming into his hands as factor: '*Coming into* his hands as factor,' — of course that means, after the balance claimable by the factor has arisen, and after the goods in respect of which the balance is claimed have passed, or the price of them, out of his hands. . . .

"On the large transaction as to the oats, a commission was due. That is admitted. It is not pretended that the claim for commission was abandoned or waived. It is admitted that it continued good and effectual as an unsettled item or balance on the accounts of factor and consigner, although there was a dispute as to the amount of commission legally claimable. . . .

"The right of retention . . . has no analogy to a special lien on the goods of another, for labour and skill, or outlay on these particular goods. If the factor's right were to be so considered, a general right of retention for any former transaction against goods coming into his possession, he never could have, if he has remitted the whole price of that sale — and yet the right is given really in order to apply to, and enforce the claim against, other goods subsequently coming into the factor's hands."

LORD COCKBURN (at p. 223): "The whole case is settled when we get possession of the legal rule; — that is, that a factor has a right of retention not only on each individual transaction, but that he is entitled to retain on subsequent consignments, in payment of prior unsettled transactions. . . . The retention of a factor covers his right to commission, not only in the goods in his hands, but on prior consignments, unless some special agreement can be shewn as to the way in which he was to account for the goods, which would have the effect of preventing his retaining his commission, or the two transactions were separated by such a distance in point of time as to show an abandonment of it."

LORD MURRAY (at p. 223): "It is a clear rule, that where a party acts as factor for a commercial house, he has a right of retention for his balance, over what comes into his hands in that capacity. This has been the case since Lord Stair's time, and I should be sorry to throw any doubt upon it."

LORD WOOD (at p. 224): "The fact to be looked to is, that the factor parts with the goods in his possession, in reliance on his right of retention over any balance that may remain in his hands. There is nothing to take the case out of the ordinary rules as to a factor's retention."

NOTE

*Cf. Gairdner* v. *Milne and Co.* (1858) 20 D. 565.

Currie & Co., grain merchants and millers in Glasgow, employed M. & Co., also grain merchants in Glasgow, to purchase grain on commission. The course of dealing was that M. & Co. paid the price to the sellers, and drew bills of exchange on Currie and Co. for the price plus commission and charges.

The last of several transactions was a purchase of wheat from Boston, in Lincolnshire, to be shipped to Glasgow on board the "London". M. & Co. insured the wheat in their own name through an insurance-broker for £1,500, and the policy remained in the hands of the broker.

Currie & Co. accepted a bill of exchange for the price plus commission and charges, and M. & Co. endorsed the bill of lading to Currie & Co.

The "London" with its cargo was lost at sea. Currie & Co. became bankrupt. M. & Co. received payment of the £1,500 in the policy.

M. & Co. held bills of exchange to the amount of £14,198 accepted by Currie & Co. in respect of transactions during the three previous months.

M. & Co. claimed a lien over the proceeds of the policy for the general balance due to them as factors.

*Held* that (1) the transactions, though for purchases, not for sales, were proper factorial transactions; (2) the possession of the policy by the broker was possession for the factors; (3) the factors were entitled to a lien over whatever property of their principals was in their possession in security of any general balance due on factorial transactions; and (4) the right of lien had not been waived by the making over of the bill of lading to the principals.

Lord Cowan (at p. 570): "There are *three* things which the defenders must establish to support their right of lien, — (1), that they stood, as regards their connection with Currie and Company, on whose sequestrated estate the pursuer is trustee, in the relation of factors, and entitled as such to a right of general lien over the property of their principals; (2), that the policy of insurance in question, with the consequent right to claim the sum insured from the underwriters, was under their control and in their possession, so as to be subject to their right of lien; and (3), that there is a general balance due to them as factors by their principals, to secure which the lien may be pleaded. . . .

"1. The first point is, whether the parties occupied the relative position of principal and factor to give rise to the lien claimed by the defenders.

"I do not think this can be reasonably disputed. An agent or factor is a person authorised to do some act or acts in the name of another, who is called his principal or constituent; and mercantile agents or factors are employed in sales or purchases, — their duties or responsibilities depending upon the nature of their employment, and of the instructions transmitted to them by their employers. I see no reason in principle or authority for holding the right of lien to belong merely to agents or factors for the sale of commodities, and not to those employed to effect purchases. . . .

"No doubt the more general case is that of lien claimed by a factor holding the property of his principal for sale or on consignment; but every reason that can be stated in support of the general lien possessed by such factor applies with equal force to factors employed to purchase goods for their principal, and undertaking obligations in carrying out their agency. The property of the principal coming into their possession legitimately in the course of their employment must be subject to the right of lien for the general balance due to them on their factorial accounts.

"And this being so, it seems to me impossible to dispute that, in the admitted statements on the record, the defenders did act as the agents and factors of Currie and Company in effecting purchases for them on commission, and that the particular transaction which gave rise to the insurance in question was entered into by the defenders in course of that employment. . . .

"2. The next inquiry is whether the policy of insurance was in the possession of the defenders, so as to be available to them under their lien as factors.

". . . The argument has been taken entirely on the footing stated at the outset, viz. whether the policy of insurance, holding it to be still in the hands of the broker, is to be held under the control and in the possession of the defenders, so as to give them right to the sums exigible from the underwriters in respect of the loss, to the effect of bringing the amount within the operation and scope of their general lien.

"The insurance was effected in name of the defenders, and it is not to be doubted, under the authority of the cases referred to in the argument, . . . that the possession of the broker who effected the insurance was, apart from specialties, possession for behoof of the defenders, by whom the insurance was ordered on account of their principals, Currie and Company. Is there, then, in the facts relied on by the pursuer, relevant ground for disturbing this view as to the possession of the policy being with the defenders?

"The bill of lading for the goods which were the subject of the insurance was indorsed by the defenders to their principals, and a bill was drawn for the amount of the goods upon the principals, the proceeds of which, when discounted, the defenders admit to have been received by them. But these facts can afford no answer to the plea of general lien. Had the bill of lading gone into the hands of an onerous third party, with a transference of the right, express or implied, to the policy of insurance opened on the goods, there might have been room for contending that the right to the policy was a mere sequence of the right to the goods, and that the defenders could not have asserted their right of lien against such onerous third parties. There is no case of that kind here. The question arises with the principals themselves and the trustee on their sequestrated estate. The factors, therefore, must be entitled to hold this part of the property of their constituents, which is legally in their possession through the insurance broker, subject to their lien for their general factorial balance.

"But then it is contended by the pursuer, and is made the subject of averment in the record, that the underwriters could not be called upon to pay for the loss by a party merely holding the policy of insurance unless he was holder also of the bill of lading for the goods insured. It is obvious that this proposition is not an averment in fact to be the subject of proof, but is matter of law for the Court. The question is, whether the indorsation of the bill of lading by the factor to his principal deprives the former of his lien over the policy of insurance still in the hands of the broker, and through him legally in possession of the factor? I do not think this can be maintained. The underwriters are liable to pay only under the policy of insurance. That is the written constitution of the debt against them upon the occurrence of loss. As in a question between factor and principal, — no onerous third party being interested, — the transfer of the bill of lading to the principal gives no right to the policy of insurance, unless the general balance due to the factor in whose possession it is be provided for. The insurance is to be recovered under the policy by the factor in whose name it stands, for behoof, no doubt, of his principals, the holders of the bill of lading, but all whose effects, and the amount recoverable under this policy *inter alia*, in possession of the factors, are subject to their general lien. The mere possession of the bill of lading, therefore, by the pursuers can be of no avail in obviating this right of the factor.

"3. The remaining question is, whether a general balance is due to the defenders, in security of which they are entitled to plead the right of lien?

"As the state of the account between the parties is matter of dispute in the record, it may be necessary, as proposed, that there be inquiry under a remit from the Court, but the remit need not prevent a judgment now sustaining the claim of lien for whatever balance, if any, may ultimately be found due to the defenders as factors."

*Retention and lien: auctioneer*

**Miller v. Hutcheson & Dixon**
(1881) 8 R. 489

H. & D., a firm of auctioneers in Glasgow, received horses from Neilleay, horse-dealer, Beith, to sell on commission. H. & D. kept the horses in their stables until the date of the sale and made advances against them to Neilleay.

There had been a previous course of dealing between H. & D. and Neilleay, on which a balance had arisen in favour of H. & D.

Neilleay became bankrupt.

*Held* that H. & D. were entitled to a lien over the horses in their stables for the general balance due to them on all their transactions with Neilleay.

LORD JUSTICE-CLERK (MONCREIFF) (at p. 491): "The real question is, whether these stable keepers have a lien for a general balance due to them over the horses consigned to them for sale? Over moveables, putting aside hypothec, no security can be constituted without possession. But possession there was here beyond question. Again, a security may be constituted with possession by contract over the goods of a person who is a party to the contract. Thirdly, lien is presumed in certain commercial relations without any express contract. In my apprehension the question for decision here is, whether these stable-keepers are within any of the categories known to law in which a lien can be constituted in their favour? and I think that they are, because they are in the position of a factor selling the goods of a principal for him, and claiming a lien for a general balance, and a factor is entitled to retain goods coming in ordinary course of dealing into his hands until a general balance due to him be paid. If, then, the defenders here are ordinary commercial agents, there is no doubt. But it is said that they are only auctioneers . . . and that . . . they are not general commercial agents, and therefore not entitled to any general lien. Now . . . I do not know what an auctioneer is if he be not a commercial agent. Goods are sent to him that he may turn them into money by public sale, and he may, if he chooses, advance money on the goods consigned to him. These defenders made advances on the horses consigned to them, sold the horses, and retained so much as would pay the balance due them, or when they had other horses in hand they said, 'We have a lien on these horses until the balance due us is discharged.' I do not see how they were in any different position from commercial agents in this sense. I do not see how this conclusion can be, as has been contended, any extension of the law of lien, and in my humble opinion these defenders are just in the position of factors having a general lien. . . .

"I am therefore of opinion that the defenders were commercial agents, and entitled to retain for a general balance horses consigned to them."

LORD YOUNG (at p. 492): "Lien is just a contract of pledge collateral to another contract of which it is an incident. If the principal contract be about a horse — that it is to be fed and kept by one man for another, — to that contract there is the incident called lien — that is, an agreement that the person to whom the possession of the horse is committed shall have right to retain the possession till his claim for the food and attention given to the horse shall be satisfied. That is a special lien, and it stands like general lien . . . upon contract, express or implied. The law always, in the absence of evidence of an agreement to the contrary, assumes that the owner of the horse shall not reclaim possession till he has satisfied the claim of the other party for what he has done under the contract.

"There is also general lien, which is this, that a factor possessing goods, having that possession as a lawful contract, may retain that possession until the general balance due to him by the owner of the goods is satisfied. Such a lien may in any case be constituted by contract. It stands on contract. The contract may be expressed, or it may be implied from the course of dealing of the parties, or from the usage of trade. . . .

"People can contract as to liens as they please, and these stable keepers can refuse to take in horses except on such terms as they choose, and can . . . contract that there shall be a general lien over the goods entrusted to them for the balance owing to them at the time. . . .

"In this case I am of opinion that the proof shews that while reasonable advances were to be made by the auctioneers the horses which might be in the stables were not to be removed by Neilleay without leave from the auctioneers. I therefore agree that there was a general lien."

NOTE

See also *Mackenzie* v. *Cormack* (p. 128, below).

*Retention and lien: stockbroker*

**Glendinning v. Hope & Co.**
1911 S.C. (H.L.) 73

See p. 20, above.

*Retention and lien: solicitor*

**Paul v. Meikle**
(1868) 7 M. 235

Mrs Duncan by her will conveyed heritable property in Linlithgow to her son. The will had been prepared by Mrs Duncan's solicitor, M., who had been her legal adviser for many years and to whom Mrs Duncan was indebted to the extent of £35.10.2d for professional services.

On Mrs Duncan's death, her son conveyed the property to P. by disposition containing the usual assignation of writs clause.

M.'s representatives claimed that they were entitled to retain Mrs Duncan's will until the business acount was paid.

P. brought an action against M.'s representatives for exhibition and delivery of the will.

*Held* that M.'s representatives were entitled to retain the will.

LORD DEAS (at p. 237): "There are two questions in this case — the first is, whether there is a subsisting account? . . .

"It seems to me . . . impossible to hold that there is no existing debt.

"The second question is, whether there is a hypothec in security of the debt?

"It appears that the late Mr Meikle was agent for Mrs Duncan, and that he prepared, by her instructions, the deed of which exhibition and delivery is sought to be enforced by this action. The deed was executed, and was returned to Mr Meikle to have the testing-clause completed, and it thereafter remained in his custody. This account was in course of being incurred at the time, and his representatives maintain that the deed was hypothecated to him in security of that account. . . .

"Mrs Duncan might undoubtedly have executed another deed superseding this one which was in her agent's possession, but that deed, I think, he was clearly entitled to retain, *quantum valeat*, against all the world, until he got payment of his account.

". . . The question is as to the real right of hypothec, and not as to personal liability for the debt. . . . I cannot agree with the Lord Ordinary that James Goodlet Duncan would have been entitled to get the deed delivered to him without paying the account. It happens not unfrequently that even an onerous purchaser, when he goes to pay the price of the subjects purchased by him, and to get delivery of the titles, finds that these or some of them are hypothecated for a debt due to a law-agent by the seller or his predecessors, and it has never been questioned that the agent's account must be paid before he can be compelled to part with the title-deeds. The seller will be personally responsible for the consequences of not being able to deliver these title-deeds to the purchaser, but so far as the law-agent is concerned, it is just the necessity for getting them out of his hands which constitutes the value of his hypothec over them. I am therefore of opinion that this interlocutor must be altered."

NOTES

1. The early case which is regarded as having established the solicitor's right is *Ranking of Hamilton of Provenhall's Creditors* (1781) Mor. 6253, in which the "hypothec" of Wilson, a writer to the signet, on the papers of a bankrupt was found to be preferable to another creditor's infeftment on the bankrupt's lands, although the infeftment was prior in date to the writer's account; by the law of Scotland, title-deeds or other writings in the custody of an agent were held to be pledged in security of his account.

2. See also *Macrae* v. *Leith* (p. 18, above).

3. In *Christie* v. *Ruxton* (1862) 24 D. 1182, the solicitor's right was held not to give him security for cash advances made to his client, as distinct from the business account due by his client.

4. In *Liquidator of Grand Empire Theatres Ltd.* v. *Snodgrass*, 1932 S.C. (H.L.) 73, the House of Lords held that a solicitor's lien did not extend to accounts incurred by the solicitor on his client's behalf to English solicitors and auctioneers, at least where the solicitor had not paid the accounts or become personally liable to pay them.

S. had acted as solicitor to G. Ltd., which went into liquidation. One of the transactions undertaken by S. had been an attempted sale by auction of one of the three English theatres owned by G. Ltd. In that connection S. had engaged Carlisle solicitors who in turn had used the services of English auctioneers. The property failed to find a purchaser.

On liquidation there were no assets available for the ordinary creditors. G. Ltd.'s title-deeds were in S.'s possession, and S. claimed a lien on them for his own account of £42 (which was admitted), the Carlisle solicitors' account of £31 and the auctioneers' account of £65.

Lord Macmillan (at p. 17): "In my opinion the lien of a law agent does not extend to accounts incurred on behalf of his client which he has not in fact paid and for which he is not personally liable. To hold otherwise would, in the result, be to confer a preference, not on the law agent, but on the persons to whom such accounts had been incurred, and to give protection to those persons and not to the law agent."

5. Accountants are contrasted with solicitors in that they do not have a general lien, though in appropriate circumstances they have the normal, *i.e.*, a special, lien.

*Meikle & Wilson* v. *Pollard* (1880) 8 R. 69:—Smith, a merchant in Kirkliston, employed M. & W., accountants and business agents in Edinburgh, to recover debts for him. For this purpose books and documents belonging to Smith were delivered to M. & W.

M. & W.'s account for the work which they performed amounted to £16.1.10d.

Smith became bankrupt, and his trustee, P., applied to M. & W. for delivery of the books and documents. M. & W. refused to deliver them until their account was paid.

*Held* that they were entitled to do so.

Lord Justice-Clerk (Moncreiff) (at p. 70): "It is certainly not a question of a law-agent's lien. The real question is whether, when documents or any other article are put into the hands of a professional man to enable him to do any particular piece of business, he is bound to part with those documents or other articles until he is paid for having done the work, and that in a question with the person who employed him. . . . These circumstances do not raise the general question of lien, but the general case of counter obligations under a contract, and on that consideration I am of opinion that there is no necessity for the man to give up the documents till the other party has performed his obligation under the contract."

Lord Gifford (at p. 71): "If I thought that by this decision we were extending directly or indirectly the legal right of law-agents and others, or extending the number of old liens, I should require more argument and further consideration before I took part in it. But I agree that this is not a case of lien. It is simply a case of the retention of a subject put into a person's hands for a special purpose, and resolves itself into a case of the relative duties of parties under a contract. The one party to it is bound to perform his part of the contract just as much as the other. The counterpart here of the duty of the one party to do the piece of business is that the other shall pay the price, and I think that until the latter is done the party employed need not hand over articles which were put into his hands to enable him to fulfil his part of the contract. The effect of this judgment is not to extend general lien."

Lord Young (at p. 71): "There is certainly here no case of general lien. If it is a lien at all it is a special one. All liens arise primarily from contract, and the name is not an inconvenient one to express the right of certain parties to keep articles belonging to a person with whom they have contracted, until he has fulfilled his part of the contract.

". . . All the people who carry on lawful businesses under which the property of others comes into their possession are . . . entitled to retain possession of that property until the true proprietor performs his part of the contract. That is just the case here. These accountants were employed by a baker to do something which he thought would be useful to him. To that end his business books were handed over to them to enable them to collect the debts, and in the course of this employment the baker incurred debts to these accountants to the amount of £16. . . . On no exceptional rule, but on the ordinary rule of law, I think that these persons are not bound to part with these documents which came to them under a contract until their claim under the same contract is satisfied. There is a counterpart in every contract, and here it is that the man of business is not entitled to get his money until he gives up the books, and his employer is not entitled to get his books till he pays the money. These are obligations *hinc inde* prestable by both parties."

This case was followed in *Robertson* v. *Ross* (1887) 15 R. 67, in relation to a bank-agent in Dingwall who had acted as factor for a landed proprietor and who had in that capacity obtained possession of documents relating to the estate.

Lord Justice-Clerk (Moncreiff) (at p. 70): "This is not a case of hypothec in the true and strict sense of the word, but is a right of retention arising out of mutual obligations under a contract. We had occasion to consider the question in an almost precisely parallel case, viz., *Meikle & Wilson* v. *Pollard*. . . . We were there very clearly of opinion that the accountant's right to retain the papers was not a right of lien, but a right of retention rising out of the conditions of the contract, one of which was, that the accountant was bound to restore the documents when the employment came to an end, but was not bound to do so until the other party fulfilled his part of the contract. That is precisely the case here."

*Meikle & Wilson* v. *Pollard* was also referred to in *Findlay (Liquidator of the Scottish Workmen's Assurance Co. Ltd.)* v. *Waddell*, 1910 S.C. 670, in which the liquidator in a voluntary winding up was held entitled to an order under a provision of the Companies (Consolidation) Act 1908 for the delivery of books and papers "without prejudice" to any lien which the accountant who was in possession of them might have.

Lord Johnston (at p. 674): "Whether Mr Waddell was merely an accountant employed by the Company to do certain work, or was in the full sense of the term auditor of the Company, or whether he was auditor of the Company and something more, the authority of the case of *Meikle & Wilson* v. *Pollard* appears to be directly in point. I do not think that an accountant employed to audit or do any other piece of work, whether for an individual or a company, has any general lien such as a law-agent. But he has a right of retention of papers put into his hands for the purposes of the work on which he is employed until he is paid the counterpart of his employment."

## CHAPTER 7

# THIRD PARTY'S RIGHTS AND LIABILITIES

NOTE

The general principles illustrated by the cases in this chapter were concisely stated by Lord Anderson in *A. F. Craig & Co. Ltd.* v. *Blackater*, 1923 S.C. 472, at p. 486:

"The rights and obligations of agents, principals, and third parties, with reference to contracts made by agents, are well settled and are not recondite. If A contracts as an agent for a disclosed principal, A cannot competently sue or be sued with reference to the contract. Again, if A contracts for an undisclosed principal, A may sue and is liable to be sued as a principal, the third party having no knowledge that he is anything but a principal. If, however, A contracts for an undisclosed principal who is subsequently disclosed to the third party, the latter may sue either agent or principal. He cannot, however, sue both. If an action is raised against the third party he may insist that it be at the instance of the disclosed principal. All this is elementary."

*Principal named: general rule: agent not liable to third party*

**Stone & Rolfe Ltd. v. The Kimber Coal Co. Ltd.**
1926 S.C. (H.L.) 45

The "Allie," owned by S. Ltd., was chartered to the Atlantic Baltic Co., Copenhagen, to carry a cargo of coal from Grangemouth to Denmark.

The charterparty was negotiated in Glasgow by G. T. Gillie & Co. for the owners and by K. Ltd. for the charterers. The document was a printed form with blanks filled in before signature. At the end of the printed clauses a manuscript clause was added: "Freight and demurrage (if any in loading) to be paid in Glasgow by K. Ltd." The signature on behalf of the charterers was adhibited by Jamieson, the manager of K. Ltd., and was in the following form:

"For the Atlantic Baltic Co., Copenhagen,
J. B. Jamieson of K. Ltd."

S. Ltd. brought an action against K. Ltd. for £335.16.9d as demurrage incurred at Grangemouth.

*Held* that K. Ltd. was not liable because (1) the form of signature showed that K. Ltd. had signed as agent only and (2) the manuscript clause was not sufficient to rebut the inference drawn from the form of signature.

LORD SUMNER (at p. 49): "The first issue, therefore, was the familiar one whether, by reason of the form of the signature, the Kimber Coal Co. had been made liable upon the charter. The issue arises in a very simple form, which makes immaterial many of the authorities commonly cited in such cases. The Kimber Coal Co. are nowhere named in the body of the charter as charterers, while the Atlantic Baltic Co. are so named throughout. . . . The form of the signature was simple. No words of limitation were added after the name which was taken to be the company's, but there were prefixed to it the words 'for the Atlantic Baltic Co., Copenhagen.'

"The defenders argued that to say 'we sign for the company,' who are named 'charterers,' is the same as to say 'we sign as their agents. He who signs "for" another does so as his agent to sign.' In itself I think this contention is correct, nor was this point very stoutly contested. The authorities support it on the whole. . . .

"The second point taken on the charter I think may be put thus. The words in manuscript, 'to be paid by the Kimber Coal Co.,' in themselves import a personal promise by the named payers, sufficient to rebut any inference to the contrary from the form of the signature. Still more is this clear when it is borne in mind that the named charterers were abroad. . . .

"I do not think it necessary to go into the question how far evidence might have been called to add a party — namely the Kimber Coal Co. — as chargeable on the contract, for the manuscript words do not in themselves import a promise by any other party than the charterers. They bind the charterers to make payment in Glasgow by the hands of agents, whom the charter names in advance, and to be answerable for seeing that this is done."

NOTE

*Cf. Fenwick* v. *Macdonald, Fraser, & Co. Ltd.* (1904) 6 F. 850, in which the Lord Ordinary (Kyllachy) held that an auctioneer, acting for a named exposer, incurred no liability to a person who claimed to be a purchaser and brought an action for implement or damages.

Lord Kyllachy (at p. 851): "I am of opinion that as against the defenders Macdonald, Fraser, & Company, Limited, the action is excluded by the fact, which is not disputed, that they acted in the matter in question as agents of a disclosed principal, and that the pursuer does not allege that they exceeded their authority."

The decision in the Inner House was on another ground.

*Principal ascertainable: general rule: agent not liable to third party*

**Armour v. Duff & Co.**
1912 S.C. 120

A., a ship store merchant and ship chandler, received from D. & Co., who carried on business as "steamship owners and brokers," the following order: "Please supply the s.s. 'Silvia' with the following stores to be put on board at Port-Glasgow. . . ."

A. delivered the goods, and rendered an account to D. & Co., whom he believed to be the owners of the vessel. D. & Co. were not, and had never been, the owners, and they refused to pay the account.

*Held* that, as A. could, by examining the Register of Shipping, have discovered who the owners of the "Silvia" were, D. & Co. were not liable since they had been acting as agents for a disclosed principal.

LORD GUTHRIE (at p. 123): "It is said by the pursuer that he was entitled when he went to Duff & Company . . . to assume that they were owners of the steamship 'Silvia.' . . . The position of parties was that Duff & Company held themselves out in two capacities — as steamship owners no doubt, but also as brokers. It is quite certain that brokers are in the habit of acting as managers for steamships belonging to others. That being so, I am of opinion that the pursuer was not entitled, simply because he found that T. L. Duff & Company were willing to give him an order, to assume that they were owners of the ship. . . .

"Now, it so happens that there would have been no difficulty in ascertaining from the register how things stood, because the excerpt which has been lodged shows that not only does the register contain full information as to the owners of the ship, but it shows that the ship was subject to a mortgage, it tells who the mortgagees were, and it shows that these mortgagees were in possession. In these circumstances I think the Sheriffs were right in holding, without in the least impugning Mr Armour's *bona fides* in the matter, that he had no right to raise this action against Duff & Company, either on the footing, which is now abandoned, that they were the true owners, or on the footing, which is still maintained, that although not the true owners they held themselves out as the true owners."

LORD SALVESEN (at p. 125): "I think the Sheriffs have reached a sound conclusion. The Sheriff expresses his view in a single sentence. He says, — 'The order is in these terms:—"Please supply the s.s.

'Silvia' with the following stores." If a firm of brokers gives an order in these terms it seems to me that they are acting on behalf of the owners of the ship, and, as these can be discovered, the principals of the broker are disclosed.' I think that is a substantially accurate statement of the law applicable to a contract of this kind, with this qualification that the owners of the ship are not bound unless the firm of brokers who gave the order had their authority to place it. In this case it is perfectly evident that the defenders had a mandate from the legal owners of the ship for the time being — that is, the mortgagees in possession. This was disclosed upon the face of the register, and it was on the owners' behalf that they gave the order."

*Principal named: general rule: agent not liable to third party: foreign principal*

**Millar v. Mitchell, &c.**
(1860) 22 D. 833

Mitchell & Co. of Leith, acting as agents for Cordes and Gronemeyer of Hamburgh, entered into a contract with Millar of Musselburgh for the supply of a quantity of bones to be shipped from Denmark in March and April 1854. The bones were not shipped in accordance with these terms, and Millar brought an action of damages against Mitchell & Co. for the loss sustained as a result.

*Held* (by a majority of the whole court) that there was no *presumptio juris* that an agent acting for a named foreign principal incurred personal liability.

LORD JUSTICE-CLERK (INGLIS), LORD WOOD, LORD COWAN, LORD BENHOLME, LORD ARDMILLAN, LORD MACKENZIE, LORD KINLOCH, and LORD JERVISWOODE (at p. 844): "We understand . . . that our opinion is asked whether there is any *praesumptio juris*, or rule of law, that where an agent in this country sells for a foreign house to a merchant in this country, he is personally liable to fulfil the seller's part of the contract, though he contract expressly *factorio nomine*, and disclose his principal at the time of contracting.

"We are of opinion that there is no such presumption or rule in the law of Scotland. . . .

"In the absence of any authoritative recognition of this presumption, it is difficult to understand how it can have any place in our jurisprudence as a proper presumption of law. A *praesumptio juris* may be introduced, either by statute or custom; it may have its origin in some strong natural probability assented to by the general voice of mankind, or in some usage of trade, drawing uniformly the same inference from a certain fact or combination of facts; but before it can have the authority of a proper *praesumptio juris*, it must be recognised, and take its place as a part of the system to which it belongs. Till it has been so recognised it is fact and not law. . . .

"It is a fixed rule of general jurisprudence, in the law of principal and agent, that where one contracts *factorio nomine* for a disclosed principal, he binds his principal alone, and not himself. The cases in which the agent becomes personally answerable are exceptional, because the liability is rested on circumstances not of usual occurrence in the conduct of such business. The best known exceptions are, where the principal is undisclosed, or where the credit of the agent is specially interposed. The grounds of these exceptions are self-evident. But shall we add to these established exceptions the case where the disclosed principal is abroad?

"It is contended, that this is the fairest rule as regards the interest of the home merchant; because, as the foreign merchant is of unknown character and credit, and inaccessible, it is reasonable the home merchant should have some one on the spot, or within the jurisdiction of the courts of his own country, to be answerable to him. But in the first place, there is no hardship in the opposite rule; for where the foreign principal is disclosed, the home merchant is at liberty to enter into the transaction or not, according to his knowledge and estimate of the principal. And, in the second place, it is a purely gratuitous assumption to say, that the foreign merchant is in all cases, or even in a majority of cases, either of unknown character and credit, or inaccessible. Inaccessibility is a quality infinitely varying, both in kind and degree. If an agent should contract in this country to sell and deliver a certain number of horses to a home-purchaser, and should disclose as his principal a wandering Arab, or should represent himself as the agent of a native of Japan in the sale of bronzes, the character and position of the principal would be a circumstance of the strongest weight in determining the question of fact, whether it was the intention of the contracting parties that the agent should be personally bound. But if, on the other hand, the agent being himself a man of no great wealth or resources, represents one of the first houses in Calcutta or New York, the probability certainly is, in the absence of any other specialty, that the purchaser will prefer the obligation and liability of the principal to that of the agent.

"It thus appears, that the presumption arising from the fact of the principal being a foreigner, is nothing more than a presumption of fact. It is a presumption which will constantly vary with the varying circumstances of each particular case. In the case of an agent who buys for a foreign principal — especially if the payment is stipulated to be immediate, or the credit given is short — the presumption may be strong, that the seller looked to the agent for the price of his goods. The presumption will be weaker where the agent is not a purchasing but a selling agent, and merely takes orders for goods to be supplied by a foreign house; for, practically speaking, there is less reason for supposing that the agent in such a case undertakes a guarantee that the goods will be furnished. Yet, in this last case, it may make a difference if, in place of the goods being only expected from abroad, they are actually in the hands of the agent, and sold for immediate delivery. The presumptions in all such cases, weaker or stronger as the circumstances may be, are all mere presumptions of fact; and presumptions of fact are nothing else than pieces of evidence. The legal relation between the parties, and the onus of proof, remain in all cases the same. There is no presumption of law against the agent of a foreign principal more than against the agent of any other party. Every agent, avowedly acting for a disclosed principal, is presumed to bind his principal, and not himself, till the contrary is proved by the party maintaining the liability of the agent.

"We are, therefore, in this case, of opinion that Mitchell, Cadell, and Company, the advocators, must be held to have occupied the ordinary position, and undertaken no more than the usual liabilities of agents, unless it be shown, on the evidence, that their personal responsibility was interposed.

"We are of opinion, on the evidence, that the interposition of such personal responsibility has not been established."

LORD PRESIDENT (M'NEILL) (at p. 848): "In this case we asked the opinion of all the Judges upon the question whether the defenders are personally liable for this breach of contract. They have given their opinions. The majority of the consulted Judges are of opinion that, in a question of this kind, there is no rule of law as to the liability of an agent, that there is no presumption of law properly so-called, but that there may be a presumption of fact, more or less strong according to circumstances. In the circumstances of this case, and looking to the evidence, I think that judgment ought to go for the defenders. I concur in the opinion of the majority of the consulted Judges, that it is a question of fact as to the intention of the parties in making the contract. I think that there may be a presumption of fact, and that the presumption may be more or less strong according to circumstances; that there may in certain circumstances be no presumption at all, and in many cases a very slender presumption indeed. The rule seems to be fixed that an agent not disclosing his principal is held to oblige himself, and that the party with whom he transacts relies on him, the agent, knowing nothing of any other person. On the other hand, it is a general rule that the agent for a party, in this country at least, disclosing his principal transacting *factorio nomine*, is held not to oblige himself, and the party with whom he transacts is held to look to the principal alone. That is the general rule.

"Then, in regard to the agent for a foreign purchaser, the same rules do not in all respects apply. In that case generally there is perhaps a presumption of fact that the seller relies on the purchaser's solvency, and the responsibility of his agent in this country, with whom he transacts, and therefore that the agent, if he means not to be liable, must take care to make that clear, so as to overcome that presumption of fact.

"Then, in regard to the agent for a foreign seller, that is not, in my opinion, quite the same case as when the agent acts for a foreign purchaser. There is a difference, and not an immaterial difference, in my view of it. In the case of a foreign purchaser, the fulfilment and proper solution of the contract on his part is payment of the money. In the case of a foreign seller, fulfilment is by specific performance. In the one case the obligation is payment; in the other case the obligation is performance. Payment can be made by any solvent party. The agent may implement the obligation. He may have funds in his hands, or he may, as agent, make advances for his principal. That is within the ordinary business of an agent in a mercantile transaction. But specific performance by a principal, especially a foreign principal, is often and generally not within the power, and certainly not within the ordinary scope, of an agent. . . . In the present case, it appears to me that if there is any presumption at all that the agent undertook liability, it is of the most slender kind possible, and the evidence is, to my mind, much more than sufficient to overcome any permissible presumption of that kind. The principal was disclosed. The sale was made on behalf of the principal, and the parties were made aware of that at the time. . . . Therefore I concur with the majority of the consulted Judges, and on the import of the evidence also, and I think judgment should go for the defenders."

LORD IVORY (at p. 849): "In point of legal principle, I can see no distinction between the case of a domestic principal and a foreign principal. A man who acts, *factorio nomine*, and discloses the principal, naturally is to be held as saying, I do not undertake anything in my own person; and the general principle in such a case is that the agent is to be free, and the onus lies upon the party with whom he deals to prove that the transaction was entered into on the footing that the agent was to be liable. Nor is there any stronger reason for holding the agent liable for an obligation of guarantee. It is not said that an agent acting for a foreign principal receives an additional commission for undertaking additional risk; and it has not been said here that the agent received any such commission. Why, therefore, should there be a larger responsibility? There is not a *presumptio juris* of the agent's liability. . . . I am perfectly satisfied, on the face of this evidence, that there was no personal undertaking or guarantee on the part of the agent."

NOTE

In this case there were comments on a possible difference between English and Scots law in relation to the liability of an agent acting for a foreign principal.

The consulted judges (at p. 844): "The law of England and the law of America have been appealed to by both parties in argument, but we can find nothing in either system of jurisprudence to support the alleged presumption of law. On the contrary, whatever fluctuation of opinion there may have been in these countries on the question under our consideration, we think it is clear that the latest and best authorities, both in England and America, distinctly negative the existence of any such presumption."

Lord Ivory (at p. 849): "There is not a *presumptio juris* of the agent's liability. There has been some misunderstanding on that point, especially in England, arising from a misreading of certain *dicta* that fell from the Judges. But now any misapprehension of them has been corrected in various cases in England, and in the best of the American authorities, and the result of all the authorities is that it is a matter for a jury to deal with, taking all the surrounding circumstances into consideration."

Lord Curriehill (at p. 850): "Nor does it appear from the authorities of the law of England, if I rightly understand them, that there is now any such exception, in that country, to this general rule of the law of principal and agent. The later decisions appear to be conclusive on this point. In that country, it appears now to be held that in law there is no such exception to the general rule; that even in a question whether or not an agent has, *de facto*, undertaken a conventional liability for his principal, there is not such a legal presumption to this effect as to throw the *onus* on the agent; and that the circumstance of the principal being resident in a foreign country, and not subject to the jurisdiction of the Court of the country in which the transaction takes place, is only one of the elements of evidence to be taken into consideration in ascertaining whether or not any particular transaction has been entered into on that footing."

In *Girvin, Roper, & Co.* v. *Monteith* (1895) 23 R. 129, opinions were reserved in the Inner House as to whether on the question of the liability of a foreign principal the laws of England and Scotland were identical.

M., who was resident in British Columbia, instructed Younger & Monteith, grain-merchants, Edinburgh, to purchase a cargo of Californian wheat on his behalf. Younger & Monteith purchased a cargo from G. & Co., London. G. & Co. knew that Younger & Monteith were acting as agents for a foreign principal, but the principal's name was neither asked nor given. The contract provided that disputes which might arise under the contract were to be settled according to the law of England.

Younger and Monteith failed to pay the price, and G. & Co. resold the wheat. G. & Co. then brought an action against M. for the loss sustained on the resale. M. pleaded that he was not liable to be sued since he had not given Younger & Monteith authority to make him a party to the contract.

*Held* that (1) the question whether M. was liable to be sued on the contract was a dispute arising under the contract, and fell to be determined according to the law of England; (2) according to that law M., being a foreign principal, was not bound by the contract of his agents unless he had given them authority to make him a party to the contract; and (3) there was nothing amounting to such authority in this case. M. *assoilzied.*

Lord Ordinary (Stormonth-Darling) (at p. 131): "The first question thus comes to be, whether the law of England is to rule. If in this, as in so many branches of the law merchant, the laws of England and Scotland were identical, the question would be one of merely academic interest. But I am by no means satisfied that they are. After a careful examination of the *dicta* in *Millar* v. *Mitchell* . . . and of the judgment of the First Division in *Bennett* v. *Inveresk Paper Company*, it rather seems to me that the law of Scotland admits to a very modified extent the presumption which exists in England, that the credit of a foreign principal is not pledged in a contract made by an agent at home. The latter case in particular (as I read it) practically comes to this, that the presumption (if it exists at all) is displaced by evidence of the mere fact of agency. It therefore becomes a question of practical importance to determine which law is to be applied."

Lord M'Laren (at p. 135): "While my opinion on all essential points is in entire agreement with the judgment of the Lord Ordinary under review, I should desire to reserve my opinion on the question first considered by his Lordship, viz., whether on the question of the liability of the foreign principal the laws of England and Scotland are identical. The Lord Ordinary observes, under reference to the cases of *Millar* v. *Mitchell*, and *Bennett* v. *Inveresk Paper Company*, that the law of Scotland 'admits to a very modified extent the presumption which exists in England that the credit of a foreign principal is not pledged in a contract made by an agent at home.' Now, there can be no doubt that the known principles of the law of Scotland in relation to mercantile agency are largely founded on the decisions of the English Courts of law; and it was certainly not my intention, nor, so far as I know, the intention of any of my colleagues who took part in the decision of the case of *Bennett*, to introduce a new distinction between the laws of England and Scotland in relation to principal and agent. In the judgment the question of the principal's title to sue is treated as a question of general mercantile law or usage. It was not a case of singular employment like the present; there was a standing agreement in writing between the principal in Australia and his agent in London, under which the powers of the agent were carefully limited, and his accountability to his principal defined; and we were of opinion that in such a case the principal was in the position of a party to the contracts made for him by his agent, although his name was not immediately disclosed. It may be inferred from my opinion in *Bennett's* case that I am not prepared to subscribe to an expression attributed to Lord Blackburn to the effect that there is a presumption of law against the foreign principal being bound. But, on a reconsideration of the English authorities, I see no reason to believe that the case of *Bennett* would have been decided differently in England supposing the law of England were applicable. . . . If there be any divergence of view in this class of cases I think that at most it is no more than such as occasionally occurs where co-ordinate Courts of the same country have to apply known principles of law to different states of fact."

Recent English cases have tended to treat the fact that the principal is foreign as just one of the circumstances to be taken into account in the determination of whether the agent assumed personal liability and had no authority to pledge the foreign principal's credit by establishing a privity of contract between the principal and the third party. The leading case of *Teheran-Europe Co. Ltd.* v. *S.T. Belton (Tractors) Ltd.* [1968] 2 Q.B. 545 declared the special "foreign principal" rule out of date. Of this case, *Bowstead on Agency* states (14th ed., at p. 234):—

"In *Teheran-Europe Co. Ltd.* v. *S.T. Belton (Tractors) Ltd.*, where air compressors were ordered for use in Iran, the Court of Appeal held that the presumption itself no longer exists, for 'the usage of the law merchant are not immutable.' But the fact that the principal is foreign is not irrelevant. Diplock L.J. said (at p. 558):

'The fact that the principal is a foreigner is one of the circumstances to be taken into account in determining whether or not the other party to the contract was willing, or led the agent to believe that he was willing, to treat as a party to the contract the agent's principal, and, if he was so willing, whether the mutual intention of the other party and the agent was that the agent should be personally entitled to sue and liable to be sued on the contract as well as his principal. But it is only one of many circumstances, and as respects the creation of privity of contract between the other party and the principal its weight may be minimal, particularly in a case such as the present where the terms of payment are cash before delivery and no credit is extended by the other party to the principal.' "

From this it would appear that in principle English law does not now differ from Scots law as established in *Millar* v. *Mitchell, &c.*

*Principal named: exception to general rule: agent voluntarily undertaking personal liability*

**Stewart v. Shannessy**
(1900) 2 F. 1288

Shannessy was appointed sales manager for a cycle company and also for a tyre company, under separate agreements, each of which authorised Shannessy to appoint travellers at the expense of the respective companies.

Shannessy wrote a letter, on paper headed with the name of the cycle company, to Stewart, appointing Stewart as representative for the two companies on stated terms as to salary and commission. The letter was signed "J. J. Shannessy."

Stewart raised an action against Shannessy for payment of commission.

Shannessy maintained that Stewart's only claim lay against the two companies, Shannessy having acted as agent for them in appointing Stewart.

*Held* that Shannessy was personally liable, since he had signed the letter in his own name without qualification and without indicating that he did not intend to bind himself as principal.

LORD KINNEAR (at p. 1292): "The pursuer was engaged by the defender to act as traveller for the sale of goods belonging to two companies . . . and the question is, whether the defender is liable personally to make good the terms of the engagement, or whether that liability attaches only to the companies. The question depends upon the meaning and effect of a written contract which is embodied in the letter. . . .

"What is the meaning of the letter he wrote? . . . He signs the letter in his own name, without qualification of any kind. The letter does not purport to make an engagement by the defender in the character of sales manager to the companies, and as binding them. It is an engagement by the defender in his own name. Now, the general rule as to the construction of such documents is . . . that 'where a person signs a contract in his own name without qualification, he is *prima facie* to be deemed to be a person contracting personally, and in order to prevent this liability from attaching it must be apparent from other parts of the document that he did not intend to bind himself as principal.' That is stated as the law of England, but there is nothing technical in it; it is a statement of the reasonable and just inference to be deduced from documents expressed in ordinary language, and passing in the ordinary course of business, and I have no hesitation in accepting it as a correct statement of the law of Scotland also.

"Now here I cannot find in any part of the document any indication that the defender did not intend to bind himself. . . . There is in the substance of the engagement a condition which seems to me to necessitate the application of the general rule, and to exclude the exception; and that is the condition as to remuneration. The payment of commission, being on the sale of all goods, is distributed between the two companies, but the weekly salary is a lump sum for the whole services rendered. There is nothing to infer the joint liability of both companies for the entire salary, or the separate liability of either to pay for the services rendered to the other, and there is no means of apportioning the liability between the two, so as to make each liable for its own share. It is quite clear that the pursuer can look to nobody but the defender for payment of the salary which the defender undertakes shall be paid. I think therefore that the substance of the agreement is in accordance with the general rule of law. . . . I think . . . that [the letter] is conclusive, and that it puts an end to the whole question."

NOTES

1. In this case Lord Kinnear treated the question as depending solely on the true construction of the letter. He said (at p. 1292): "When the true construction of that letter has been determined I do not see that the result can be affected one way or the other by any extrinsic evidence."

This point received further attention in *Lindsay* v. *Craig*, 1919 S.C. 139.

L. purchased from C., a chartered accountant, 150 shares in Iron Ore Processes Ltd. for £150. L., on paying the £150 to C., received a receipt which mentioned that a transfer would be sent to L. in due course and which was signed "C."

L. brought an action against C. for delivery of a valid transfer of the shares, or, alternatively, for payment of £150.

C. pleaded that, as to L.'s knowledge he had acted merely as agent for Houldsworth in selling the shares, he was not liable to L.

*Held* that on the terms of the receipt C. was personally liable to implement the contract of sale, and that it was incompetent for him to adduce parole evidence to show, in contradiction of the terms of the receipt, that he was merely an agent. Accordingly decree was pronounced against C.

Lord Ordinary (Hunter) (at p. 141): "There is nothing in the contract to indicate that the pursuer ought to sue anyone else except Mr Craig; and, if a person puts a contract in writing without a qualification, I think he must answer for it. . . . The position is summed up by Lord M'Laren, I. Bell's Com. (7th ed.) 540. In dealing with that matter he says: 'In the case of written contracts, the question who is the party to, or personal obligant directly bound by, the contract is determined by the writing, which cannot be contradicted or varied by extrinsic evidence. The general presumption is, that the party executing the contract intends a personal liability, unless it appear expressly on the face of the contract that he does not contract personally; and words of description merely, denoting his character of agent, and not exclusive of personal liability, are insufficient for this purpose.'

"In the present case, there are not even such words of limitation on the face of the document. On the contrary, there is nothing to suggest here that anyone else than the defender is liable in respect of this money which he received from the pursuer. He did not receive the money on the footing of its being a gift or anything of that sort; he received it in payment for shares, a transfer for which was to be sent. As no transfer has been sent, I think the pursuer is entitled to decree in terms of the conclusion of the summons."

Lord President (Strathclyde) (at p. 142): "The writing . . . founded on by the pursuer in this action is not, in my opinion, a simple receipt but fully and accurately expresses a contract of sale. It contains all the essential requisites of a contract of sale clearly set out. There is the subject-matter of the contract — 150 fully-paid shares of the Iron Ore Processes, Limited; there is the purchase price — £150 sterling; there is the name of the buyer who has paid the purchase price — the pursuer in this action; there is the name of the seller who received the purchase price — the defender in this action; and there is finally, as I read this writing, an obligation on the part of the seller to deliver the shares to the pursuer, who is the buyer.

"Now, it is said by the defender that he cannot, or will not, deliver the shares. Be it so. Then he must repay the money which he has received as the purchase price of the shares. In my opinion, the defence stated here is irrelevant. It is nothing to the purpose to say, as the defender does, that he does not possess the shares; that X possesses the shares; that X is the seller of the shares; and that X will not deliver. It appears to me that he (the defender) has, in the writing before us, undertaken all the obligations of the seller; and it is neither here nor there that he is not in possession of the article which he professed to sell.

"The passage quoted in the Lord Ordinary's opinion from Lord M'Laren's note in Bell's Commentaries appears to me to be a correct and apposite statement of the law of Scotland applicable to the subject-matter in hand. If this defender, who has undertaken to deliver the goods, is unable to do so, he must, I think, return the money."

Lord Mackenzie (at p. 143): "In my opinion the terms of that document are sufficient to impose upon the defender the obligations of a seller under a contract of sale. . . . There is no trace in the writing of any suggestion that the defender was binding himself merely as an agent. Even if it be the case that the pursuer knew he was acting for a disclosed principal this would not, in my opinion, entitle the defender to say that he was not liable. On the terms of the document it is a final and conclusive expression of a complete transaction between the parties.

"Even if the writing be not regarded as the constitution of a contract of sale, there is an alternative view under which the defender is liable, and that is because of the words 'the transfer for which will be sent you for signature in due course.' By this I think the defender undertook personal responsibility for the forwarding of the transfer. As he failed to do so, he is liable in damages."

Lord Cullen (at p. 146): "The pursuer had paid the purchase price in anticipation, without receiving the shares in exchange for his money. It was therefore only proper business dealing that he should be given, not only a receipt for his money, but also an obligation for future delivery of the shares of which he could demand fulfilment. I think the words in the latter part of the document were intended to, and did, give him such an obligation.

"*Esto*, however, that the document contains such an obligation, the defender avers that he acted in the matter, within the knowledge of the pursuer, as selling agent for a Mr Houldsworth, who was disclosed to the pursuer as his principal, and that the contract of sale of the shares was thus made between the pursuer and Houldsworth. But an agent acting for a disclosed principal may interpose his own personal credit and obligation in the transaction. . . . The document, if I have construed it aright, expresses the obligation on the vendor's side to make delivery in respect of the price already . . . paid; and this written obligation delivered to the pursuer is signed by the defender in his own name without any qualification, either *in gremio* or adjected to his signature, expressing a limitation of his capacity to that of an agent merely. This being so, I think the defender is bound personally to answer to the pursuer's demands for implement of the obligation given by him."

2. In *Brebner* v. *Henderson*, 1925 S.C. 643, personal liability was held to have been undertaken by a director and secretary who had signed a promissory note on which their company's name appeared.

The promissory note was in the following form:—

"Fraserburgh, 7th March 1923.

"£175 Stg.

"Four months after date we promise to pay to Mr James Brebner, Retired Builder, Fraserburgh or Order, within the Office in Fraserburgh of the Clydesdale Bank Limited, the sum of one hundred and seventy five pounds sterling, value received.

JAS. R. GORDON, Director
ALEX. HENDERSON, Secretary
The Fraserburgh Empire Limited."

On payment having been refused, Brebner brought an action against Henderson and Gordon. The defenders averred that the promissory note was one of a series granted to Brebner for joiner work in the erection of a picture house at Fraserburgh for the Fraserburgh Empire Ltd., which had gone into liquidation. They pleaded that, as they were not the makers of the promissory note, they were not liable to pay the sum contained in it.

*Held* that Henderson and Gordon were personally liable, the words added to their signatures being merely descriptive.

Lord President (Clyde) (at p. 645): "In this case the creditor in a promissory-note sues the two signatories for the amount of the note. Their defence is that their signatures were intended to bind, and do actually bind, a limited company of which they were director and secretary respectively, without implying any personal obligation on their part. This defence rests on certain words in the note partly opposite to and partly underneath their signatures.

"The question thus raised is truly one of the construction of the promissory-note as a whole. Words which are appended to a signature, while they may be nothing more than descriptive, or designative, of the signatory, may be (and in the case of commercial documents often are) such as to express the capacity in which the signatory puts his name to the deed, and so to qualify (and indeed control) the effect of the signature. In this way they may have the result of making the obligation in the document exclusively binding on a third party who had conferred upon the signatory the representative capacity in which he signed. But in all such cases the appended words are truly part of the document itself; and the test is whether — fairly construed along with the rest of the document — they make the equivalent of a clause which, being embodied in the deed, would have the effect of making the signatures bind, not the signatories themselves, but a third party. The note runs simply, 'we promise' and so on. *Prima facie* 'we' refers to the two individuals who sign the note. The question is whether the words appended to their signatures, construed along with the rest of the document, are equivalent to some such clause as 'we, the limited company, promise,' or again, 'we, for the limited company, and as authorised by the said company, promise.' . . .

"The first aspect of the question arises under section 26 of the Bills of Exchange Act 1882; for the primary question in the case is whether the two people who put their signatures to the note are personally liable on it or not. . . .

"According to section 26 of the Act of 1882, where a person who signs a bill 'adds words to his signature, indicating that he signs for or on behalf of a principal, or in a representative character, he is not personally liable thereon; but the *mere addition* to his signature of words describing him as an agent, or as filling a representative character, does not exempt him from personal liability.' Plainly then, if the words appended to the two signatures to the promissory-note in this case were merely words describing the signatories as filling a representative character, the signatories remain (notwithstanding those words) personally and exclusively liable on the note. The argument for the defenders was based, in the main, upon the view that the name of the company written at the bottom of the note was truly the signature of the company. If that could be made out, the description of the signatories as director and secretary of the company might possibly be held — I do not say it would — to involve no personal liability on their part. But I am unable to understand how the name of the company written by the clerk who drew out the bill under the two spaces reserved for the signatures, and under the words 'Director' and 'Secretary' opposite those two spaces respectively, can be said to constitute a signature by the company. . . . It is intelligible that the written name of the company might be regarded as the equivalent of the signature of the company, if written on the bill by somebody who, by the authority, or according to the ordinary business practice, of the company was in the habit of executing deeds for the company by signing its name and appending his own signature in a representative capacity. But I cannot bring my mind to regard the name of the company written on this bill by the clerk who prepared it, underneath the designations of 'Director' and 'Secretary,' as constituting in any sense whatever a signature by the company; it seems to me to be nothing more than an appendage to the designations of 'Director' and 'Secretary.' . . .

"The appellants presented a further argument on section 77 of the Companies (Consolidation) Act 1908. They maintained that this note was so executed and signed as to bring it within section 77 — that is to say, that it was executed in such a fashion as to bind the company within the meaning of section 77. The section says that a bill shall be deemed to have been made by a company if made 'in the name of, or by or on behalf or on account of, the company by any person acting under its authority.' . . . No doubt the bill or note could be made to bind the company, if it was actually made in the name of the company. . . . If the bill had read 'we, the [limited] company, promise,' it might have bound the limited company exclusively. So also, if it had borne to be made 'on behalf or on account of' the company, the authorised signatures would have bound the company and not the signatories. . . . It seems to me to be plain, on the terms of this note, that it is neither expressly nor by implication made in the name or on behalf or on account of the limited company. In the case of a commercial document like a bill or promissory-note, which passes freely from hand to hand, it is a reasonable requirement that, if the actual signatory is to bind a third party and not himself, the obligation should unambiguously bear that meaning. Hence the statutory requirements of 1882 and 1908. The note with which this case is concerned binds, in my opinion, the signatories and not the limited company of which they designed themselves as director and secretary. . . .

"I . . . proceed . . . upon the construction of this particular document; and, in my opinion, if one has regard to section 26 of the Act of 1882, it does not absolve the signatories from personal liability; and, if one has regard to the Companies Act of 1908, it does not impose liability on the company."

*Principal named: exception to general rule: custom: alleged custom not proved: agent not liable*

**Livesey v. Purdom & Sons**
(1894) 21 R. 911

M'Donald, contractor in Hawick, was a client of P. & Sons, solicitors, Hawick.

P. & Sons introduced M'Donald to M'Keever & Son, solicitors in Carlisle, who, along with L., their successor in business, conducted an action in the English courts on behalf of M'Donald.

L. brought an action against P. & Sons for £604.15.7d, as the balance of the account incurred in connection with the action. In thus attempting to make M'Donald's agents liable, L. relied on the custom in England to the effect that a solicitor employing another solicitor on behalf of a client was liable for the costs of the action, unless he expressly stipulated to the contrary.

*Held* that L. had failed to prove that that custom extended to the situation where the solicitor conducting the action was employed by a Scots law-agent.

LORD ORDINARY (KYLLACHY) (at p. 913): "It is not disputed that the contract being to be performed in England its construction and effect must be determined according to English law; and as to that law English counsel have been examined on both sides. There does not, however, appear to be any real controversy as to what the law of England is. It is, on the one hand, admitted that by the general law of England an agent contracting on behalf of a disclosed principal binds his principal and not himself. On the other hand, it is also admitted that to this rule there is in England an exception established by custom, and judicially recognised, to the effect that an English country solicitor employing a London solicitor on behalf of a client becomes personally liable for the latter's costs, and that the result is the same as between English country solicitors when they employ one another. The point to be decided is whether the present case falls within the rule or within the exception.

"It appears to me that the parties here must be held to have contracted with reference not to the exception but to the general rule. In other words, I do not think it is proved that the exception in question extends beyond the case of solicitors practising and entitled to practise in England. It is clear upon the evidence that the exception depends not upon any general principle of jurisprudence, but what seems properly described as a custom judicially recognised; and I do not, I confess, see how that custom can be extended so as to include a case which can never come within it. The defenders here are no doubt solicitors, — that is to say, they practise the profession of the law; but they are not required to practise as solicitors in England, and in any question with English solicitors they are, I apprehend, simply laymen.

"On the whole, therefore, I have come to the conclusion that, according to the law of England, the defenders are not liable, and are entitled to absolvitor."

LORD JUSTICE-CLERK (J. H. A. MACDONALD) (at p. 914): "A great deal has been said as to an alleged custom in England to the effect that where an English solicitor employs another solicitor in a litigation on behalf of a client, the first solicitor becomes liable for the costs incurred by the second solicitor. . . . An attempt was made to shew that this custom applied to the case of a Scottish solicitor who was the means of an English solicitor being employed. I see no ground whatever for that. That custom applies to a defined class, viz., English solicitors *inter se*. There is no such custom between law-agents in Scotland and solicitors in England. . . . I think that the result arrived at by the Lord Ordinary is the correct one."

LORD YOUNG (at p. 914): "There are two grounds upon which it is sought in this action to make the defenders liable.

"It is said, in the first place, that a certain custom has grown up, and now prevails among solicitors in England, and is applicable to the facts of this case. That custom happens to be — there are customs like it in trade, and in that of shipbuilding especially — that if one solicitor introduces a client to another solicitor in order that a specific piece of business should be carried out, there shall be understood to have arisen a certain relationship between the two solicitors; the first solicitor shall be held, unless he expresses himself to the contrary, to guarantee that the client he has introduced is a good and paying client, and in return he is to receive for his services in effecting the introduction one-half of the profits of the business to be performed.

"Now, I am of opinion that that custom, which I assume has grown up and reigns among English solicitors, has no application to the facts of this case, which is not one between English solicitors. If the solicitors in Carlisle intended to hold Messrs Purdom & Sons liable to them for the account, they should have taken a guarantee from the latter to that effect.

"The law of Scotland recognises established customs provided they are honest and expedient, and will enforce them as furnishing the terms of a contract in regard to matters where nothing is expressed. But custom is matter of fact which requires to be established to the satisfaction of the Court, although when the custom is of such a nature as is here alleged the Courts come to recognise and apply it without evidence. But the idea that the custom upon which the pursuer here founds has been shewn to apply to the facts of this case cannot in my opinion be entertained.

"The second and other ground upon which liability is sought to be established against the defenders is that they so communicated with the pursuers as to justify them in taking up and conducting the piece of business under the belief that they were to look to the defenders for payment of the account.

"I am of opinion that here also the pursuers must fail, because I think the parole evidence and the correspondence do not establish any such case."

*Principal named: exception to general rule: interest conferring on agent title to sue third party*

**Mackenzie v. Cormack**
1950 S.C. 183

M., an auctioneer of Wick, acting on the instructions of Knight, the owner of Keiss Castle, Caithness, conducted a sale of the furniture and plenishings of the castle in the castle.

C. was the successful bidder for a blue Wilton carpet knocked down to him at the price of £59.

C. alleged that the carpet had not been delivered to him, and when M. brought an action against him for payment of the price he pleaded that M., being an agent for a disclosed principal, had no title to sue.

*Held* that as M. was a mercantile agent with a lien over the price for his charges and commission he had a title to sue C. for the price.

LORD JUSTICE-CLERK (THOMSON) (at p. 187): "The defender has not obtained the carpet, and we are not told what has happened to it. The pursuer now brings this action for the price at which the carpet was sold. The defender takes the plea that the pursuer has no title to sue, in the sense that the pursuer has no right to enforce the obligation to pay.

"The parties are agreed that the pursuer was acting for a disclosed principal in carrying through the sale, and the present case is said to come under what is described as the general rule that an agent acting on behalf of a disclosed principal has no title to sue on the contract between his principal and the other party to the contract. . . . The basis of this general rule would appear to be that in the ordinary case an agent is a mere intermediary with no patrimonial interest of his own, but the rule admits of exception in certain circumstances where the agent is more than an instrument and where he can qualify some interest of his own, and indeed the exception in the case of factors and mercantile agents has in many ways become as important as the rule itself.

"That an auctioneer falls within this exception is well established by a series of English decisions which has been very fully brought before us. . . .

"In Scotland, there is no case in the Court of Session which expressly decides the point now before us. . . .

"It was argued to us that the English cases were an unsafe guide, as there was no guarantee that the terms used to describe an auctioneer's interest in England were applicable to the position of an auctioneer under our law. But there can be little doubt that an auctioneer's functions and duties are substantially the same in Scotland and in England and that in each country the same relationship exists among the seller, the buyer and the auctioneer. Accordingly, although the English definitions of the interest which confers a title to sue are couched in somewhat unfamiliar terms, I can see no reason for thinking that that interest is any different in the two countries. That interest is simply an interest to be paid commission and to have any charges that the auctioneer may incur refunded. . . .

"That such an interest confers a title to sue in Scotland seems to me independently of any English authority to be quite clear on principle and to be amply vouched. It is well established that a factor or a mercantile agent enjoys a general lien. . . .

"The argument chiefly pressed on us was that, if this interest springs from lien, there must be possession, and, while it might be possible to say that there was possession where the auctioneer actually takes the goods into his own premises, that could not be said when all that the auctioneer does is to attend at the exposer's premises and carry out an auction there. . . . It seems to me that any such distinction is far too fine to be practical, and I am prepared to say that the auctioneer, when he is carrying through the sale even in the premises of the exposer, is ceded possession for the purpose of carrying through the sale and that that possession is sufficient to support his lien. . . . If then an auctioneer has possession when he puts the articles up to auction, the lien flowing therefrom extends over the price due by the buyer of the article after it is sold. . . . Accordingly, I entertain no doubt, independently of any English authority, that an auctioneer in the position of the pursuer has a title to sue for the price of an article sold by him."

LORD MACKAY (at p. 191): "I . . . think it very important to settle this broad issue both on precedent and in principle.

"While I have worked out, in common with your Lordships, the Scottish century of legal progress upon the authorities, I prefer here to follow out and express the answer to the question as one solvable by two broad principles. The first question of principle, as I see it, is this:—The English law of public auctions and the specific question of the position of an auctioneer towards the bidders having now been completely settled, is there any ground whatsoever, or any suggestion of any principle, or any authority within Scottish *dicta*, for endeavouring at this stage and at this time of day to set up the Scottish law in opposition to the earlier settled and unshaken English law? Now, the English law, as do your Lordships, I regard as completely settled by four cases, dated from the year 1788 onwards. . . . These cases leave no doubt that in appropriate circumstances the auctioneer has a right, when the price bid to him by his preferred bidder has not been paid during the progress of the sale, to sue for that price, and the ratio given seems to me in principle to be so strong that we ought certainly not to refuse it, even if it were only offered here for the first time. The authority steadily pursued from 1788 onwards has covered two supposed difficulties again argued to us — (*a*) what if the name of the so-called principal — the exposer of all the lots — has been advertised, published, or known? (*b*) does the same law apply to auctions conducted under the flag at the houses, farm or premises of the exposer, as applies in the special more urban premises of the professional auctioneer?

"As foundation, various English Judges have put emphasis on the element of an 'interest' held by the auctioneer. Sometimes the phrase is 'interest and possession'; sometimes it is 'a special property'; often all three words are put to use together. To me the ratio seems statable in still clearer and more compelling form. The ratio is that the possession of the goods as they pass down is put into the public auctioneer's hands in order that he may have such possession and control as to make present sales by the action of the hammer to that person to whom his judgment assigns the last and perfect bid, and that the possession, if desired, can be so delivered direct from the hands of the auctioneer during the sale . . . on the sale being completed either of one lot, or of the whole lots; he then passes the delivery by possession over to the successful bidder, and it is the general rule both of early auction law and of the Sale of Goods Act 1893 that the duty of passing over the money to the maker of delivery arises at that same moment. . . .

"The channel by which the goods must necessarily pass down in order from auctioneer to bidder must necessarily again be the channel by which the counterpart, the price, passes up. The channel by which the price can reach the exposer, whether cash be promptly paid or not, is through the auctioneer. And why is that, as I conceive, the necessary reverse channel? Just because the auctioneer has got a right to satisfy himself for his expenses and all charges out of the price, and is under no obligation to pay over the price to the exposer *in globo* and in full, but only the net residuum, that is to say, after payment or deduction of his own commission or charges, as well as of the appropriate expenses of the auction's working. . . . It must be the auctioneer's books or record that can constitute the price bid, and the source of that bid; and the keeper of these books it must be who alone can sue for it, and not the owner. The owner looks to the auctioneer as the only source for him for recovery of the price. . . . In short and without reliance whatever on an English conception of 'special property,' my opinion is that Scots law should, and indeed does, agree with its English counterpart. The doctrine should hold both in principle, and for simplicity; and indeed for sheer common sense the law in this matter in Scotland ought to be the same as the well-settled law of England.

"The next point concerns what is to be said on the authorities. . . . I have found the authorities in Scotland to be sufficiently clear, even as early as Professor Bell's Commentaries. . . . Nor do I feel it to be still open to serious discussion. . . .

"Has an auctioneer, in the circumstances stated, a right to go to the bidder and ask him to pay? . . . Yes, he has a right to have any payment passed through his hand in order to operate his lien for his charges and expenses."

LORD PATRICK (at p. 195): "Mercantile factors or agents have a general lien over all property in their possession belonging to the principal. . . . I think it is settled, and rightly so, that in the normal case an auctioneer is a mercantile factor, and entitled as such to a general lien over his principal's property so far as coming into his possession.

"Moreover the factor's lien extends not only over the goods themselves, but over the price of the goods sold by the factor if the price be payable to him, and still unpaid. . . . A factor's lien covers prices still unpaid and held by buyers. In section 1415 of the *Principles,* Bell is quite definite on the matter. He says 'the possession of goods by a factor who sells and delivers them is transferred to the price unpaid, so as to extend his lien over it,' and gives other exceptional instances where the lien subsists after the person in right thereof has parted with the goods. . . .

"It follows that, in cases where the factor's lien extends not only over the goods entrusted to him for sale but also over the unpaid price of the goods, the factor is entitled to sue the buyer for payment of the price. This is settled in England, as Bell points out, and, in my opinion, this is necessarily the law of Scotland also. The factor's right of lien over the price cannot be made effectual against the principal unless the factor is entitled to sue for and recover the price out of which he will then deduct the sums due to him and covered by the lien. . . .

"Lastly, the defender submitted that, when the goods are sold by the auctioneer in the premises of the principal, as contrasted with a sale in auction rooms, no such possession is conferred on the auctioneer as to entitle him to any lien. . . . The pleadings in this case show that the auctioneer was to receive payment of the price, and was to deliver the articles sold to the buyer. A lien was therefore conferred on him over the goods, and consequently a title to sue for payment of the price."

NOTES

1. In *Johnston* v. *Little*, 1960 S.L.T. 129 (O.H.), J., a solicitor acting for a purchaser of heritable subjects, was held to have a title to sue L., the solicitor acting for the seller, for implement of a letter of obligation to deliver writs. L. had contended that as J. had been acting for a disclosed principal, the principal alone was the contracting party.

Lord Guest (Ordinary) (at p. 130): "This was an inter-solicitor transaction in which the two contracting parties were the respective solicitors."

Similarly, in *Laing* v. *Taylor*, 1978 S.L.T. (Sh. Ct.) 59, the drawer of a cheque was held not entitled to object to the title of the payee to sue on the cheque, although the circumstances pointed to the probability that the payee had been involved in the transaction only on behalf of a disclosed principal — the gaming club at which he was employed as a croupier.

Sheriff Principal (G. S. Gimson) (at p. 59): [After referring to *Johnston* v. *Little*] "In principle, the present case is similar. It does not appear to me that one who signs a cheque in exchange for cash (or goods) can object to the title of the payee of the cheque to sue on the transaction — and it seems to me to make no difference whether the drawer inserted the payee's name or left it to others to do so, or what further relationships might lie in the background."

2. Contrast *McIvor* v. *Roy*, 1970 S.L.T. (Sh. Ct.) 58, in which an agent was held to have no title to sue for repayment of a sum of money conditionally paid out by him on behalf of his named principal to a third party, even although the condition on which repayment became due had been purified.

McI. was branch manager of an industrial insurance company, and in that capacity he paid out to Mrs Jessie Roy £19.14.3d, the proceeds of a policy of assurance on the life of her deceased father-in-law. Mrs Roy was not entitled to these proceeds, and as a result McI. had to pay a further sum of £19.14.3d to a son of the deceased who was entitled to them.

McI., claiming that he was bound to reimburse his principals for the sum which he had wrongly paid out to Mrs Roy on their behalf, brought an action against Mrs Roy for repayment.

*Held* that, as the claim was truly a contractual one, only a party to the contract could sue, and accordingly that, since McI. had acted on behalf of named principals, he had no title to sue.

Sheriff-Substitute (A. B. Wilkinson) (at p. 60): "I turn now to what, in my opinion, is the true character of the transaction between the pursuer and the defender. The pursuer's evidence is . . . that the money was paid under a condition as to repayment. If that is so and the condition under which payment was made has been purified, the party who made the payment has a contractual right to repayment. . . . The immediate difficulty, however, facing the pursuer on this branch of his case is that of title to sue. The remedy is a contractual one and therefore, in the absence of a *jus quaesitum tertio* (and there is no suggestion of that here), only a party to the contract can sue. The pursuer was not a party, having expressly made payment on behalf of his principals. Accordingly, in my opinion, only the pursuer's principals can enforce an action on this ground.

". . . The pursuer's evidence certainly was that the condition attached to payment had been purified (*i.e.*, that another claimant had come forward and had been paid). . . . I should perhaps add in relation to the question of title to sue that I do not overlook that in England, at any rate, it appears to be settled that an agent may sue for repetition of money in certain circumstances other than those of error . . . but that has no bearing on purely contractual remedies."

Had McI.'s claim been a quasi-contractual one under the *condictio indebiti*, it seems that he might have been held to have had a title to sue. The sheriff-substitute said (at p. 59): "I am . . . inclined to the view that were it necessary for me to decide this question, the pursuer's title to sue could be upheld so far as this ground of action is concerned."

It was, however, unnecessary for the sheriff-substitute to form a concluded view on that point, since he held that the *condictio indebiti* was not applicable to the situation — McI. had not paid under error; he was in possession of the full facts; he had known that the defender was not entitled to the money, and had apparently known of the existence of other possible claimants:—"The pursuer took a risk with results that proved unfortunate but there was no error in the sense necessary to found a *condictio indebiti*."

The sheriff-substitute also rejected the other ground on which McI.'s case had been based — that of recompense — holding that the payment to the defender had had the character of donation.

The English law as stated in *Bowstead on Agency* (14th ed., p. 408) is:— "Where an agent pays money on his principal's behalf, under a mistake of fact, or in respect of a consideration which fails, or in consequence of some fraud or wrongful act of the payee or otherwise under such circumstances that the payee is liable to repay the money, the agent may sue the payee for its recovery."

*Principal undisclosed: agent known to be an agent: agent's failure to disclose principal: agent liable to third party*

**Gibb v. Cunningham & Robertson**
1925 S.L.T. 608 (O.H.)

G. was a shareholder and director in a family company which carried on a flax-spinning business at Johnshaven in Kincardineshire. C. & R., a firm of solicitors in Stonehaven, acted as law agents and secretaries of the company.

G. entered into negotiations with C. & R. for the sale to them of his 1,000 shares in the company and of his dwelling-house known as "The Bungalow." The negotiations ended in missives, by which a price of £5,000 was agreed. Previous and subsequent correspondence showed that C. & R. were acting for others (in fact for the other directors in respect of the shares and for the company itself in respect of the heritable property), but the missives themselves did not refer to any principals.

C. & R. paid part of the price to G., but a hitch occurred in the payment of the balance of £3,750. An agent for G. wrote to C. & R. inquiring whether they had been acting as secretaries of the company or as agents, and adding: "If the offer was made by you as agents then I shall be glad to know on whose behalf the offer was made. Failing my hearing from you in reply in course of post the proceedings will be laid against you as the parties who actually signed the contract." No answer was made to that letter.

G. raised an action against C. & R. for implement of the bargain so far as not implemented, and, failing implement, for payment of £3,750 as damages.

C. & R. pleaded that, to G.'s knowledge, they had contracted as agents and not as principals, and should therefore be assoilzied.

The Lord Ordinary (Constable) *repelled* that plea.

LORD CONSTABLE (at p. 610): "For the pursuer it was argued that the defenders' averments with regard to agency are not relevant because, having signed the missive offer without qualification and having also failed to state, in answer to the pursuer's request, who their principals were, they are personally liable to the pursuer for the fulfilment of the contract. The general rule applicable where a person has signed a contract in his own name and maintains that he was acting as agent for another was thus stated by Lord Kinnear in *Stewart* v. *Shannessy* . . .: 'The general rule as to the construction of such documents is . . . "that when a person signs a contract in his own name without qualification he is *prima facie* to be deemed to be a person contracting personally, and to prevent this liability attaching it must be apparent from other parts of the document that he did not intend to bind himself as principal." ' The rule is stated more fully in Lord M'Laren's note in Bell's Comm. (I. 540): 'In the case of written contracts the question who is the party or personal obligant directly bound by the contract is determined by the writing, which cannot be contradicted or varied by extrinsic evidence. The general presumption is that the party executing the contract intends a personal liability, unless it appear expressly on the face of the contract that he does not contract personally; and words of description merely denoting his character of agent and not exclusive of personal liability are insufficient for this purpose. Where an agent contracts in writing in such a way as by the form of the writing to make himself personally liable, he cannot relieve himself from liability by evidence that he contracted as agent for a principal, or even that the other party knew he was acting as an agent at the time of contracting, for such evidence would tend to contradict the written agreement.' . . .

"Turning to the missives in the present case I fail to see anything in them which expressly or impliedly qualifies the defenders' liability, and in my opinion it is not competent to qualify them by parole evidence. It is perhaps more open to doubt whether the correspondence is not admissible in order to construe the missives. I am not prepared to say that the part of it following on the missives is wholly inadmissible. I prefer to rest my judgment on the ground that even if the correspondence is admissible it does not suffice to establish the defenders' plea. It shews that the defenders were acting and were understood by the pursuer to be acting, on the instructions of clients, but it does not shew precisely who the clients were. In the case of the heritable property it appears from the disposition that the clients were the company; but the company could not lawfully acquire its own shares. And when the defenders made no reply to the pursuer's request that they should disclose their clients, I think that the pursuer was entitled to treat the case as one where the principal had not been disclosed and to sue the agents."

NOTE

For *Stewart* v. *Shannessy*, see p. 120, above.

*Principal undisclosed: agent known to be an agent: principal suing third party: third party not entitled to plead compensation of debt due to him by agent*

**Matthews v. Auld & Guild**
(1873) 1 R. 1224

M., a merchant in Dundee, instructed Henderson, stockbroker there, to sell certain securities and purchase other securities for him.

Henderson employed A. & G., stockbrokers in Glasgow, to carry out the transaction. He did not disclose M.'s name to A. & G., but represented throughout that he was acting for a client.

On completion of the transaction a balance of £83.13/- remained in the hands of A. & G.

Shortly afterwards, Henderson absconded, leaving a large balance due by him to A. & G.

In answer to a letter from M., A. & G. stated that they intended to hold the balance in their hands against the much larger debt due by Henderson to them.

M. raised an action of count and reckoning against A. & G.

*Held* that A. & G. were not entitled to plead compensation, since they had known that Henderson was acting for a client, although the name of the client was not disclosed.

SHERIFF (GLASSFORD BELL) (at p. 1226): "On the one hand if a factor or broker sells goods as his own, and the buyer knows nothing of any principal, the buyer may set off any demand he has on the factor or broker against the demand for the goods or their price made by the principal; but . . . on the other hand, if a person buys goods of another whom he knows to be acting as agent, though he does not know who the principal is, he cannot set off a debt due to him by such agent in an action by the principal for the price of the goods. . . . It follows that, in the circumstances of this case . . ., the pursuer, as Henderson's principal, has a sufficient title to insist, and . . . the defenders cannot compensate or set off the debt due to him by any general balance resting owing to them by Henderson."

LORD JUSTICE-CLERK (MONCREIFF) (at p. 1227): "I do not find much difficulty in adhering to the interlocutor of the Sheriff.

"The general rule as to the position of an agent in a sale is well settled. . . . If a person buys goods of another, whom he knows to be acting as an agent for another, though he does not know who the principal is, he cannot set off a debt due to him by the agent in an action by the principal for the price of the goods. That is the general rule, and if there is nothing to take this case out of the general rule it is not disputed that the judgment of the Sheriff is sound. But it is said that a different rule must be applied between stockbrokers on the Stock Exchange, and that a different rule is actually in use among stockbrokers. There is, however, no allegation to that effect on record, and no proof of such a practice. It is sufficiently clear that Henderson, in the transaction in question, acted as an agent. It is also proved that he so represented himself to Auld and Guild, and the fact that the shares were held by the Commercial Bank must of itself have led to that inference. Auld says that he would not have contracted with Henderson except on the assumption that he had a client. Besides, a broker is a person who acts for a principal, and individual transactions between stockbrokers on their own account do not seem to be within the ordinary practice of the Stock Exchange. I should rather have inferred, although we have no general evidence on the subject, that a stockbroker is generally understood to act for a principal, and not on his individual account. This therefore appears a clear case for the application of the rule. I cannot see any ground for allowing what Henderson owes Auld and Guild to be paid out of Matthews' money, for that would be the result of giving effect to the contention of the defenders. I am therefore of opinion that we should adhere to the judgment of the Sheriff."

NOTE

This aspect of the law of agency was also considered in *Lavaggi* v. *Pirie and Sons* (1872) 10 M. 312.

P. & Sons, paper-manufacturers, Aberdeen, had extensive dealings with Wood, commission agent in Aberdeen. The transaction out of which the case arose was a sale of ten bales of cotton rags by Wood to P. & Sons. Wood had obtained these goods from Lavaggi, a merchant in London. Wood was credited in P. & Sons' books with the value of the rags as fixed by P. & Sons, and the rags were then converted into paper by P. & Sons.

Wood became bankrupt and insane.

L. claimed that the rags had been his property and that he had sent them through Wood as his agent to P. & Sons merely for examination with a view to an offer being made for them.

L. raised an action against P. & Sons for payment of £50.7/-, as the market price of the rags.

*Held* by the Second Division (reversing the judgment of the sheriff-principal) that Wood had been a principal, and not L.'s agent, in the sale to P. & Sons.

Sheriff (Smith) (at p. 314): "The question in the present case is, whether the defenders are at liberty to keep the goods of the pursuer in payment of a debt due to them, not by him, but by an insolvent named Joseph Wood, who carried on business as a broker and commission merchant, and to whom the goods in question had been consigned for the purposes of sale.

"When an agent or factor sells the goods of his employer as his own, the purchaser, being ignorant of the fact that he is only an agent, is entitled, in an action by the principal for the price, to set off a debt due to himself from the agent or factor. The reason is, that a vendor who allows another to deal with his goods as if they were his own cannot deprive the vendee of the equities which he has against the apparent vendor, by resuming his character of principal and reducing the seller to the position of a mere agent. But if the seller was known to possess a purely representative character, no such set-off can be pleaded against the principal, even although the buyer did not know who the principal was. . . .

"Thus the first point for decision in this case is, whether the defenders dealt with Wood as principal in the transaction, and had reason to believe that the rags in question were his property. The Sheriff is inclined to think that this can hardly be maintained in the face of the letter of 1st October 1870, which opens with the statement that the rags had 'been sent by the same party who sent the former lot, and who specifies them as cotton rags, No. 2.' The plain meaning of this is, that this unnamed person had sent the rags to Wood for disposal on commission, not that Wood had acquired or purchased them from the same collector. The language used is just what an agent would have employed under the circumstances, and the defenders, as men of business, must have known quite well Wood's position in the matter. If that be so, the pursuer, as principal in the transaction, is still in time to come forward and claim the price of his property."

Lord Justice-Clerk (Moncreiff) (at p. 315): "The first question is, whether the defenders dealt with Wood as a principal. . . . I am of opinion that the defenders did deal with Wood as a principal. The law on which the Sheriff relies is sound enough in cases which admit of its application; but we have here a long course of dealing, to a very large amount in point of value, between the defenders and Wood as principal, and accounts settled from quarter to quarter on that principle. In these accounts all the transactions are entered as the individual transactions of Wood, and the balances are calculated and carried on without any reference to anyone else. From the nature of the business, the defenders knew that Wood had correspondents elsewhere; but they had no reason to know, and they were in no degree bound to inquire, on what terms they dealt with him. In these circumstances I have no doubt that the same principle of compensation which is given effect to throughout the whole of their mutual accounts must apply in the present case. . . .

"I am of opinion that the judgment of the Sheriff is wrong, and that we should return to that of the Sheriff-substitute."

Lord Cowan (at p. 316): "I concur in thinking that the case raises no question of law, and that its solution depends on the application of undisputed law to the facts of the case. The Sheriff has found that 'the pursuer having, for the purposes of sale, consigned to the bankrupt, Joseph Wood, the ten bales of rags libelled,' the same were sent by him to the defenders, 'with a request that they should sort them, and state what price they would give for them'; and farther, 'that, though the said Joseph Wood did not disclose who his principal was, the defenders knew that in said transaction he was acting as an agent.' I agree with your Lordships in holding that these findings are not well founded on the facts. I cannot hold it to have been proved that Pirie and Sons knew that he acted as agent in this particular transaction. Wood had a long series of transactions, extending over years, with the Piries, as principal, and no attempt has been made to show that on this occasion he acted in a different character or capacity from what he did in the other transactions."

Lord Benholme (at p. 316): "If the purchaser knows that the seller acted as agent, though he did not know for whom he was agent, he cannot have the benefit of compensation. But it will not be enough to say if he knew or might have known, for the alternative can only be introduced if there is a duty to know. There was no duty in the purchaser to inquire. If there was a duty, it was the duty of the agent to disclose that he was acting for another.

"If the transaction was made between Pirie and Son and Wood as principal the benefit of compensation must be conceded."

*Principal undisclosed: agent contracting ostensibly as principal: principal, on disclosing himself, has a title to sue the third party*

**Bennett v. Inveresk Paper Co.**
(1891) 18 R. 975

B., a newspaper proprietor in Sydney, Australia, through Poulter & Sons, his London agents, entered into a contract with the I. Co. for the supply of paper which was to be shipped to him in Australia. At the time of the making of the contract, the I. Co. did not know of B.

The paper was duly paid for, but on arrival at Sydney was found, owing to bad packing, to be damaged and spoiled.

B. brought an action of damages for breach of contract against the I. Co.

*Held* that B. had sufficient title to sue the action.

LORD M'LAREN (at p. 982): "This is an action at the instance of a commercial firm trading under the name of Bennett, whose domicile is in Sydney, and who sue the Inveresk Paper Company on a contract arising out of an order by Bennett for a large quantity — I think 3,600 reams — of printing paper. This order was given to or through their correspondents in London, Messrs Poulter & Sons. Messrs Bennett sue the Inveresk Paper Company for breach of contract, in respect that the paper when it arrived in Australia was found to be damaged, as they allege, through insufficient packing. One of the defences to the action is that the pursuers have no title to sue; and this defence is founded on a legal proposition which I think may be expressed in this way — that in all transactions between a seller in the home country and a foreign purchaser effected through a middleman, it is a presumption of law that the middleman contracts as an independent contracting party with the seller and the ultimate purchaser respectively; and that as matter of law the intermediary is not and cannot be the agent of either party; or, as it is otherwise put, that in the foreign trade there is and can be no privity of contract between the seller and the buyer, unless they are in direct communication. . . .

"Before considering whether there be such a rule of law regarding foreign transactions as the defenders maintain, it may be convenient in a few sentences to review the general rules of the law of principal and agent in relation to questions of title to sue and liability to be sued. Supposing that the parties were within the jurisdiction, I apprehend there can be no doubt that a seller to the agent of an undisclosed principal, may elect to sue the principal for the price. But, if he takes advantage of this right, he is disabled from maintaining any plea that would alter the relations of the principal and the agent to the disadvantage of the principal. . . .

"A corresponding rule exists that a principal, if he has occasion to sue for fulfilment of a contract, may come forward and disclose himself, and may sue the other party in his own name. But he also, if he elects to sue in his own name, will be affected by counter claims that might have been pleaded against his agent. This qualification of the principal's right of action is very distinctly stated in Bell's Commentaries. . . .

"Now, the rule in question applies to cases where the principal at the time of the purchase is undisclosed; and it is plain enough in principle that, if the seller knew who the principal was from the beginning, the election is held to be made at the time of making the contract, because the seller is bound to elect whom he is to take as his debtor, as soon as he comes to know who is the principal to whom the goods are sold. . . .

"But it is contended . . . that . . . a rule of law has been established, that in all foreign transactions the broker or commission-merchant is deemed to be an independent contracting party and not an agent; and reliance is placed on certain judicial observations — especially those of Lord Blackburn — in the series of cases that were cited. . . . Now, I can only read this passage, and those of a like nature which have been cited, as a statement by Lord Blackburn of what is known to be a general usage (not necessarily universal) in the foreign trade. For reasons of convenience, it is found better that the commission-merchant should, in such cases, contract as purchaser on his own account, and should resell to his correspondent abroad. The inconvenience resulting from entering into such transactions on the footing of agency is such that a practice has grown up under which the commission-merchant acts as an independent contracting party towards those from whom he buys, and to whom he sells. But Lord Blackburn never said, and I do not think he intended to say, that, if a foreign or colonial house chooses to appoint an agent in London for the management of its business, including the sale of its goods or the purchase of goods on its account, the law will not give effect to such an arrangement. To say so would be to place a restriction on the freedom of contract, which could not emanate from any authority other than the Legislature, and which is certainly not warranted by any legal principle that I have been able to discover in the judicial opinions to which I am referring. But I think perhaps this also may be inferred from Lord Blackburn's opinion, that, in the absence of evidence to the contrary, it is a reasonable presumption of fact that the commission-merchant contracts as an independent party and not as agent for the foreign trader. . . . Accordingly, if there had been no documentary evidence in this case defining the position of the London house, I should have agreed with the Lord Ordinary in thinking that it was a proper subject for inquiry by proof whether the London house acted as Messrs Bennett's agents or as merchants. But it appears to me that this matter is really not open to dispute, because if we refer to the letter constituting Messrs Poulter the agents of Bennett I think its terms are very clear. They admit of no other construction than that Poulter's relation to Bennett was, in the strictest sense, that of an agent to a principal. The letter begins, —'I herewith appoint you my sole agents and representatives in the United Kingdom for the term of five years from January 1st, 1886, for the purchase and forwarding of all papers,' &c., 'and for the transaction of all my business generally, as per instructions.' . . . I do not think it can be disputed that, as matter of construction, this is an appointment of Messrs Poulter as agents for the Australian house, and that all orders given in execution of the mandate given by this letter, followed by this special instruction, are to be regarded as orders given by Messrs Bennett through their agents.

"In these circumstances it appears to me that this must be treated as an exception to what we are told on high authority is the general usage of the foreign trade. Parties may make their own contracts and are not bound to conform to usage, and as in this case Messrs Bennett have chosen to act through agents in London, the relations of these agents with the manufacturers from whom the paper was purchased must be subject to the known and settled laws of principal and agent. For these reasons I am of opinion that Messrs Bennett are entitled to declare themselves, and to sue the Inveresk Paper Company for fulfilment of their contract. It does not appear from the proof that they were known to be principals at the time when the first orders were given, but they certainly came to be known afterwards. That is a circumstance more material to the election of the vendor when the option lies with him as to which party he will sue, and would not, in my judgment, amount to a limitation on the right of the purchaser, when he thinks proper, to declare himself, and to sue in his own name. As he will be affected by any counter claims or pleas pleadable against his agents, no possible injustice can be done to the Inveresk Paper Company. The objection is a purely technical one, and I am of opinion that it is not well founded in law."

NOTE

In *Girvin, Roper, & Co.* v. *Monteith* (1895) 23 R. 129, at p. 136, Lord M'Laren commented on the opinion which he gave in *Bennett's* case: see Note to *Millar* v. *Mitchell, &c.* (p. 118, above).

*Principal undisclosed: third party's election to sue principal or agent: third party held to have elected to sue principal: agent not liable*

**Ferrier v. Dods, &c.**
(1865) 3 M. 561

D., an auctioneer, advertised a sale by auction of certain horses, all warranted good workers. At the sale F. bought a grey mare for £27 and paid for her by cheque.

A few days later, F. informed D. that the grey mare was utterly unsound and unfit for work. D. admitted F.'s right to return the mare if unsound, but he requested F. to return her direct to her former owner, Bathgate, whose name had not been disclosed at the auction.

F., having accordingly returned the mare to Bathgate, brought an action both against D. and against Bathgate for repayment of the £27.

*Held* that F. had elected to sue Bathgate. The action as against D. was dismissed.

LORD JUSTICE-CLERK (INGLIS) (at p. 564): "I am willing to assume that the pursuer has averred that Dods sold the mare to him as agent, and did not disclose his principal. He was known to be an agent; an auctioneer is presumably an agent. Soon after the sale he did disclose his principal. This was the position which the pursuer then occupied. He was entitled to go against either Dods as seller, because the principal had not been originally disclosed, or against the true owner, now disclosed. But he was not entitled to go against both. What the law gave him was an election or option. He was entitled to have his choice of action against the ostensible or the real seller. But here he proposes to go against both. Not only so, but he proposes to go against the agent, though, in my opinion, he has already elected to go against the true owner. This I gather from that article of the condescendence, where the return of the mare to Bathgate is set forth. No doubt he says he returned her to the owner at Dods's request, but it is not the less true that it was to the owner he returned her. He was not entitled to get back the money unless he returned the mare, nor from any one, except the person to whom he returned her.

"I think, therefore, that Dods is liberated, and all that remains is the case against Bathgate."

LORD COWAN (at p. 564): "As regards Dods's position, I do not dispute the general doctrine that an auctioneer who warrants the thing he sells without disclosing his principal is to be treated as responsible personally. As affecting this matter, however, there are facts stated on the record by the pursuer himself which are most material. The pursuer avers that he tendered back the mare to Dods; that, on the suggestion of the latter, he sent her to Bathgate; and that Bathgate received her. It seems to me that the fact of the pursuer having directed the conclusions of this action against Bathgate, taken along with that statement explanatory of Dods's connection with the transaction, frees Dods from the personal responsibility libelled. Bathgate and Dods were not joint sellers; the pursuer must sue either the agent or the principal, — if he selects the principal, he cannot go against the agent. The action cannot be directed against both principal and agent, and I think, therefore, Dods is entitled to be assoilzied."

LORD NEAVES (at p. 564): "The pursuer says that he returned the mare to Bathgate, and that Bathgate accepted her as unsound. How is it possible after this statement for the pursuer to maintain that he has an action on warrandice against the auctioneer?"

NOTES

1. Contrast *Meier & Co.* v. *Kuchenmeister* (1881) 8 R. 642, according to which the third party may sue the agent and then sue the principal provided

he has not obtained judgment against the agent.

M. & Co., shipbrokers in Newcastle-on-Tyne, had made certain disbursements for the German vessel "Jacob Rothenburg," which was owned by K., and had been stranded near Shields in November 1878. The disbursements had been made on the authority of Captain Wilde, the master of the vessel, and without K.'s consent or knowledge. As payment, Wilde drew bills of exchange on K., but K. returned the bills unaccepted.

M. & Co. raised an action against Wilde, as the drawer of the bills, in the German court of his domicile. M. & Co. obtained judgment against him in the lower court, but on appeal that judgment was reversed on the ground that by German law the suit against the drawer ought to have been brought within three months from the date when the bills fell due and this had not been done.

M. & Co., with jurisdiction founded on arrestments, then sued K. in the Court of Session. K. pleaded that M. & Co., having elected to take the master as their debtor, were barred from suing the owner.

*Held* that the doctrine of election did not apply, because M. & Co. had not obtained a judgment against the master.

Lord Justice-Clerk (Moncreiff) (at p. 644): "The action is by a Newcastle firm of shipbrokers against a shipowner in Rostock, for furnishings said to have been made to a vessel by order of the master. Jurisdiction has been founded by arrestments in Scotland. The answer to the claim is that the master granted bills of the amount to the shipbrokers, and that they have sued him on them in Germany. It is not denied that the master is liable along with the owner, but the master is said to have been successful in the German Courts. This action is now brought against the owner, and he pleads that there cannot be an action both against him and the master, and that the shipbrokers having sued the master, although without success, must be held to have elected to accept him as the debtor, and cannot now sue the owner. . .

"Election is no doubt recognised in our law. In the case of a shipmaster and shipowner, where the master is sued on his own obligation and decree is given against him, he having relief against the owner, there is no doubt that the owner cannot be sued also for the same debt. That is common sense. But where the master has not been sued to judgment, or the action fails from some technical reason or another, the case is different. The fact of the pursuer having sued the wrong man will not bar him from suing the right one. And the same rule must apply if he have failed to recover. . . .

"On the whole it seems to me that here we have no case of election truly, and that no plea has been stated to exclude the action."

Lord Young (at p. 646): "The general rule is that if a person really acting for another goes into the market and buys as if for himself, he binds himself; but if the party from whom he buys finds out his true position then he can treat him as an agent only. He cannot have two principals to deal with, and no double remedy is allowed. The only other rule is that an agent acting for a disclosed principal does not bind himself at all."

2. In *The Hill Steam Shipping Co. Ltd.* v. *Hugo Stinnes Ltd.*, 1941 S.C. 324, the question was considered whether H.S. Ltd., a coal exporting company, described in a charterparty as "agents to charterers," and signing

the charterparty "as agents only," were entitled afterwards to maintain that they were themselves the principals under the charterparty with the result that they would have had the benefit of a cesser clause in the charterparty, which provided:—"The charterers' liability shall cease as soon as the cargo is shipped, and the advance of freight, dead freight and demurrage in loading (if any) are paid." The question did not require to be decided, however, because H.S. Ltd. were also shippers, were sued as such, and were held liable as such since the bills of lading did not incorporate the cesser clause.

Lord Justice-Clerk (Aitchison) (at p. 330): "The cargo duly arrived at the port of destination and was delivered. War was declared before the amount of freight was remitted. The shipowners now claim payment of the freight amounting to £883 from the defenders as shippers of the cargo under the bills of lading.

"The defenders maintain in answer that they were in fact principals under the charter-party, that it was entered into by them to fulfil a contract by which they sold a quantity of coal to Messrs Hugo Stinnes G.m.b.H. Berlin, to be shipped during the years 1938, 1939 and 1940 and that the shipment of coal was in implement of this contract. Their contention is that, being in fact charterers notwithstanding their designation and signature, the only contract between them and the shipowners is to be found in the charter-party, and that as principals in that contract they are entitled when sued for freight to the protection of the cesser clause. . . .

"The first question, therefore, is whether the defenders are to be allowed to prove that they themselves were the principals in the charter-party although professing to enter into it as 'agents only.'

"The general rule where a person enters into a contract for a principal who is undisclosed is that the principal may come forward and take the benefit of the contract, or be made liable under it at the suit of the other contracting party, and the rule in general obtains, not only where the agent contracts nominally as such, but also where he contracts without reference to agency at all, provided always that the person who claims, or is alleged, to be the undisclosed principal can bear that character consistently with the terms of the contract. . . . This, I think, furnishes the criterion by which questions of this kind are to be tested: Is the assertion by a person that he is an undisclosed principal consistent with the contract? In this case, is the assertion by the defenders that they are the undisclosed principals consistent with the description of themselves in the charter-party as 'agents for charterers' and their signature 'as agents only.' This is not the same question as whether an agent for an undisclosed principal who refuses to disclose his principal may not be liable on the contract, as, for example, for the price of goods sold where the agent refuses to disclose the buyer's name. Such a case may raise different considerations.

"If in this charter-party the principal had been named, the defenders, it is plain, could not have shifted their character. The rule enunciated by Lord Ellenborough, C.J., in *Bickerton* v. *Burrell* ((1816) 5 M. & S. 383, at p. 386) would apply:—'Where a man assigns to himself the character of agent to another whom he names, I am not aware that the law will permit him to shift his situation, and to declare himself the principal, and the other to be a mere creature of straw.' Does the same rule apply where the principal is unnamed, so that it cannot be said that the identity of the principal is a material element of the contract? That is the case which the defenders make. They say:—Under this contract the obligation on the shipowners was to carry someone's cargo, and it does not matter whose cargo, so long as a cargo was furnished and freight was earned. They say, therefore, that it is open to themselves, although professing to contract as agents, to assume the character of principals with all the right effeiring thereto without contradicting the real substance of the contract.

". . . I can conceive of such cases where there is a usage or custom, either local or general, affecting a particular class of transaction or mercantile dealing, which is accepted by the commercial community, and can be assumed to be understood by the contracting parties, and with reference to which the contract would fall to be read. In such cases the express contract would have a term added to it agreeable to the common understanding of merchants. But, in the absence of any proved or admitted usage, I have difficulty in understanding how a shifting of character is possible to persons who contracted 'as agents only.' 'As agents only' are words of qualification and not merely of designation, they are a representation that the defenders had a principal other than themselves, and that they intended to assume neither the liabilities nor the rights of a principal under the contract. It was an unambiguous intimation that it was not their contract but somebody else's contract. That is the plain meaning of the words. I should therefore entertain the greatest doubt, in the absence of averment and proof of custom, whether evidence to show that the defenders were themselves principals did not contradict the contract. It is, however, enough in the present case to say . . . that a party to a contract who shifts his character can never do so to the prejudice of the other party to it. . . .

"The liability of the defenders as shippers is to be found in the bills of lading. . . . Under the bills of lading the primary liability for freight is on the shippers. . . . This cesser clause . . . is for the protection of charterers, and not for the protection of shippers. The fallacy of the defenders' argument lay in assuming that, if they could show themselves to be charterers, they would escape their liability as shippers. That is surely a *non sequitur*. As already pointed out, if a party who contracts as agent shifts his character, he cannot alter the situation to the prejudice of the other party, either by increasing the obligations of the other party, or by securing for himself a release from his own obligations under that contract, or any other contract. At best he has the double character; the different capacities do not merge into one but remain distinct. . . . The contention of the defenders that the pursuers can suffer no prejudice because they contracted in the charter-party with persons unnamed is, in my opinion, unsound. There was no disclosure to the pursuers when the bills of lading were presented for the master's signature that the shippers were also the charterers. If the defenders were repudiating the character of agents, the pursuers should have been apprised of the fact. . . . The defenders, however, allowed the deception to continue, concerned, I have no doubt, to obtain their brokerage on shipment which they had contracted to be paid under clause 22."

*Principal undisclosed: third party electing to sue agent: agent entitled to counter-claim against third party*

**A. F Craig & Co. Ltd. v. Blackater**
1923 S.C. 472

C. Ltd., engineers and boilermakers in Paisley, supplied two marine boilers to B., shipowners of Glasgow, at a price of £5,900. The full price was not paid, and C. Ltd. brought an action against B. for the unpaid balance of £2,412.0.5d.

B., averring that the boilers had been disconform to contract, brought a counter-action for £9,897.11.5d in name of damages alleged to have been sustained through C. Ltd.'s breach of contract.

The two actions were conjoined, and a proof was led.

In the course of the proof it transpired that B. were not the registered owners of the ship in question, but merely managing owners, the registered owners being the Cadeby Steamship Co. Ltd.

Both parties in the action then amended their records, and C. Ltd., as defenders in the counter-action, pleaded that B. had no title to sue, and had sustained no loss through any breach of contract on C. Ltd.'s part.

*Held* that, by prosecuting their own action to decree, C. Ltd. had elected to treat B. as their debtors in the contract, and, accordingly, that B. were entitled to counter-claim for damages.

LORD JUSTICE-CLERK (ALNESS) (at p. 481): "But Blackaters . . . maintain that when a contract is made by an agent for an undisclosed principal and the principal is afterwards disclosed, the other party to the contract can elect to sue either principal or agent, but that, if he sues one of the two and follows the suit to judgment, he must be taken to have made a deliberate election, and must treat his adversary as not only liable under the contract, but also as in right of it and entitled to sue upon it. In other words, applying the doctrine to this particular case, Blackaters maintain that, when the Cadeby Steamship Co. was disclosed as principal, Craigs could then have said, 'We were misled; we will begin proceedings anew' — a course well within their rights, although probably unnecessary — but that they are not entitled to enforce Blackaters' liability under the contract, and at the same time deny them the right to recover under it. This would appear to be common sense as well as rudimentary law.

"What is to be said against it? Mr Robertson, as I understood his argument, admitted that Blackaters have a title to sue, but he maintained that they could not recover damages because they had themselves sustained none. But if Blackaters sue, it must surely be in their principal's interest. Though they have suffered no damage, they represent a person who has. Why should they not enforce their principal's right? That is precisely what they are endeavouring to do. They do not propose to put a penny in their own pocket. They sue, so they aver, for and on behalf of the Cadeby Co., and that averment, be it observed, Craigs deny. Why should Blackaters not have an opportunity of proving their statements, and of recovering damages for their principal on whose behalf they claim to act? . . . The representational capacity in which Blackaters defend the action against them by Craigs provokes no comment by the latter; but when it is, as I think, logically contended that the same representational capacity should avail Blackaters in their action against Craigs, the doctrine becomes an offence to the latter. . . .

"I accordingly propose that the interlocutor reclaimed against should be recalled, and that the case be remitted back for the assessment of the damages due in the action by Blackaters against Craigs."

LORD ORMIDALE (at p. 484): "It appears to me that, when it became patent that the Messrs Blackater had entered into the contract merely as authorised agents and the name of their principal was disclosed, Messrs Craig were entitled to follow one or other of two courses — either to continue to treat Messrs Blackater as the party liable to them under the contract to all intents and purposes, or to abandon their action against Messrs Blackater and take proceedings against the Cadeby Steamship Co. The logical sequence of that would, no doubt, have been the replacement in the second action of the Messrs Blackater by the Cadeby Steamship Co. . . .

"But I cannot think that it was open to Messrs Craig & Co. at once, as it were, to approbate and reprobate the fact of the disclosure of the principal, ignoring it to the effect of forcing the price of the boilers from Messrs Blackater, as the parties liable therefor under the contract, but calling it in aid to disentitle the Messrs Blackater from stating any counter-claim otherwise competent to them under the identical contract. To do so would have been to violate the principle underlying the rule of law according to which, in the case where an agent contracts for a principal who is afterwards disclosed, the other party to the contract may sue either principal or agent but cannot sue both. Here Messrs Craig & Co. have elected, for their own purposes, to treat and sue the Messrs Blackater as principals, and consequently the latter are, as principals, entitled to counter-claim. Further, the counter-claim of damages as made by the Messrs Blackater is, in my opinion, competent. No doubt, they have suffered no personal loss by the breach of the contract. The same would be true if the principal had not been disclosed, and that is, in effect, the position here, because of the election made by Messrs Craig & Co. to treat the Messrs Blackater as the parties bound by the contract; and I see no reason why, if they are to be saddled with the obligations of debtors under the contract, they should not also enjoy the rights of creditors thereunder. In neither case is their interest a personal one."

LORD ANDERSON (at p. 486): "As matters stand, . . . Messrs Craig . . . hold a decree against Messrs Blackater, to which the latter, apart from the claim made in the counter action, have no answer. . . .

"The rights and obligations of agents, principals, and third parties, with reference to contracts made by agents, are well settled and are not recondite. If A contracts as an agent for a disclosed principal, A cannot competently sue or be sued with reference to the contract. Again, if A contracts for an undisclosed principal, A may sue and is liable to be sued as a principal, the third party having no knowledge that he is anything but a principal. If, however, A contracts for an undisclosed principal who is subsequently disclosed to the third party, the latter may sue either agent or principal. He cannot, however, sue both. If an action is raised against the third party he may insist that it be at the instance of the disclosed principal. All this is elementary; the difficulty of applying these principles to the present case arises from its unusual facts.

'When the two actions were raised the principals were undisclosed. It was only during the course of the proof in the conjoined actions that it was casually divulged that the Cadeby Steamship Co. were the principals in the contract. When this fact became known to Messrs Craig they were, in my opinion, put to their election. They had to determine whether or not they would proceed to decree against Messrs Blackater or against their true debtors the Cadeby Co. There was no necessity for commencing proceedings *de novo* and so rendering useless the procedure which had taken place. There would have been no difficulty, by our procedure, in substituting the one party for the other in both actions. . . . But no proposal to this effect was made by Messrs Craig. They elected to continue the action in which they were pursuers against the agents, but in the counter-action they declined to submit themselves to a decree for damages in respect of their breach of contract. They thus prevented the application of the principle of compensation or set-off to the counter-claims. This is plainly inequitable; it is, moreover, a result which is against all legal principle and which is supported by no decided case. If the principals had remained undisclosed, Messrs Blackater's title to sue for damages for breach of contract could not have been challenged. Their title would then have been good, because they were *understood* to be principals. Why should it be otherwise when they have been *treated* as if they were principals? It seems to me to be in accordance with sound principle that Messrs Craig, suing Messrs Blackater as their debtors in a contract, must admit to any counter-claim in respect of the same contract as to which *they* are debtors. It is urged that Messrs Blackater are not the true creditors under the contract in respect of the claim of damages. That is doubtless true, but neither are they true debtors under the contract in respect of the price. If Messrs Blackater are to be saddled with the liability of the contract as *quasi* principals they are surely entitled to maintain, in order to diminish or wipe out this liability, any claims under the contract which are open to the true principals. Their pleadings show that they have no claims as individuals under the contract against Messrs Craig, and that they are claiming damages on behalf of their principals. Messrs Craig are thus certiorated that, if decree for damages passes against them, they thereby obtain a complete discharge of their contractual obligations both as regards principals and agents."

LORD HUNTER (at p. 489): "As Craig & Co. chose to continue their action against the agents after they ascertained who the undisclosed principal was, they were bound to allow these agents to plead any breach of contract that they had committed. Liability to be sued on the contract was accompanied by the right to plead as a counterpart the pursuers' failure to implement the contract. The fact that recovery of such damages is made in a representative capacity, or as *quasi* trustees for the undisclosed principals, does not constitute an effective plea of no title to sue."

NOTE

A similar case relating to a building contract is *James Laidlaw and Sons Ltd.* v. *Griffin*, 1968 S.L.T. 278.

L. Ltd., building contractors, entered into a contract with G. for certain structural work at the Griffin Hotel, Bothwell. The hotel was owned by Griffin Hotel (Bothwell) Ltd., of which company G. was a director. In making the contract G. was acting as agent for the company, but this was not then known to L. Ltd.

A term of the contract was that L. Ltd. should be responsible for all damage to "property of employer," arising out of the contract, and in the interpretation clause of the contract the "employer" was stated to be G.

L. Ltd. came to know that G. had been acting on behalf of the company.

L. Ltd. raised an action against G. for payment of certain sums certified as due by the architect for works executed by L. Ltd. under the contract. G. counter-claimed on the ground that in carrying out the work L. Ltd. had caused serious damage, amounting to £20,000, to the hotel. L. Ltd. argued that the only damage claimable under the contract was damage to the property of the "employer," namely G., and that the property alleged to have been damaged belonged to the company and not to G.

*Held* that, as L. Ltd. had elected to sue G. as agent for the company, "employer" in the contract was not G. personally but G. in his capacity as agent for the company, and the averments in support of the counter-claim were therefore relevant.

Lord President (Clyde) (at p. 280): "The pursuers in this case are a firm of builders who contracted to carry out certain structural work on an extension of the Griffin Hotel at Bothwell. The contract was entered into with the defender, Mr Griffin. The hotel is in fact owned by a limited company, Griffin Hotel (Bothwell) Limited, in which company the defender is a director and a principal shareholder. The pursuers sue in this action for the amounts in certain certificates issued by the architect and the defender has counter-claimed for certain damage which he contends is due under the contract. . . .

"The pursuers have . . . contended to us that the averments in support of the counter-claim are irrelevant and that they should, at this stage, accordingly, be dismissed. They do not challenge the Lord Ordinary's allowance of a proof before answer on the pursuer's own claim.

". . . The heritable property on which the hotel and its extension are situated is owned by the limited company. The contract was, therefore, one made by the defender as an agent for an undisclosed principal and in accordance with well settled law the other party to the contract can, when the disclosure of a principal takes place, elect to sue either the principal or agent and 'if he sues one of the two and follows the suit to judgment he must be taken to have made a deliberate election and must treat his adversary as not only liable under the contract but also as in right of it and entitled to sue upon it.' (See *Craig & Co.* v. *Blackater*, 1923 S.C. 472, *per* Lord Justice-Clerk, at p. 481, 1923 S.L.T. 240.) In the present case the pursuers have elected to sue the agent and not the principal and it follows that for the purposes of this litigation the agent and not the principal is liable under the contract and is also entitled to the rights conferred by the contract which could otherwise have been enforced by the principal under it.

"The defender's counter-claim which he seeks to enforce is a counter-claim under art. 9 (2) (i) of the conditions of contract for building works which was incorporated in the present contract. . . .

"The pursuers concede that the defender has a title to counter-claim under this contract as they have elected to sue the agent and not the principal and they have consented in the course of the argument before us to their second plea to title in their answers to the counter-claim being repelled. They have, however, maintained before us that the averments made in support of this counter-claim are irrelevant, and that in consequence they should not be sent to proof. This was the only issue argued before us.

"The argument was that the only damage claimable under art. 9 (2) (i) was 'damage to property of the employer': that under the contract the employer was Mr Griffin personally and that as the hotel did not belong to Mr Griffin but to the limited company he had no claim under this article for damage to a building which did not belong to him. In my opinion this argument is unsound. Once it is disclosed that the defender is not contracting on his own behalf, but as agent for the limited company, then both parties are made aware of the fact that the property does not belong to the defender personally, and that he is contracting on behalf of a third party, who owns that property. The damage for which art. 9 (2) (i) makes the pursuers responsible is damage to the same property whether the pursuers choose to sue the principal or the agent. It is damage to the subjects which they have been engaged in extending. If they elected to sue the agent on the certificates by the architects they are suing him not for work done on his property but for work done on the limited company's property and similarly, in that case, he can counter-claim in respect of damage to the limited company's property on whose behalf he is involved throughout the contract. Once it was disclosed that Mr Griffin was an agent for a principal, and once the pursuers had elected, as they had, to sue the agent, then 'the employer' in the contract is not Mr Griffin personally, but Mr Griffin in his capacity of agent for a now disclosed principal. In my view, therefore, the attack on the relevancy of the averments in the counter-claim has failed."

Lord Guthrie (at p. 282): "The pursuers have maintained that the averments in support of the counter-claim are irrelevant in the following circumstances. While the defender ostensibly contracted as a principal when the contract was entered into in February 1964, he disclosed some months later that he was in fact acting as agent for a principal, namely Griffin Hotel (Bothwell) Limited, a company which owns the hotel on which the works were done. The pursuers submitted that in these circumstances the defender was the employer in terms of the contract, and that, therefore, as he did not own the hotel, the hotel was not 'property of employer' to which condition 23 referred. This argument really means that the defender has no title to sue for decree in terms of his counter-claim, which is based on condition 23, although, strangely enough, the pursuers did not support their plea of 'no title to sue.' Their counsel explained that they did not maintain that plea in view of the decision in *Craig & Co.* v. *Blackater*. . . . They rested their argument on their plea to the relevancy, maintaining that the defender had not relevantly averred breach by them of condition 23 in respect of their alleged failure to make good damage to the hotel in the course of the works, because he was the employer and the hotel was not 'property of employer.'

"In my opinion this argument, whether presented under the plea to the relevancy or a plea of no title to sue, is negatived by the ratio of the decision in *Craig & Co.* v. *Blackater*. . . . Both parties have averred on record that the hotel is owned by the company, and that the company carried on the business of the hotel. It is therefore agreed that, when the defender entered into the contract, he did so as agent for an undisclosed principal, now disclosed.

". . . In the circumstances of the present case, when the existence and identity of the principal were disclosed, the pursuers were entitled to elect whether to sue the defender, who had entered into the contract, or the principal. They have elected to sue the defender. Therefore, the defender is entitled to rely upon the principle stated by Lord Hunter in *Craig & Co.* v. *Blackater*, at p. 489:—'Liability to be sued on the contract was accompanied by the right to plead as a counterpart the pursuers' failure to implement the contract.' The defender, as agent, is therefore entitled to counter-claim under condition 23 in respect of damage to property of his previously undisclosed principal, the true employer, since the true employer under the contract is the company. The pursuers founded in argument upon the definition of 'the employer' in the contract as meaning 'William Griffin, Esquire,' that is the defender. But when the existence and identity of the undisclosed principal have been revealed, the definition of the employer must be taken as meaning 'William Griffin, Esquire, as agent,' and therefore the property of the employer referred to in condition 23 (1) must be taken as referring to the property of the agent's principal. Accordingly, when the pursuers elected to sue the defender, he acquired the right to plead their failure to implement condition 23 (1) by making good the damage to the property of his principal."

Lord Cameron (at p. 283): "In my opinion . . . the distinction which the reclaimers sought to draw between the present case and *Craig & Co.* v. *Blackater* . . . is without substance. In that case, Lord Hunter said at p. 489:—'As Craig & Co. chose to continue their action against the agent after they ascertained who the undisclosed principal was, they were bound to allow this agent to plead any breach of the contract they had committed. Liability to be sued on the contract was accompanied by the right to plead as a counterpart the pursuers' failure to implement the contract.' That statement of law appears to me to fit the circumstances of this case."

## *Principal not a legal person: agent personally liable to third party*

### **M'Meekin v. Easton**
(1889) 16 R. 363

Repairs had been carried out on the Reformed Presbyterian Church at Stranraer, and M'M., a farmer, had lent £300 to pay for them. In security of this loan, M'M. received a promissory note for that amount, signed by the minister, Rev. Thomas Easton, and two other persons. The promissory note stated:—"... We, the undersigned, in the name and on the behalf of the Reformed Presbyterian Church, Stranraer, promise to pay Mr Robert M'Meekin . . . the sum of £300 sterling, value received."

Some years later, M'M. raised an action for payment of £290, as the balance due on the note.

*Held* that the three persons who had signed the note were personally liable for payment of it.

LORD YOUNG (at p. 364): "The persons who signed this promissory-note, two of whom are now dead, were connected with the congregation of the Reformed Presbyterian Church at Stranraer. Money had been borrowed from a bank for purposes of the congregation, and when it was paid up to the bank the pursuer M'Meekin stepped in and advanced it. When he did so he received this promissory-note signed by the three gentlemen whose names it bears, Mr Easton, David Easton, and Peter Lusk.

"Is this a worthless document, and did he receive it as such? The idea that this Reformed Presbyterian Congregation was the proper debtor in a personal obligation is, of course, absurd. A congregation could not be debtors on a promissory-note, and there is therefore no personal obligation on them. Well, did not these three gentlemen become the debtors? They were legally capable of being so, and they signed it. They refer on the face of it to its being signed in the name and on behalf of the congregation. That is, it was a debt which the congregation would feel it to be their duty to provide for. They can do that, though they are not capable of being the debtors or creditors on the note, out of good feeling and the conviction that they are morally bound to relieve those who became debtors, for their behoof. On the face of the note, then, that is the position of the debtors. It is the only thing that could be meant, unless we suppose they meant to give and M'Meekin meant to take a worthless document. The only legal view of M'Meekin's position is that he must be taken as saying to those who signed the note that he could not take the congregation as his debtors, but would look to them, and they on their part would look to the congregation for their relief."

NOTES

1. For the personal liability of "agents" for a company not yet incorporated, see *Tinnevelly Sugar Refining Co. Ltd.* v. *Mirrlees, Watson, & Yaryan Co. Ltd.* (p. 8, above).

2. *Thomson & Gillespie* v. *The Victoria Eighty Club* (1905) 43 S.L.R. 628

(O.H.) gives an instance of the same personal liability in the case of persons who contract on behalf of a club.

T. & G., wine merchants, raised an action against (1) the V. Club, (2) the members of its committee, and (3) the known members of the V. Club, for payment of £120, as the balance which they alleged was due to them for liquor supplied to the V. Club.

*Held* that the members of the committee, but not the club itself or its ordinary members, were liable.

Lord Pearson (Ordinary) (at p. 629): "It was formed on 31st May 1899. . . . At the close of the first year there were one hundred and seventy members. In pursuance of the rules, there was a committee of twenty-one, consisting of three office-bearers and eighteen members, one-third retiring annually. The committee had the management of the whole affairs of the Club, with full power to provide and alter the furnishings, to provide periodicals, and to purchase liquors. They had power to appoint sub-committees. The pursuer supplied liquors to the Club from about March 1900. . . .

"The account now sued on is for liquor supplied between 6th September 1902 and 8th August 1903, under deduction of certain payments to account. . . . All the orders were given through the clubmaster personally, and were upon a printed form and signed by him. It does not appear what the precise form of order was. In so ordering supplies the clubmaster acted upon the instructions of the committee to this extent, that they told him what tradesmen to employ, and instructed him to order supplies as necessary; and the invoices from the tradesmen were laid before the committee, who passed them for payment, the cheques being signed by two of the office-bearers. . . .

"I consider first the claim made against the ordinary members. This is an action on contract for the price of goods sold and delivered by the pursuer, and the question is, who the other contracting party was. The question who is in law liable to pay for supplies furnished to a club has not been much canvassed in Scotland. The course of the English decisions, of which there are now a good many, shows the necessity of having careful regard to the circumstances of each case, including the rules of the particular club. But subject to this . . . they have also resulted in establishing what I may call the *prima facie* legal view of such contracts as are here in question, as determined by the known practice of social clubs. To begin with, it is impossible to affirm the liability of the Club as such, for that is not a legal entity, capable of contracting or of being sued. The liability must rest either with the members as such, or the committee-men, or some of them, or the clubmaster. Circumstances might be figured in which it was the clubmaster alone; but in the normal case this view has never been received with favour, any more than has the argument, submitted in some cases, that there was really no contract at all, and that the tradesman must be deemed to have relied merely on an honourable understanding that he would be paid. In the ordinary case the clubmaster is regarded as having acted as an agent, and not as principal, in such a contract. But unless there is something special in the circumstances he is not regarded as having acted as agent for the ordinary members as such.

. . . Of course there may be exceptional cases either way. There may be cases where certain ordinary members have intervened and pledged their own credit for the goods. There may be cases on the other hand where the rules of the club emphasise and strengthen the view that ordinary members were not to be liable. . . .

"The pursuer pleads alternatively that in any event those who were members of the managing committee during the currency of the account cannot escape liability. . . . Eighteen of the defenders called are alleged to be in that position; and of these, seventeen have not appeared to defend the action. The remaining one, the defender Robert W. Millar, is, of course, quite entitled to raise the question of his liability as a committee-man. . . . The weekly supplies were being obtained from the pursuer; and although Mr Millar says he was not aware of the particular orders or of their amount, he was aware generally that fresh orders were being given and that the Club could not be kept open unless fresh supplies of liquor were got. I cannot doubt that all this implies liability on the part of the members of committee to see the account paid, and that on the facts the clubmaster gave the orders as their agent. It is no sufficient answer to point to the pursuer's evidence as showing that he thought the Club and all its members were liable to him, and that it was on their credit that he relied. It is, of course, of some importance to ascertain who it was to whom the pursuer thought he was giving credit. But the mistake made by the pursuer was in a sense a mistake in law and does not alter the facts. The true principal can be sued when he is discovered, notwithstanding that credit was erroneously given to another. . . . No doubt there are cases in which certain selected committee-men have been found liable on grounds special to themselves, *e.g.*, the personal giving of orders or the signing of cheques for payment of specific accounts to the same merchant. But it does not follow that where no such specialty exists the members of committee are not liable as such. That depends upon the course of dealing and the practice of the committee of which they are members. If the system of orders and payments adopted by the committee is such as to fix the members of committee with the general knowledge that supplies necessary to the existence of the Club were being obtained from a particular tradesman, and his accounts were passed by the committee for payment as part of their ordinary business, then I hold that the committee-men are liable, with such relief as they can obtain from the Club funds, or from the members by way of contribution. Nor do I think that there is room (in such a case of continuous weekly supplies) for distinguishing between those committee-men who were present and those who were absent from any particular meeting, as if only those who attended a meeting were liable for the accounts passed at that meeting. . . . Further, I think it clear that the liability is not merely *pro rata*, and that the proper course is to decern against the compearing defender Mr Millar for payment, reserving any right of relief competent to him."

*Breach of warranty of authority: agent liable to third party*

**Anderson v. Croall & Sons Ltd.**
(1903) 6 F. 153

At the Musselburgh race meeting held on 3rd October 1902, a mare "Ethel May," which had come second in a race, was, by an innocent mistake, auctioned by C. Ltd., auctioneers. The mare was knocked down to A. for £36.15/-. A. paid the price, and received a delivery-order.

The owner refused to give delivery of the mare, on the ground that the sale had been wholly unauthorised by him.

In May 1903, the mare was sold by auction at York for 70 guineas.

A. claimed damages of £136.15/- from C. Ltd.

*Held*, on the ground that an auctioneer warrants his authority to sell, that A. was entitled to damages of £26.5/- in addition to the return of the purchase money.

LORD ORDINARY (STORMONTH-DARLING) (at p. 154): "The pursuer here seeks damages for loss of bargain. He was present at the Musselburgh Races held on 3d October 1902 when a mare called 'Ethel May,' described as the property of 'J. Cast,' ran second for the Carberry Selling Handicap. After the race the winner and two other horses, which had been named as for sale on the card, were sold by auction; and then the defenders, who acted as auctioneers at the meeting, put up 'Ethel May' for sale, and knocked her down to the pursuer for 35 guineas. The pursuer at once paid the price at the office of the Clerk of the Course, and obtained a delivery-order for the mare; but delivery was refused at the trainer's stable on the ground that she had been sold by mistake. . . . The pursuer . . . refused to accept repayment, and insisted on delivery or damages, asserting that the mare was worth much more than he had paid for her.

"He now sues the auctioneers for damages on alternative grounds:—(1) That they, having sold the mare as agents for an undisclosed principal, are liable on the contract as if they had been themselves the sellers; and (2) that, having sold without authority, they are liable on the ground that a person who so acts, even in good faith, and induces another to deal with him as an agent, is held to warrant the authority which he professes to have.

"On the first of these grounds I am against the pursuer. The principal was not undisclosed, for the owner was correctly said to be 'J. Cast,' which was the racing name, and known by the pursuer to be the racing name, of a certain Mr M'Lauchlan, of Glasgow, now deceased.

"But, on the second ground, I have come to be of opinion that the purchaser is entitled to succeed. At first sight, it seemed to me a little hard that auctioneers, acting in good faith and without negligence except of a very venial kind, should incur this responsibility to a disappointed purchaser, especially when the mistake was so soon discovered and explained. The circumstances which led to the mistake were of the simplest character. The stable-boy in charge of the mare rightly brought her back to the paddock after the race, until the weighing-out was done and the result of the race declared. Then he ought to have led her away. But, instead of that, he kept her in the paddock while the winner and the other two horses were being sold, and the auctioneers, seeing a horse standing close to the ring, and jumping to the conclusion that she was intended for sale, asked the lad for her name and, on getting it, told him to lead her round, which he, believing the auctioneer to have authority from his master, the trainer, proceeded to do. In all this, there was nothing but a misunderstanding between the lad and the auctioneer, betraying, perhaps, some haste and want of caution on the part of the latter, but nothing worse. Plainly, on these facts, it is impossible to represent that the mistake, so far as the lad contributed to it, in any way bound the owner. . . .

"While I own that my first impression was rather unfavourable to the pursuer's demand, I cannot resist the authority of a whole series of English cases on a branch of commercial law in which there is no difference between the law of England and the law of Scotland. The authority of some of these cases was recently recognised by the Second Division, in circumstances no doubt very different from the present, in the case of *Salvesen & Co.* . . . And the principle which the cases embody, as explained in the leading case of *Collen* v. *Wright* (1857) 8 E. and B. 647, at p. 657, is that 'a person professing to contract as agent for another, impliedly, if not expressly, undertakes to or promises the person who enters into such contract, upon the faith of the professed agent being duly authorised, that the authority which he professes to have, does, in point of fact, exist.' . . . This rule extends to cases of innocent misrepresentation. . . .

"Now, an auctioneer is, in law, nothing but an agent for the seller down to the fall of the hammer. Indeed, the only respect in which he differs from some other commercial agents is that he is obviously and confessedly nothing else. Accordingly, he never can be made liable on the contract as a principal, except in the single case of his acting for an undisclosed principal. But, with respect to the undertaking or warranty of authority which all agents are held to give, I see no reason why he should receive exceptional treatment.

"If so, the only remaining question is as to the measure of damages. Here also the rule in England is fixed by authority. . . . Now, what would the pursuer here have gained if the contract had been made with authority and, therefore, had been enforceable? He would have become owner of a mare worth more than he paid for her. It is not easy to say how much more, for his own witnesses admit that the value of a racehorse is a very uncertain quantity. But we know that seven months later the mare fetched 70 guineas by auction at York, not having raced or done anything remarkable in the interval. That seems to me the safest guide to value in the evidence. . . . Something must come off for cost of keep and transit, for I suppose it may be assumed that York at the beginning of a racing season was a better market than Musselburgh at the end of one. But I think I shall not be far wrong if I assess the damages, both for loss of bargain and for any trouble and outlay to which the pursuer was put before the action was raised, at 25 guineas. That is the sum for which I shall give decree, with expenses; besides which the defenders undertake, through their counsel, to return the price of 35 guineas paid by the pursuer."

LORD TRAYNER (at p. 158): "I do not see my way to differ from the Lord Ordinary. The defenders sold the mare in question to the pursuer, and were bound therefore to deliver it on payment of the price, which the pursuer made. The defenders admitted in their letter of 9th October 1902 that they had made a mistake in exposing the mare for sale without the authority or instructions of the owner. If that mistake resulted in damage to the pursuer the defenders must answer for it."

LORD MONCREIFF (at p. 158): "Although this is rather a hard case for the defenders I am of opinion that the judgment of the Lord Ordinary is right. The reclaimers' counsel did not dispute the general law upon which the Lord Ordinary proceeds, namely, that an agent who, though innocently, contracts without authority of his principal, is liable in any damages which the other party to the contract can instruct that he has sustained through loss of the contract when absence of the authority is discovered. In the case of *Salvesen & Company* I fully stated my views on the decisions and the law applicable to this case.

"With that admission the defence, in my opinion, fails, because —

"First, an auctioneer is simply an agent for the seller till the fall of the hammer, though his duties are restricted, and rapidly performed. If he has the seller's authority he binds the seller, and through him (the auctioneer) the successful bidder is bound to the seller. But if he sells without such authority I agree with the Lord Ordinary in thinking that he is entitled to no higher immunity than any other agent.

"Secondly, in this case it is not proved that the auctioneer had authority from the owner, or from anyone entitled to bind him, to sell the 'Ethel May.' Under the rules of racing the winner in a selling race must be offered for sale by auction immediately after the race; and therefore in such a case the auctioneer is probably entitled to assume that he has the owner's authority to sell. But horses which are not winners are in a different position. They are sold entirely on the responsibility of the auctioneer on the instructions of the owner or his trainer. On such sales the auctioneer receives a commission of five per cent, and he receives the price and gives the purchaser the delivery-order. Now, the 'Ethel May' was not a winner, and therefore the auctioneer should not have proceeded to sell her without the authority of the owner or some responsible representative. But what he did was this; he saw the 'Ethel May' standing outside the ring near the door of the weighing-room in charge of a stable-boy, and erroneously assuming that it was there for sale he called to the boy to bring the mare into the ring to be sold. The boy, naturally supposing that his master had told the auctioneer that the mare was to be sold, did what he was bid; and the auctioneer, without any communication with the owner or trainer, knocked the mare down to the pursuer. I cannot acquit the auctioneer of rashness in acting as he did, though the misunderstanding is quite intelligible.

". . . Defenders' counsel admitted that if damages were to be awarded the sum named by the Lord Ordinary, twenty-five guineas, is not excessive, and good reason is disclosed in the evidence for the defenders not objecting to the award."

NOTES

1. The Lord Justice-Clerk (J. H. A. Macdonald), while he saw "no ground for holding [the Lord Ordinary's] judgment to be wrong," reached the same conclusion as the majority in the Second Division, on the ground that the defenders had failed in their duty "to take reasonable care that in what they did they were truly acting for the owner, so that they had a right to sell, and give delivery on payment of the price."

Lord Young dissented.

2. The case of *"Salvesen & Company"* referred to was *Rederi Aktiebolaget Nordstjernan* v. *Salvesen & Co.* (1903) 6 F. 64. That case was, however, subsequently taken on appeal to the House of Lords — *Salvesen & Co.* v. *Rederi Aktiebolaget Nordstjernan* (1905) 7 F. (H.L.) 101 — and the House of Lords altered the judgment of the Second Division.

R. of Stockholm were owners of the steamship "Oscar II." S. & Co. were shipbrokers in Leith.

S. & Co. applied to Ireland & Son, coal merchants and exporters in Dundee, with a view to negotiating a charter for the carriage of 5,000 tons of coal from an east coast port to Stockholm. S. & Co. acted as intermediaries without disclosing to either principal who the other principal was.

S. & Co., finding that their two principals would not agree to one another's terms, and being anxious to earn their brokerage for the trouble which they had taken, informed each principal that agreement had been reached on his own terms.

Ireland & Son, having lost their intended market in Stockholm, repudiated the charterparty with R., and when sued for damages by R. stated in defence that S. & Co. had not been authorised to conclude the charterparty on their behalf.

R. then sued S. & Co. for damages including the expense incurred in raising the action against Ireland & Son through the fault of S. & Co. in representing to R. that Ireland & Son had authorised S. & Co. to enter into the contract.

The Second Division held that R. were entitled to recover as damages the difference between the profit which would have been made on the abortive contract and the best terms which could be obtained in the market when the misrepresentation was discovered.

The House of Lords held that R. were entitled to the actual damage sustained by their having been led to believe that a contract had been completed, but that R. had no claim for loss of profit.

Lord Moncreiff (at p. 69): "It must be kept in view throughout that the question is not whether there was a contract between the pursuers (the shipowners) and the charterers — undoubtedly there was not — but whether the defenders without authority represented that there was, and thereby caused injury to the pursuers. . . . It is immaterial whether the defenders, the shipbrokers, are regarded as having acted as agents for both parties or as agents for the pursuers alone. They acted as intermediaries; all communications passed through them, and they were undoubtedly bound to transmit those communications with strict accuracy. If they failed to do so, and especially if they failed to do so intentionally, they are equally in law liable in damages if damage resulted. . . .

"If, then, there would have been a completed contract if telegram No. 41 had been authorised by the charterers, the next question is whether the defenders are in law liable in damages if damage was sustained in consequence of their misrepresentation. No Scottish decision directly in point was referred to; but authority is scarcely required. I cannot doubt that if an agent, whether acting for both parties or only for one, falsely represents that he has authority to contract and loss results to either party in consequence of their relying upon the representations, the agent will be personally liable in damages. If, for instance, it had been here the charterers' interest to found on the contract which the defenders professed to make and the pursuers had repudiated it, they would have had a good claim against the defenders, and the latter would certainly not have had relief against the pursuers. It happens that it is the pursuers who have sustained loss, and I see no reason why they should not equally recover from the parties who caused it. In short, in such a case ultimate liability must rest with the agent who exceeds his authority.

"In the absence of Scottish decisions the pursuers rely upon the class of cases in English law of which *Collen* v. *Wright* and *Simons* v. *Patchet* ((1857) 7 E. and B. 568) are leading examples. By these cases it seems to be settled in the law of England that 'where a person, by asserting the authority of the principal, induces another person to enter into any transaction which he would not have entered into but for that assertion, and the assertion turns out to be untrue, to the injury of the person to whom it is made, it must be taken that the person making it undertook that it was true, and he is liable personally for the damage that has occurred.' . . . It is also established in these cases that the measure of damages is what was lost by the party with whom the contract was made in consequence of not having the valid contract which the agent professed to make — that is, the difference between the profit which would have been made on the abortive contract and the best terms which could be obtained in the market when the misrepresentation was discovered. . . .

"Those decisions no doubt are not binding upon us, but on a mercantile question like the present it is desirable that as far as possible the same rule should be applied in both countries. . . .

"I have no hesitation in following the law there laid down in so far as it applies.

"On the question of damages . . . the main item is the loss of anticipated profit under the contract which the defenders professed to have made for the pursuers, under deduction of the profit actually realised on a substituted voyage, the freight in which was 5s. instead of 7s. 6d. Now, from 5th December onwards freights fell rapidly. The pursuers lost their opportunity of getting equally good freight, and ultimately 5s. a ton was as much as I believe they could have obtained under a suitable charter.

"As to the minor item of the expenses of the action against Ireland & Son . . . I think the pursuers were entitled to proceed against the charterers until defences were lodged."

Lord Chancellor (Halsbury) (at p. 101): "The proposition of law laid down . . . in *Collen* v. *Wright* must, I think, . . . be held to be law. But one must see what that proposition is, and how far it is applicable to the case before your Lordships. The proposition is this — that a person who induces another to contract with him as the agent of a third party by an unqualified assertion of his being authorised to act as such agent is answerable to the person who so contracts for any damage which he may sustain by reason of the assertion of authority being untrue. This is the authority upon which the Court below have given damages, but it really has no application to the facts in proof here.

"A firm applies to a shipbroker in Scotland to obtain freights for a vessel of theirs. The shipbroker, in consequence, opens a negotiation with Messrs Ireland, who state certain terms which they will accept, one of which is what the appellants' principals will not agree to. The appellants nevertheless untruly report that the bargain is complete, whereas the bargain, in fact, went off altogether. Now, I quite agree that, if in consequence of their misstatement the respondents changed their position and suffered damage, the appellants would be liable for any actual damage arising from the acting on that erroneous statement . . .; but it appears to me there is absolute failure to make out any such damages as are claimed, though I think £33 odd has been justly suggested as enough to cover all actual damage sustained."

Lord Davey (at p. 102): "It is not necessary for the purposes of this decision to have recourse to the doctrine of *Collen* v. *Wright*. The appellants, the shipbrokers, were undoubtedly agents of the respondents for the purpose of finding a charter for their ship. But I am not satisfied on the evidence that the appellants were employed by Messrs Ireland & Son to find a ship for their requirements. It appears to me that the negotiations were carried on between the appellants as agents for the respondents with Irelands as principals acting on their own behalf. No doubt the appellants were intermediaries between the two firms, but that always is so where the agent of one party is negotiating with the other party. Wherever a person misrepresents a fact relative to a third party, he, in a sense, impliedly represents that he is authorised to make the statement. But I do not think that he is thereby asserting that he is clothed with an authority or fills a particular character within the meaning of the doctrine of *Collen* v. *Wright* . . ., or that the doctrine ought to be extended to such a case as that now before your Lordships.

"But the appellants were guilty of a breach of their duty to the respondents, their principals, in giving them incorrect information as to their business, and are liable in damages for such a breach of duty. The measure of damages in such a case . . . [is] the loss actually sustained by the principal in consequence of the misrepresentation, and . . . [does] not include the anticipated profit which he might have made if the representation had been true. . . . With regard to the expenses of the abortive action against Ireland & Son, the question is whether they were reasonably incurred. On this point . . . I think the respondents are entitled to recover these expenses subject to taxation. The only other head of damage claimed is a general charge for telegrams and trouble and inconvenience. I think the sum of £33, 1s. 3d. which has been awarded by the Court below will be an ample compensation and solatium to the respondents on this head."

Lord Robertson (at p. 103): "In the view which I take of it this case is one of great simplicity both in fact and in law.

"A foreign shipowner (the respondents' firm) employs a Leith shipbroker (the appellants) on the usual terms of remuneration to find freight for a steamship. The appellants take the business in hand and report that they have concluded a bargain. In fact no bargain had been concluded. . . .

"That the appellants, by making this misstatement, acted in violation of their duty as agents for the respondents admits of no doubt; and the respondents have a good claim of damages for whatever loss has been caused them. If, for example, acting on the faith of the alleged contract, the respondents had incurred expense, or if, misled into inaction, they had missed other chances for the ship, these and the like would be heads of damage.

"The facts in the present case are not of this kind. The respondents, in furtherance of their theory of their case, have been at pains to prove that at this particular time no other advantageous freights were to be had, and, when informed that the bargain was off, they made no efforts to look for them. They found employment for the steamer in a quarter where it was easily to be had (under a current contract) although at a low rate, 5s. per ton.

"The claim of the respondents is for the difference between this rate and 7s. 6d. per ton, the rate in the bargain which was not concluded; and their theory is that they are entitled to take the appellants at their word, and demand from them fulfilment of the charter or damages. To this the short answer is that the appellants (who dealt with Ireland at arm's length) did not in point of fact assume to act for the alleged charterers at all, and they purported to report the agreement of the charterers as matter of fact. The central and crucial fact in the case is that the appellants did not represent to the respondents that they acted for Irelands. The case is therefore not within the scope of *Collen* v. *Wright*.

"The practical result is that in my opinion the main part of the claim of damages is untenable. But I think that the respondents are entitled to something for certain damage which they have proved, to wit, trouble, outlays on telegrams, and the like; and in the Court of Session this has been fixed at £33, 1s. 3d. They have been also held entitled to the expenses incurred by them in the action against Messrs Ireland down to the closing of the record, and I think that they are entitled to this."

The case is commented on by David M. Walker, *The Law of Civil Remedies in Scotland*, p. 489, as follows: "In *Salvesen* v. *Rederi Aktiebolaget Nordstjernan* it was held by the House of Lords that, where an agent mistakenly represented to his principal that he had concluded a contract with a third party on the principal's behalf, he was liable to the principal for the expenses incurred by the latter's actings, proceeding on the belief that the contract had in fact been completed, but not liable (altering on this point the decision of the Second Division) for the loss of profit which the principal would have made on that same basis, in respect that he was not acting and had not represented himself to be acting for the third party. He could not be liable for breach of warranty to the person who granted the authority and knew its extent, as that party must, if anyone, have known the true extent and limits of his authority."

3. *Irving* v. *Burns*, 1915 S.C. 260, was an unsuccessful claim for damages for breach of warranty of authority.

B., the secretary of The Langside Picture House Ltd., accepted an offer made by I. for the execution of certain plumber-work in connection with a hall or theatre which the company was about to erect.

After the work had been executed and I. had ascertained that the contract was not in fact binding on the company, I. brought an action against B. for damages for breach of warranty of authority. In this action I. averred that the company had no assets.

*Held* that as it appeared from this averment that I. would have been in no better position had the contract bound the company, he had suffered no loss from, and therefore could not recover damages for, B.'s breach of warranty.

Lord Salvesen (at p. 265): "The Langside Picture House, Limited, was a private company incorporated on 14th December 1911. The defender appears to have been the chief promoter. . . .

"The nominal capital was £4,500; but in the course of its brief and inglorious existence only a fraction of the capital was subscribed. . . . Nevertheless contracts were entered into to the amount of £2,500 for building a picture house on a site the company had secured on lease. After these contracts had been partially implemented the company found itself unable to meet its liabilities; and eventually the directors renounced the lease, and the proprietors are now in possession of the ground and the buildings that had been so far erected upon it. The company has no assets; and the pursuer has not received a penny to account of the contract work which he did to an amount which he estimates at the sum of £164, 13s. 8d. It is not surprising that in these circumstances he should have looked about for some person who could be made responsible to him for payment of his account. . . .

"The pursuer's second ground of action is . . . to the effect that 'the defender having falsely professed to have the authority of the directors of the company to contract with the pursuer and to accept the pursuer's offer, and having thus induced the pursuer to believe he had such authority, the defender is personally responsible for the loss suffered by the pursuer.' . . . The import of the numerous cases cited to us on this subject is that the agent who acts without authority on behalf of his principal does not become liable on the contract which he professes to make, but only warrants his authority. Now, it is part of the pursuer's case that if he had had a good contract with the company he could have recovered nothing, as the company has no assets. In the case of *Firbank* [*Firbank's Executors* v. *Humphreys* (1886) 18 Q.B.D. 54, at p. 62], in dealing with the liability of directors who issued debenture stock on the implied representation that they had authority to do so whereas they had none, Lindley, L.J., said, 'if genuine debenture stock of the company had been worthless, the measure of damages would have been nil.' The defender, no doubt, warranted his authority to contract on behalf of the company. If he had in fact had authority the company would have been bound; but as it has no assets the damage arising from a breach of the warranty is nil."

This case is commented on by David M. Walker, *The Law of Civil Remedies in Scotland*, p. 487, as follows: "It would appear on principle that an award of nominal damages would have been appropriate in this case, but does not appear to have been suggested to the court, though in this respect the decision is contrary to the general rule that any infringement of a right sounds in damages."

4. See also *Royal Bank of Scotland* v. *Skinner* in Note to *Sinclair, Moorhead, & Co.* v. *Wallace & Co.* (p. 33, above).

## CHAPTER 8

# TERMINATION OF THE RELATIONSHIP

*Expiry of the time for which constituted*

**Brenan v. Campbell's Trustees**
(1898) 25 R. 423

B., a civil engineer and architect in Oban, was employed by C. to be factor on C.'s estate of Lochnell for four years from Martinmas 1890 on the express condition that B. should take C.'s stepson, M'Clement, as an apprentice for four years from Martinmas 1890 and pay M'Clement a yearly salary of £50. B. was not restricted by the agreement from carrying on business in addition to the Lochnell factory. He accordingly continued to practise as an engineer and architect in Oban, but the Lochnell factory was his main business.

In October 1894 B. was informed that his services would not be required on the Lochnell estate after Martinmas 1894.

B. claimed that he was entitled to six months' notice of termination of his factory, and raised an action against C. for six months' pay in lieu of notice.

*Held* that, as B. was not a servant but a professional man employed by a number of clients, he was not entitled to notice of the termination of his employment, and further that the special contract limited the period of his factory to four years.

LORD ORDINARY (LOW) (at p. 425): "The pursuer, besides being factor upon the Lochnell estate, carried on business at Oban as an engineer and architect, and so long as he duly performed the duties of factor he was free to engage in any other business he chose. At the time of his dismissal he was engaged under an agreement for a specified period of four years, and it was on the expiry of the four years that his employment was terminated. . . .

"In these circumstances, I am of opinion that the pursuer is not entitled to a money payment in lieu of notice of the termination of his employment. There is no case in the books in which the rule as to reasonable notice has been applied to the case of a person employed under agreement for a definite period, or of a person who did not give his whole time to his employer, but who also carried on other business. The principle upon which the rule is founded appears to me not to apply to such a case, that principle being that a servant ought not to be unexpectedly deprived of his sole means of support, but should receive reasonable warning that his employment is to be terminated, so that he may have an opportunity of obtaining other employment."

LORD PRESIDENT (J. P. B. ROBERTSON) (at p. 425): "I think the Lord Ordinary is right. The pursuer's claim depends on his making out that he was entitled to notice on the expiry of his contract of employment, if that employment was to be brought to a termination. Now, I think it is more than doubtful whether the doctrine of tacit relocation applies to a gentleman circumstanced as he was in relation to the estate of Lochnell. I do not think that Mr Brenan can be described as the servant of the Lochnell trustees, even in the wider sense in which that term is used in legal phraseology. He was in truth a professional man, qualified by his training for the management of estates, and the evidence shews that he resided in Oban, and held himself out as open to employment by landlords for the work of factoring and rent collecting. He had employment as a factor not only from the Lochnell trustees but from another proprietor, and the circumstance that his professional business was not large does not alter his true relation to those whose employment he accepted. To adopt a popular expression used in another connection, he went out factoring and was not the factor of the Lochnell trustees. I think that is an important distinction, because if the other view were adopted all professional men who are employed to factor estates, or, for that matter, houses, would fall within the class entitled to notice on termination of their employment. . . . I think the facts of this case shew that Mr Brenan was not the servant of the trustees of Lochnell estate in the true sense of the term, but that they were only one of the clients who employed him in his business of factor.

"Then another point which I think is even more decisive against the pursuer's claim is, that he was employed under a very special contract. The agreement with which we are concerned seems to me expressly to ascribe the duration of the factorship for four years to the condition that Mr Brenan should take Mr M'Clement, a relative of Mr Campbell of Lochnell, as apprentice for the same period, because the words are, that it was 'resolved to continue the factory of the said George Woulfe Brenan for a period of four years from the term of Martinmas 1890, upon the express condition that the said George Woulfe Brenan should enter into an indenture with Mr Richard M'Clement, stepson of the said Archibald Argyll Lochnell Campbell, for a period of four years from the said term of Martinmas 1890.' The two things are therefore identical in duration, the one being the inducing cause of the other. . . . I think, therefore, that when the contract came to an end Mr Brenan was entitled to no notice."

NOTE

For an instance of implied agency terminated by lapse of time and change of circumstances see *Ferguson and Lillie* v. *Stephen* in Note 5 to *Barnetson* v. *Petersen Brothers* (p. 13, above).

*Death of principal*

**Life Association of Scotland v. Douglas**
(1886) 13 R. 910

A bond and disposition in security was granted to the Life Association of Scotland by the Athole Hydropathic Co. Ltd. and the directors of that company. The deed had been signed by the several granters of it on different dates, between 11th May and 23rd July. One of the directors, D., had signed on 11th May. D. died on 4th July. The secretary of the company continued to hold the bond until, having been signed by all the granters, it was delivered to the Life Association of Scotland on 24th July in exchange for the sum advanced.

There was failure to pay the whole sum in the bond, and the Life Association of Scotland raised an action against certain of the co-obligants, including D.'s executor.

*Held* that the executor was not liable, because the implied authority given by D. for the delivery of the bond once all the signatures had been obtained had fallen by D.'s death.

LORD PRESIDENT (INGLIS) (at p. 912): "It must always be kept in mind, in considering such questions, that the delivery of a deed is not a matter of law, but a matter of fact. The condition of the deed here was that it had been subscribed by Mr Douglas, and probably by some others, but it was held by the secretary of the Hydropathic Company — *i.e.*, by the agent of the borrowers — and no money had been advanced on it. Therefore, *de facto*, it was an undelivered deed at the date of Mr Douglas's death.

"No doubt the secretary for the company would have been entitled, if nothing had intervened, and the money had been advanced, to deliver the deed, because he had a clearly implied mandate to that effect. But Mr Douglas died before that was done, and the mandate by Mr Douglas to deliver the deed in exchange for the money fell. No one can dispute all that, and therefore Mr Douglas cannot be bound, and his executors cannot be bound."

NOTE

In *Campbell* v. *Anderson* (1829) 3 W. & S. 384, an agent who had contracted in the *bona fide* belief that his principal, who had died abroad, was still alive was held to have bound his principal.

A. was factor for Gordon of Draikies, an estate in Inverness-shire. C. & Co., of Glasgow, were Gordon's commercial agents in connection with Gordon's West Indian possessions.

On leaving to visit his West Indian estates, Gordon granted to A. in September 1808 a factory conferring on A. extensive powers for the management of Draikies, including power to borrow money and to draw bills of exchange on his account.

On 11th November 1809, A. drew a bill of exchange for £500 on C. & Co., and discounted the bill. On 22nd November A. informed C. & Co. that he had just received notification that Gordon had died on 25th August. There was a large balance due by Gordon to C. & Co. who, when the bill of exchange became due, refused to pay it. The holder of the bill raised an action against C. & Co. to compel payment (*Shepherd* v. *Campbells, Frazer, and Co.* (1823) 2 S. 346), and was successful.

C. & Co. assigned their claim to their partner C., and he raised an action against A. concluding for reduction of the bill, for repetition of the amount, and relief of the expenses in the action on the bill. The ground of the action was that A.'s powers as factor had necessarily ceased from the time of Gordon's death, whether he knew of it or not, and that in any event A.'s letters imported an individual liability. A.'s answer was that as he had acted on the *bona fide* belief that Gordon was alive and as the bill had been drawn expressly *factorio nomine* he could not be made personally liable.

*Held* that A. was not personally liable.

Lord Ordinary (Medwyn) (at p. 386): "The fourth reason is the only proper ground of reduction, that the bill is null, as having been drawn subsequent to the death of the mandant. But as this event was not known at the time in this country, the defender's having continued to act on his factory was legal, and therefore the bill cannot be set aside on that ground.

"If it be competent, under this summons, to consider whether the pursuer has any claim of relief against the defender, it appears to the Lord Ordinary to be quite clear, that the defender neither meant to undertake any personal responsibility, nor did the pursuer understand that he did. The pursuer was the chief partner in the house of Campbells, Fraser and Company, who were the consignees of the late Mr Gordon of Draikies, for his West India estates. The defender, as factor on the estate of Draikies, was authorised by the pursuer to draw upon his house on behalf of Mr Gordon. He accordingly asked leave (28th October 1809) to draw for £500; and if this was permitted, he begged the pursuer to write Mr Gordon, 'that he may have the earliest knowledge of this addition to his engagements with you, and provide accordingly.' The pursuer, on 4th November 1809, says, 'Your draft on Campbells, Fraser and Company, will meet honour to the extent you mention. . . .' The defender accordingly draws the bill under reduction for £500, 'per procuration of Robert Gordon'; and besides notifying officially to the house, he notifies also privately to the pursuer, and adds, 'By the time it falls due, I trust you will be in possession of produce to meet it, or that it can be otherwise provided for, should you find it necessary.' . . .

"Now it appears that in the whole transaction the defender was acting, and was known to be acting, as the factor of Mr Gordon, and for his behoof. The reimbursement was to come from the crop in the West Indies, all of which was consigned to Campbells and Company; and the utmost that the defender was asked to do was, if remittances did not arrive, and if Gordon's agents required it, he, as Gordon's factor, should reimburse them till the crop came round; that is, provide some temporary accommodation . . . if they really required it, till the crop arrived from which both parties contemplated that it was ultimately to be paid. . . . It appears to the Lord Ordinary that they cannot claim relief from the defender personally."

The First Division adhered ((1826) 5 S. 86). No opinions are reported at that stage.

In the House of Lords Lord Chancellor Lyndhurst said (at p. 389): "There can be no doubt what is the law of Scotland on the present point. The case resolves into a question of *bona fides*. The Court below seem to have been of opinion that there was *bona fides* on the part of Anderson; and I see no ground for drawing a different conclusion."

### *Insanity of principal*

## **Wink v. Mortimer**
(1849) 11 D. 995

Macrae had been employed as agent by Edmonstone. For a few weeks Edmonstone was insane and confined to a lunatic asylum. Macrae continued to act as his agent during that time.

Later, Edmonstone had his estates sequestrated, and Macrae claimed in the sequestration for the amount of his business account.

*Held* that Edmonstone's temporary insanity did not operate a recall of Macrae's employment as agent.

LORD FULLERTON (at p. 1002): "The objection is, that part of the account paid for business done by the agent, was so done for the bankrupt, the alleged employer, while he was confined in the lunatic assylum. The confinement was temporary and lasted only a few weeks. There is no pretence for stating that the business was not done, or was not done beneficially for the employer; and it would be of the most injurious consequences to hold that in such circumstances, an agent was bound to withhold his services during his employer's temporary disability, until he obtained some regular judicial authority for the continuance of his acting. I think in the circumstances of this case, there can be no doubt that the currency of the account was not interrupted by the very short illness of the employer."

NOTE

The effect of a principal's insanity was fully considered in *Pollok* v. *Paterson*, 10 Dec. 1811, F.C.

David Paterson had carried on business in Edinburgh for many years as a banker and insurance-broker. In 1805, on going to London, he granted a procuration in favour of his son, John Paterson, empowering him to manage his affairs in his absence.

When in London, David Paterson became insane. He was brought back to Scotland and continued to reside in his own house. Visitors of the family knew of his insanity, but no public notice of it was taken until 1811.

Meantime John Paterson carried on business on his father's account, and in the same branches of business, until the end of 1808, making use of the procuration.

In 1809, wishing to carry on business on his own account, John Paterson enlarged the sphere of his operations, entering into several mercantile and trading speculations with Kerr, a merchant in Leith. He continued to use the procuration in a number of his transactions. In 1810 his concern with Kerr became bankrupt.

Pollok, as holder of a bill of exchange accepted by John Paterson per procuration of David, claimed payment from David.

A petition was presented for David's sequestration, and the prayer of that petition was granted in 1811. The question before the court in this case was the recall of David's sequestration, "but there was a great deal of collateral argument as to the effect of the insanity of the mandant upon the powers of the mandatory, which, though it did not enter into the decision, it is deemed adviseable to preserve, from the Judges having delivered their opinions upon it at considerable length."

Lord Meadowbank (at p. 375): "This case is one of extraordinary interest. Transactions of great magnitude have been carried on for a course of years, by means of this procuration, with all the principal merchants and bankers in this city. And all those transactions are now, after the lapse of a number of years, said to be null and void by the *curator bonis*, who has obtained a verdict, finding that the person in whose name they were carried on was *non compos mentis*.

"Hardly any thing could be more fatal to mercantile transactions than bringing the doctrine of mandate into question, so as to shake such transactions on subtleties unknown to common minds. It is absolutely necessary that the nature of mercantile business, which is carried on with a dispatch which gives no time for those leisurely inquiries which take place in other civil transactions, should be attended to in settling and deciding such a question.

"On the other hand, the law is the natural guardian of an imbecile, unprotected man; and the picture was certainly most interesting that was drawn to us of a man thrown by the hand of God into a state of lunacy, and rendered incapable of taking charge of his own affairs, and, on his recovery, finding himself bankrupt and ruined by such means. . . .

"The argument for the family is, that mandate perishes by death, and by lunacy or furiosity, as equivalent to death; and, therefore, that the mandate came to an end when the insanity commenced.

"On the other hand, it is maintained that furiosity does not put an end to mandate; that neither does death; but only the execution of the business mandated, or the publication of the recall of the mandate; and that there was here no publication of the state of the mandant, but rather the reverse.

"It is maintained further, that the mandate would have been good, if it had said, in so many words, that it was to be good, and was meant to enable the mandatory to carry on business, even in the case of the mandant's insanity. That mandates, therefore, not perishing *sua natura*, and requiring promulgation of being recalled, and no promulgation of the kind having been made, but, on the contrary, the country rather kept in ignorance of the state of the mandant, we ought to find the mandate continued in force.

"On a full consideration of these arguments, my opinion is, that the plea of the creditors is well founded. The rule that mandate perishes by the death of the mandant, is liable to so many exceptions that there must be some more general principle for regulating such cases; and it is one which appears to me to lie upon the very surface of the case, — That it must continue in force till it is actually recalled. All acts of the usual conductor of a person's business, relative to that business, are complete and valid in themselves, and have effect for ever, till they meet with an obstacle strong enough to stop them.

"In the case of an ordinary mandate, a man only means to provide for the management of his affairs during his own life. The object of the mandate, therefore, in the general case, terminates with life; but then though the will that created the mandate perishes, the mandate itself does not perish by the death of the mandant. It gives place to a new will; the will of the heir, who is presumed to continue it if he does not recall it; and if it subsists in the case of death, which every person is bound to take notice of, and it continues till the will of the new party operates, by recalling it, what other rule can be followed here?

"What difference is there between the nature of mandate and the nature of trust? Trusts are mandates to be executed after the death of the granter, and they may last for many generations. There is no difference in the nature of the thing, or the universality of the principle. There is a great difference in the objects of mandates, but none at all in the nature of them. The power of the mandatory cannot be assimilated to the continuance of the willing power, or the confidence of the mandant. The loss of confidence is of no consequence if there is no recall; for there may be many things that will determine the mandant not to recall, even where he has lost the confidence he had in the mandatory. It plainly does not depend, therefore, even on the continuance of confidence. It is an act of the will to recall it; and till it is recalled, it must subsist.

"It seems to have been confounded with the notion of a perpetually renewed act. There is no ground for that idea. A man may never think of his mandate—he may have sent his mandatories to the *ultima thule*, or other places quite out of his own reach; and whatever change may take place, the person so employed may carry on his business till it is recalled. There is no continued act of the will. It is a finished act; and it is to be judged of *secundum subjectam materiam*, and not otherwise. Once given, the mandate continues *sua natura*, and does not require a continuation of mental exertion or approbation.

"Now that being my opinion of the general nature of the principles applicable to mandates, I inquire next what was the mandate in this case? Here is a mandate to John Paterson to do business for his father. Has there been any expression of a will for recalling that mandate? None. It is said that there could be none, because the mandant became incapable of expressing an opposite will, or any will at all, and that there is no will competent to recall it existing, not even the will of the *curator bonis*. That, I think, is a mistake. The *curator bonis* is the manager appointed by law for persons in this unhappy situation. Till he came to act, there was no will that could recall it. Nothing short of his will would do — but he can do it. It may have been matter of great rashness and presumption in the mandatory to have continued to act in the circumstances of this case. . . . But there was no incompetency in his so doing. There was no recall that disabled him from acting. . . .

"My opinion is, that till there was a mind capable of recalling the procuration, John Paterson was the manager for his father; that the very circumstance of the insanity prolonged his office; and that it by no means fell from the incapacity to recall it. The incapacity to recall should have been put an end to by the legal management of a *curator bonis* being introduced.

"Even if this view of the principles of the law were wrong, still I think the case acquires a great deal of strength from the effect of *bona fides* in dealing with a person who has a recalled or limited mandate; where the mandate has been circumscribed by the will of the granter of the mandate, or where it has been recalled as to certain circumstances, or where it has been recalled *in toto*.

". . . Here there was no proper *mala fides* on the part of John Paterson; he may have been guilty of great impropriety, but what have the public to do with that? They were entitled to go on transacting with the mandatory, perhaps even though they knew the situation of David Paterson, but certainly they were not bound to enquire into it."

Lord Glenlee (at p. 378): "I dont consider the true source of the claims against David Paterson as arising out of any thing done after he became insane. I dont think that there are only the two people, the mandant and the mandatory, concerned. The man who grants the procuration comes under an engagement to the public, and the risk of every circumstance whatever, not of public notoriety, falls upon himself; and that risk was undertaken by him when he was of sound mind, if he was so when he granted the mandate.

"If we were to hold that the mandate fell by insanity, what would be the consequence in all cases of mandate, and on mercantile transactions in general? The public might say, we are willing to trade with your mandatory; but how shall we be able to know whether your power has been recalled, or whether or when it may hereafter be revoked? What could the granter say? He must say it is fair, and just, and reasonable, that I should warrant what may be done; and if any bad consequences should ensue, it is much more reasonable that they should fall upon me and my family than on you, who can have nothing to do with the mandate.

"Granting that the procuration came to an end as to all who know of it, and on that head I dont mean to say any thing here; at all events, as to all who knew nothing about it, it must continue. The mandant took the risk upon himself."

Lord Gillies (at p. 379): "On its first aspect, this is a most distressing case. — Both parties here are in *bona fide*. — On the one hand we have *bona fide* onerous creditors, merely endeavouring to recover payment of just debts — on the other hand, the *curator bonis* is endeavouring to save what he can of the estate. — Both parties are struggling *de damno vitando*.

"Some blame has been thrown upon the conduct of the relations; I see no ground whatever for that; they allowed matters to continue in the state we have heard for several years; but I dont find myself at liberty to ascribe their having done so to improper motives, when it may be accounted for by good ones; and I think they lay by without any bad view, and that their silence proceeded from a very natural feeling of delicacy, which they have only broke through at last, that they may be able to save this poor man from utter ruin. . . .

"This is a petition for the recall of the sequestration; and the ground set forth for the recall is sufficient, if it were made out. It is said that there is no debt; and we are entitled to enquire into the truth of the allegation that there is no debt, and consequently no bankruptcy.

"The plea upon which this allegation is made is, that the debts were contracted under mandate, and that the mandate was expired.

"I dont think that these general propositions can be disputed; but the question is, if they are good in this case; and if they lead to the result that there is no debt.

"I hold insanity to be in a different situation, as to mandate, from death. The presumption is, that the death of a party is known, whereas the insanity is not. But the knowledge of the one fact is the same as the other. Insanity, where it is known, must have the same effect as death; and I think, that if there is a distinction, insanity should have a stronger effect than death; for, in the one case, the heir appears, or may do it; but, in the other, there is no one who can appear.

"In answer to this, the creditors say that though, in the general case, mandate expires by the death of the mandant, or by his insanity, yet third parties, ignorant thereof, are safe; and, 2d, That this was not a special mandate, but that John Paterson was an institor; and it is farther said, that it was truly granted, not only with a view to a permanent arrangement, but with the view of providing for the management, if he should become insane.

"I cannot subscribe to these arguments without some limitation. I do not think that, in the case of a special mandate, *bona fides* will have the effect that has been pleaded. For instance, if David Paterson, when he went to London, had given a mandate to sell the estate of Costarton, and his mandatory had tried to do so in the year 1809, to me it appears to be matter of very great doubt if David Paterson, or his curator *bonis*, could have been compelled to implement that sale. In the same way, if he had given him a mandate to do any other particular act, I have great doubts if he would have been entitled to execute it at the distance of years.

"Therefore I dont think that, in the case of a special mandate, the *bona fides* of the contracting party would validate the transaction. I do not think that it would entitle the *bona fide* party to insist for implement from the mandant.

"In the next place, I do not think that this was a mandate to enable the son to act in case of insanity. I think it is naturally accounted for by his journey at the time, and with a view to which it appears to have been given.

"I also doubt how far a party is entitled, in the event of his insanity, to give full powers to conduct his affairs in such a situation. The law has provided for that case, that a tutor should be served to him; and the powers of the mandatory may be superseded by him at any time. It admits of great doubt whether, where a person has been cognosced as insane, his tutor is at liberty to carry on any hazardous business in his name. And if a tutor, the legal guardian, could not do any thing of the kind, how can we hold that a simple mandatory may?

"With regard to the plea that John Paterson was not a mere mandatory, but that he was institor, and had a general *prepositura*, — that is an argument which has great weight with me, and leads to a different result, in my opinion, from that which would have taken place if this had been a special mandate; though still I doubt whether, even as an institor, he could bind the estate to parties who were aware of the insanity.

"But the existence of the insanity may not have been known to some of the friends and correspondents; for your Lordships may figure many things that would prevent it; and I conceive that all the arguments founded on the presumed *bona fides* of the parties are available to them. This man was acting for another, they may say, of whom they knew nothing, but that he had granted a power to transact *unoquoque*. The creditors were not bound to inquire into the condition of the truster, but only of the person with whom they contracted. But if they did know that condition, I conceive that the want of *bona fides* would prevent them from coming against the estate.

"Therefore, I think that though neither of the arguments of the creditors is completely well founded in itself, yet that the two together are enough to make out their case; First, That some of them were *in bona fide*; and, second, That there was a *prepositura*.

"Limited in this way, it appears to me that the rule is expedient and just; that the parties who contracted have a claim against the estate of the mandant, whether he was alive or dead, sane or insane; and, therefore, that they should be entitled to recover. It is more just that the loss should fall on the mandant than on them; and it does so not on account of any thing done by him during his insanity, but on account of want of prudence, when he was in good health, in appointing an improper person as his mandatory.

"On these grounds, I think that the sequestration should not be recalled. It is impossible to deny that some of the debts are good, and that some of them may be bad; and unless it shall be proved that, at the period of the sequestration, no debts were due by him, or that they have all been paid, it cannot be taken off."

Lord Craigie (at p. 381): "Lord Gillies has stated so clearly the views which I entertain of this case, that it is unnecessary for me to resume the argument.

"The only thing in which I differ from him is as to John Paterson being an institor. I conceive that he was not an institor; but merely a mandatory, and that of a very special kind. I think the only object of his trust was to carry on the business of an insurance-broker and of a banker. I dont think he could have sold the heritable property of his father, nor have granted leases, nor have done any thing except as an insurance-broker or banker; and he seems to have been aware of that; for he gave up the business of insurance.

"Though I do not think the limitation so absolute as that the whole transactions should fall from the time of David Paterson's insanity, yet the creditors knew, or should have known, the terms of the procuration. I conceive that the whole of them must be held as having contracted under all the limitations that are therein contained. It appears to me that, in many circumstances, the debts contracted by David Paterson will not be ultimately binding; but the present question is, if the sequestration can be recalled; and I am quite clear that *in hoc statu* it cannot."

Lord Justice-Clerk (Boyle) (at p. 381): "This is a case of a most important and distressing nature, both as to the family and as to the creditors *bona fide* dealing with the son. But, painful as the case is, and important as it may be to the family and the creditors, it is one of still more importance to the commercial interest of the country in general. And though I concur with your Lordships in thinking that there is a preliminary point which is enough to prevent the recall, yet we owe it to the country and to the parties to give our opinion on the general question. . . .

"The sequestration having proceeded regularly under the act of Parliament, on debts that have been found to be good by two judgments of the competent authority, that is enough to prevent us from recalling it *in hoc statu*.

"The general objection is stated, that the procuration was void and null from the commencement of the insanity, and that all the transactions that have been carried on, on so extensive a scale, and transactions which, it will be observed, were in the precise terms of the mandate, as being in the banking and insurance-broker business, have been from the beginning void and null, and that nothing can follow upon them. The mere discussion of such a question in this country, where the system of procuration is so extensive, is a very serious thing. Unless it is made out that no debts are due, it would never be possible for the Court to support such an action.

"It must be recollected that, down to the time of the failure, the procuration was universally acted upon, — it was received as effectual in every banking house in this city, except the Royal Bank, and, with a slight exception, Sir William Forbes's, when they became less ready to act upon it; but I see that, with the exception of the period I have mentioned, not the slightest doubt seems to have been entertained that the transactions under it were good and effectual. It seems to have been received in every quarter; the whole transactions of the house were conducted by the son without any inquiry or objection; and, if it was acted upon in that way in this city, is it possible to conceive that foreign parties were to refuse to do it? The very statement of these circumstances does carry on the face of it such an appearance of *bona fides*, that it is impossible for me to get the better of it.

"There may be circumstances, as to particular debts, where the parties knew of the insanity, and that the mandatory was exceeding the bounds of the procuration. I agree with all your Lordships that those are delicate and important points which are fit for consideration in the sequestration. I am speaking here of the general question.

"Notwithstanding all this, and when no interference took place on the part of any person in the family, (though we have evidence that two parties desired Mrs Paterson to take steps to get him cognosced, but which, from a feeling of delicacy, and dislike to expose his situation, she did not do as she should have done), we are told that mandate expires by the death of the granter, and that insanity is just in the same situation as death; and they urge that plea, forgetting that, if it was to be sustained, every thing must be restored as at the beginning.

"But, before coming to this particular case, I would observe, that the general rule of law relied on is full of most material exceptions introduced in the law of Rome, and confirmed and adopted in the law of modern Europe, and of England, if we can pay any regard to the authorities before us.

"I will not go through all the cases; but there is one which I cannot help mentioning, because I conceive, that if this man was not an institor, he approached nearer to that character than to any other whatever, and that we can apply no other rule to him than the Roman law did to institors.

"Now, it was settled in the Roman law, that even where restrictions were imposed by the party himself upon the institor, if they were not proclaimed in a public and open manner, so as to warn all the world, the acts of the institor would be good in a question with the *prepositor*. If the third party was *in bona fide*, his transactions with the institor were good and effectual.

"Is there any doubt that this rule is rooted in the law of modern Europe? We cannot doubt it, if we believe the authority of Pothier, who is most express upon the point.

"We have the opinion of an English lawyer of eminence, that the decision in that country would have been the same.

"And when the whole context of our own law is taken into view, I conceive there can be no doubt that the law of Scotland is just the same.

"Then if, in the case of an institor, due notification of the recall of the mandate, or of the ceasing of the powers of the mandatory, is indispensably necessary, is it possible to figure a case in which notification is more necessary than in that now before us?

"I agree in what was said, that if any transaction can be shown to have been *ultra fines mandati*, it will be right for your Lordships to consider it; but that must be in the sequestration, and I need not speak to it now.

"I cannot set the silence and acquiescence of the parties in any other view than that which has been taken by your Lordships, that all persons who acted fairly and *bona fide* have good claims against David Paterson. They are claims which come upon him from a deed granted by himself when he was in good health; and, in consequence of his granting such an extensive power as this, persons relying *bona fide* on their transactions are entitled to come against his estate.

"We are told that this is a grievous claim; and that here a person, who has no power of recalling his mandate, is to have his whole estate swallowed up by means of it. I lament that very much; but, in a case of this kind, we cannot extend our hand to interfere in his behalf.

"In a case of copartnery, it is not the mere dissolution of it that will liberate a man. The partner must give public notice to all the world. Is there any difference in this case? I conceive not. The very same principles enter into both of them; due care must be taken for the benefit of the public as well as of the parties; and the acts of the mandatory must be binding on the mandant till the mandate is formally recalled, at least so long as the contracting parties are ignorant of any change of circumstances."

### *Bankruptcy of principal*

**M'Kenzie v. Campbell**
(1894) 21 R. 904

On 11th October 1893 Fraser, a corn-factor in Glasgow, was arrested on various charges of forgery.

The following day, from prison, Fraser wrote to C., a law-agent in Glasgow, asking him to act in his defence. He also delivered to C. £285.5.2d, authorising C. to use the money for the defence proceedings and for paying out sums as directed by himself.

On 25th October Fraser's estates were sequestrated, and M'K., the trustee, called on C. to account for his intromissions with Fraser's estate.

On 27th December Fraser pleaded guilty and was sentenced.

According to C.'s account, the sum which he had received from Fraser on 12th October had been more than exhausted by the cost of the defence proceedings coupled with payments made on Fraser's directions.

*Held* that the mandate to C., being revocable, had fallen by Fraser's sequestration, and that C. was therefore bound to account to M'K. for all sums in his hands belonging to Fraser as at 25th October.

LORD PRESIDENT (J. P. B. ROBERTSON) (at p. 909): "On 11th October 1893 Thomas Fraser was apprehended on certain charges of forgery. When he was taken to prison he bethought himself of the necessity of looking after his affairs, and accordingly wrote to Mr Campbell asking that gentleman to act for him, and he authorised him 'to take any steps you may think necessary to preserve my estate.' Immediately afterwards, with a view to carrying out the same purpose, he wrote, on 12th October 1893, the following letter:— 'With reference to the money which I have instructed you to receive from Mr Howie, my cashier, and take possession of, I request and authorise you to use the same for the purposes of my defence in the criminal charge against me in such manner as you may think advisable, as also to pay on my behalf any sum or sums that I may direct you. — Yours truly.' Acting under this authority Mr Campbell took possession of the sum of £285, and thus became a depository for Fraser.

"Now, the letter just quoted ends with a request that Mr Campbell should pay 'any sum or sums that I may direct you.' That just means 'hold the money to my order,' and the subsequent letters contain special directions for carrying that out. Mr Campbell thereafter began to make preparations for the defence, but ultimately Fraser pled guilty, and was sentenced to a term of penal servitude. Mr Campbell thus acted in precise accordance with his instructions, assuming those instructions to have retained validity. Unfortunately, however, on 25th October, about a fortnight after the apprehension, Fraser's estates were sequestrated. There is no doubt that from the date of the sequestration the money in Mr Campbell's hands became the money of Fraser's creditors, as opposed to Fraser himself, and from that time it was Mr Campbell's duty to look not to the bankrupt but to the trustee for instructions as to its disposal. It cannot be said that the mandate to Mr Campbell was not revocable, for it was admitted in argument that there was nothing to prevent Fraser from changing his agent and directing that the money should be handed over to his new adviser. On these grounds I think there is no good defence to the claim of the trustee.

"The words of Mr Justice Wright in describing the case of *Pollitt* (L.R. [1892] 1 Q.B. 175, and [1893] 1 Q.B. 455) exactly apply to the present case, —'The money of the debtor was handed to the solicitor, who was to apply it to meet future costs. On the occurrence of the bankruptcy the authority ceased, and the money went to the trustee.' This case is precisely the case of *Pollitt*."

LORD ADAM (at p. 910): "It is clear in this case that the money in question remained at the absolute disposal of Fraser. There is no contract set forth in the correspondence that Fraser was to employ Mr Campbell to the end of the criminal prosecution, and there is no obligation on Mr Campbell to continue acting as agent. Further, the last words of the letter of 12th October are quite general, 'to pay on my behalf any sum or sums that I may direct you,' and special instructions as to the sums to be paid are given in the later letters.

"Now, if that be so, the result in law is that the sequestration put an end to the mandate, and Mr Campbell had no longer any right to dispose of what was not Fraser's money but the trustee's.... I entirely agree that this case falls under the rule of *Pollitt*."

LORD M'LAREN (at p. 911): "The employment was on the ordinary professional footing. The money was in the agent's hands, no doubt, but simply as a deposit, with an authority from the depositor to apply it in payment of services rendered and advances made *de die in diem*. Bankruptcy intervened, and the trustee quite rightly, and immediately after his appointment was confirmed, called upon Mr Campbell for an accounting, thus terminating Mr Campbell's employment as a law-agent. Thereafter the right of Mr Campbell was only to retain the money for payment of his account up to date. Subject to this qualified right of retention, he was accountable to the trustee."

NOTE

*Cf. Dickson* v. *Nicholson* (1855) 17 D. 1011.

George Brown and Sons of Arbroath had employed Osler as a traveller and were indebted to him to the extent of £295, chiefly for arrears of salary.

On 28th October 1854 the firm stopped payment, and on 30th October Osler, in full knowledge of the firm's impending sequestration, set off for England, where on 1st November he uplifted certain debts due to the firm.

On 4th November the firm was sequestrated, and on 10th November Osler was himself declared bankrupt in England.

N., the official assignee on Osler's estate, claimed from D., the trustee on the firm's estate, £163, *i.e.*, the balance of the debt of £295 left after deduction of the £132 uplifted and retained by Osler.

*Held* that Osler had not been entitled, in the knowledge of the firm's insolvency, to collect the firm's funds and retain them for payment of the debt due to himself. N.'s claim, as stated, was rejected.

Lord President (M'Neill) (at p. 1012): "I think the way to regard this case is, to look at it in the first instance in its position as at the date of the bankruptcy of Brown and Company, or as at the date of 7th November, when the demand was made on Osler to refund, he not being bankrupt. I am very clearly of opinion that the conduct of Osler in suddenly going to uplift the money, knowing the condition in which his employers were, was illegal conduct. He had no longer any authority to act for them. Knowing their condition, it was wrongous intromission with the funds of persons in a state of insolvency. The money is said to have been uplifted in the ordinary course of business. No doubt the payments made to him were so, but the act of Osler in going to get payment was not in the ordinary course of business, and therefore I think his conduct was illegal; and if the case had stood as at 7th November, and no insolvency of Osler had ensued, I have no doubt that he would not have been entitled to apply money to the extinction of his own claim, but, on the contrary, that it would have been his duty to refund that sum, and that the trustee for Brown and Company would have been entitled to apply towards the extinction of the money he refused to refund, the dividends in his hands. If, for example, the dividend on the estate of Brown and Sons had been 10s. a pound, and Osler had made his claim on their estate for the full sum due to him, he would have been entitled to receive £147. Against that the trustee would have been entitled to set off the £132, 7s. 6d., and to pay Osler the difference. But he has not stated his claim in that way. Such would have been the condition of matters if Osler had never become bankrupt. I do not think that the subsequent bankruptcy alters matters, for such were the rights of parties as at that date; and if so, I do not think that if the trustee could in that case retain the dividends on Osler's claim, Osler's assignee can acquire a greater right to these dividends than Osler himself could have."

Lord Curriehill (at p. 1013): "At the date of the sequestration the relative position of Osler and the estate of Brown and Company was this:—Osler was in possession of £132, which was part of the sequestrated estate. He had obtained that sum unlawfully. It would have been unlawfully obtained even with consent of the bankrupts. His mandate was at an end, and therefore he was an unlawful intromitter, and could have no claim of retention."

Lord Deas (at p. 1013): "On 28th October 1854 Messrs Brown had stopped payment, and granted a mandate authorising sequestration of their estates to be applied for. This was known to Osler. . . . In this knowledge he set off to England and uplifted debts due to Messrs Brown. . . . Sequestration was awarded on 4th November, and the assignee now seeks to retain the money thus uplifted in extinction *pro tanto* of Osler's current salary . . ., and to rank on their estate for the balance.

"Now, had the question been with Osler himself, I think the answer would have been good, that his mandate, assuming him to have held one, had fallen by the declared insolvency of his employers, and the authority granted by them to get their estates sequestrated. . . . The answer which would thus have been good against Osler, is, I conceive, equally good against his official assignee."

*Revocation by principal*

**Galbraith & Moorhead v. The Arethusa Ship Co. Ltd.**
(1896) 23 R. 1011

G. & Co., shipbrokers, offered to take £500 in shares in the A. Ship Co. Ltd., provided that they were appointed sole chartering brokers for the "A." The offer was accepted.

G. & Co. took the shares, and the agreement was acted on for several years. A change then took place in the management, and G. & Co., averring that the A. Ship Co. Ltd., in breach of the agreement, had failed to employ them as sole chartering brokers, raised an action against the company concluding for £600 as damages for breach of contract.

*Held* that the agreement was not terminable at the pleasure of the company.

LORD PRESIDENT (J. P. B. ROBERTSON) (at p. 1014): "The defenders' company was formed for the objects of purchasing, owning, and working the ship 'Arethusa,' and its operations were, by the memorandum of association, confined to that vessel. By the agreement, for breach of which this action is brought, the pursuers agreed to take £500 in shares of the company, provided they were appointed sole chartering brokers for the 'Arethusa,' and that all her charters were done through them, it being always understood that they were able to do as well as any other brokers regarding rates and terms.

"The defenders claim right to 'terminate the agreement at any time,' and their way of doing so is simply by giving other brokers their charters, because they so please. . . .

"First of all, what is the fair reading of the agreement so far as duration goes? I think it means simply this: that, so long as the pursuers' firm are in business, and do as well as other brokers regarding rates and terms, they shall get the 'Arethusa's' charters. To call this a perpetual contract is surely inaccurate. The conditions are the continued existence of the 'Arethusa' and of the pursuers' firm, and also the getting by them of as good rates and terms as other brokers get. The life of a ship is very far from a perpetuity; the joint lives of a ship and a firm of brokers still farther; while the condition about rates and terms still more reduces the stability of the tenure. When the employment, such as it is, is the counterpart for a substantial contribution of capital, the arrangement does not seem to call for remark or to warrant any reluctance in treating a breach of it as a breach of contract. . . .

"If the construction which I put on the contract is sound, there is, so far as I know, no rule of law which refuses it effect. There is nothing illegal in a trader engaging to give all his business, so long as he carries it on, to a broker, for any consideration he likes, if a contract to this effect be made in writing."

LORD ADAM (at p. 1015): "This case depends solely upon the construction of the agreement . . . by which the pursuers were appointed sole chartering brokers for the 'Arethusa,' and the question is, whether that agreement could be determined by the defenders on reasonable notice, or on reasonable cause only. Now, it will be observed that the pursuers paid for the appointment of sole charterers' brokers, and the consideration was their taking £500 in shares of the company, which it is not disputed they did. I have great difficulty in holding that an agreement for which consideration had been thus given could be terminated at will by the other contracting party.

". . . The agreement bears to be entered into 'on the understanding' that the pursuers are able to do as well as any other brokers regarding rates and terms. I suppose the pursuers could not do as well as any other brokers unless they exerted themselves to get charters, and that is equivalent to saying that if the pursuers do not exert themselves in procuring good charters for the vessel, the defenders would be entitled to put an end to the agreement.

"On the whole, I am of opinion that the agreement was not terminable at the will of the defenders, but only on cause shown."

NOTE

In *Walker* v. *Somerville* (1837) 16 S. 217, there were circumstances in which authority was held to be revocable at pleasure provided the principal indemnified the agent for his trouble and expenses.

W., of Dollar, addressed a letter to S., of Edinburgh, promising to S. 15 per cent of any sums which S. might recover by means of an action against W.'s father. The letter also appointed S. to act for W. in various other matters, including management of a farm which S. was to select and which it was proposed to stock out of the funds to be recovered by the action.

A summons was raised against W.'s father, but within two months after the above-mentioned letter had been written, W. and his father made an agreement, by which an annuity of £20 was settled on W., and his claims against his father were discharged.

S. then alleged that W. had had no power to settle the action to the prejudice of the stipulations in his favour in the letter, and he raised an action against W., libelling that the letter amounted to an agreement which he, S., had acted on and from which W. had not been entitled to resile, and concluding for implement or for damages.

*Held* that the agreement was truly of the nature of a letter or mandate, which W. had been entitled to recall at pleasure, subject to any claims for disbursement and remuneration for trouble which S. could prove.

*Discontinuance of principal's business*

**Patmore & Co. v. R. Cannon & Co. Ltd.**
(1892) 19 R. 1004

P. & Co., warehousemen, agents, and merchants, Glasgow and Leith, agreed with C. Ltd., of Lincoln, to act as C. Ltd.'s agents in Scotland for the sale of goods manufactured by C. Ltd., consisting of leather goods, dip, and glue, for a period of five years from 1st October 1891.

In January 1892, C. Ltd. intimated to P. & Co. that it intended to give up its fancy leather trade, and it advised P. & Co. to become agents for another principal in the same line of business. C. Ltd. also intimated that in other respects it was prepared to adhere to its agreement with P. & Co.

P. & Co. sued C. Ltd. for damages for breach of contract, and maintained also, alternatively, that C. Ltd. was bound to recompense them for their outlay in moving to larger premises in order to suit the requirements of the agency.

*Held* that (1) there had been no breach of contract, and (2) the averments in support of the alternative claim for recompense were irrelevant.

LORD ORDINARY (LOW) (at p. 1005): "In my opinion the pursuers have not set forth a relevant case of breach of contract. . . . They say that the defenders intimated that they intended to give up the fancy leather, but offered to continue the agreement in regard to other goods. If this constituted a breach of the agreement it must be because by entering into the agreement the defenders became bound to carry on all the branches of their business to which the agreement referred for the period specified in the agreement. There is no such obligation expressed, and in my judgment it cannot be implied. I do not think that the defenders bound themselves to carry on their business, or any branch of it, for five years, or for any other period, simply for the benefit of the pursuers. If the defenders found it expedient to give up any part of their business it seems to me that, so far as their agreement with the pursuers was concerned, they were perfectly entitled to do so. There is no allegation here of fraud, or that the defenders gave up the fancy leather trade for the purpose of injuring the pursuers. It is simply said that the defenders intimated that they intended to give up the fancy leather trade, but that in other respects they were willing to adhere to the agreement. In my opinion that averment does not necessarily imply, or even suggest, that the defenders did anything which they were not perfectly entitled to do. The view which I take seems to me to be consistent with the judgment of the House of Lords in the case of *Rhodes* v. *Forwood*, 1876 L.R., 1 App. Ca. 256."

LORD PRESIDENT (J. P. B. ROBERTSON) (at p. 1006): "I think that the Lord Ordinary is right. It appears to me that the case of *Rhodes* v. *Forwood* . . . applies, in so far as the action is founded on breach of contract. I think that there was no breach of contract, for I cannot read the contract as containing a stipulation that the defenders should continue in any particular branch of their business during the period named.

"The pursuers also pointed to article 5 of their condescendence as raising a separate or alternative ground of action. . . . I think, however, that their averments on record are not such as to raise this question. It appears to me that their case depends on breach of contract, or nothing at all. What they say is, that when the agreement was entered into they, at the defenders' request, arranged to change their office in Glasgow, and to remove to a larger one with greater storage and show-room accommodation in order to suit the requirements of the defenders' business, and they maintain that the defenders are in consequence liable to them in the sum of £200, which they state to be the difference between the higher rent of their new office and the rent of office which they left on becoming the agents of the defenders. I think the fair reading of this averment is that they took the larger office because unless they had made the change they would not have got the contract. That just takes us back to the question, what was the contract? and, as I have said, it was a contract which did not pledge the defenders to continue in the business which they have given up."

LORD ADAM (at p. 1007): "I am of the same opinion. To have any foundation for the alleged breach of contract the pursuers must make out that it was either an express or an implied condition of the contract that Cannon & Company, the defenders, should continue to carry on their leather business for at least a year. There is certainly no such condition expressed, and I cannot find it to be implied. All that the defenders undertake is to employ the pursuers as their agents for at least a year if they themselves continue in the business. I think the case, in so far as it is founded on breach of contract, is just *Rhodes* v. *Forwood*."

NOTES

1. Lord Adam referred to the period of "at least a year" because the contract included a provision for reconsideration of the terms for leather at the end of the first year.

2. *Cf. London, Leith, Edinburgh, and Glasgow Shipping Co.* v. *Ferguson* (1850) 13 D. 51.

In 1827 F. was appointed agent at Greenock for the L. Shipping Co., and was paid by a commission on his transactions. He continued to hold the appointment until April 1847, when the L. Shipping Co. resolved to discontinue their trade at Greenock.

F. claimed commission up to April 1848 on the ground that it had been understood between the parties that his engagement was a yearly one and that there was a custom of trade to that effect.

*Held* that F., being an agent, had not been engaged from year to year as a servant would have been, and that the L. Shipping Co. were entitled to discontinue their trade whenever they saw fit, without giving prior notice or paying compensation to F.

Lord President (Boyle) (at p. 52): "We have nothing to do with the usage of trade. There is no distinct averment about it on record; and if there were, it would be difficult to see how such a ridiculous usage could exist, as that the Company could be compelled to go on with a losing trade, in order that their agent might earn his commission. This is entirely a hypothetical charge, not for services done, but for commission which might have been earned. It is very clear from the correspondence, that at first the defender did not anticipate that he could make any such demand. There is no proof of any yearly engagement, and no distinct averment of the usage of trade."

Lord Mackenzie (at p. 52): "I am of the same opinion. It is not averred that the defender was anything more than an agent, to be paid by commission. He does not say that there was any bargain, or even any understanding, that the Company were to continue their business for any definite time. The defender was to get his commission, such as it was. I cannot see that there has been any case made out. It is in fact a claim of damages against the Company for giving up their trade, whereby the defender's expectations were disappointed."

3. *Patmore & Co.* v. *B. Cannon & Co. Ltd.* was followed in *S.S. "State of California" Co. Ltd.* v. *Moore* (1895) 22 R. 562.

The State Steamship Co. Ltd. had for many years carried on a regular series of sailings between Glasgow and New York once every five weeks.

In December 1889, certain of the shareholders agreed to form a new company, for the purpose of acquiring a new steamer of modern type to be run under agreement with the State Steamship Co. Ltd. Accordingly C. Ltd. was formed, and the two companies entered into an agreement with a firm of shipbuilders for the building of the "State of California" at the price of £97,000.

At the same time the two companies entered into a mutual agreement providing that the two ships were to have the same manager, that the State Steamship Co. Ltd. would give the "State of California" her regular turn in the Transatlantic service along with its other steamers, that the contract was to subsist for ten years from the launching of the "State of California," and that the State Steamship Co. Ltd. was to receive as remuneration a brokerage of 7½ per cent on the net amount received for ocean carriage, and a further commission of 5 per cent on the net profits shown in C. Ltd.'s balance-sheet when these profits exceeded 6 per cent of C. Ltd.'s paid-up capital.

The "State of California" was launched on 29th January 1891, but, on 4th March 1891, before the vessel was furnished, the State Steamship Co. Ltd. passed a resolution that it be wound up. M. was appointed liquidator.

C. Ltd. claimed in the liquidation for £20,000, being (i) the expenses of laying the "State of California" up for a time, and (ii) the loss of profit arising from a contract subsequently entered into with another line, which C. Ltd. alleged was less remunerative than that with the State Steamship Co. Ltd. would have been.

M. repelled the claim, and C. Ltd. appealed to the court.

*Held* that the contract between the two companies had to be construed as subject to an implied condition that it was to endure only so long as the State Steamship Co. Ltd. carried on its business, and that C. Ltd. was therefore not entitled to damages for breach of contract.

Lord Ordinary (Stormonth-Darling) (at p. 564): "In my opinion, there was no breach, for the contract is undistinguishable in principle from the contracts in *Rhodes* v. *Forwood* . . . and *Patmore & Co.* . . .

"It is quite a different case where one party contracts to employ another for a certain period at a fixed salary. That is a positive and absolute undertaking to do a certain thing, and the party failing to do it must pay damages."

Lord Adam (at p. 566): "On the 4th March 1891 . . . the State Company went into liquidation. Their fleet of steamers has since been sold, and they are no longer carrying on the Transatlantic service previously carried on by them.

"They have never worked or sailed the steamship 'State of California,' and are not in a position to do so.

"The question is whether in so failing to work and sail the steamship the

State Company have committed a breach of their contract with the 'California' Steamship Company, and that leads us to consider more particularly the terms of that contract.

"The preamble recites that it had been arranged that the State Company should work and sail the steamship in their Transatlantic service, along with their own steamers engaged in their service; and the second, and as it appears to me the leading article of the agreement, on which the other provisions depend, provides that the State Company shall give the steamship her regular turn in their Transatlantic service along with the other steamers belonging to or managed by them.

"This is the obligation which the State Company undertake as to sailing and working the steamship, and it appears to me that the breach of that obligation would have consisted in not giving the steamship her regular turn along with the other steamers belonging to or managed by them.

"But that is not the nature of the alleged breach, which is that the State Company have failed to sail or work the steamship at all, and that raises the question whether, in the circumstances which have emerged, there was any obligation on the State Company to do so.

"It appears to me that the true meaning of the contract is that the State Company were only bound to give the steamship her 'regular turn' when and so long as they were carrying on their Transatlantic service.

"It will be observed that the agreement postulates the existence of a Transatlantic service, for the 'regular turn' is to be given in their Transatlantic service. Neither is there any stipulation in the contract as to how often her 'regular turn' was to come round. It was left entirely in the option of the State Company, and dependent on the state of their business how often it should come round, whether every month, or every two months, or every six months, yet it is obvious that upon this the profits which would be earned by the steamship depended. This seems to me to point strongly in the direction that it was equally in the discretion of the State Company whether they should keep up any Transatlantic service at all.

"It appears to me, therefore, that the 'California' Ship Company cannot succeed in this claim unless they can shew that there is an obligation, express or implied, on the State Company to keep up their Transatlantic service during the whole ten years of the agreement.

"There is no express obligation to that effect, and I think the implication is the other way.

"I concur with the Lord Ordinary that the meaning of the contract was that the 'California' Steamship Company was to follow the fortunes of the State Company, and that their vessel should get a regular turn along with the vessels of the State Company, but that they did not stipulate that the State Company should work their Transatlantic service in any particular way, or at all.

"I also concur with him that the case falls within the principle of the cases *Rhodes* v. *Forwood* and *Patmore & Company*."

Lord M'Laren (at p. 567): "The impossibility that the company could have intended to bind themselves to run their line for a period of ten years, even at a loss, furnishes the strongest reason for qualifying the agreement by adding the condition that it should continue only as long as they were working their line. Therefore, as this contract has failed not by any wilful breach, but by the condition no longer existing under which it was to continue, I agree that no damages are due."

APPENDIX

## GLOSSARY OF LATIN WORDS AND PHRASES USED IN THIS BOOK

*a fortiori* (of): in a stronger position (than); clearer (than) (p. 91).
*actio contraria*: literally, opposite action; in Roman law the right which an agent had to be indemnified by his principal (p. 21).
*actio contraria mandati*: literally, opposite action of agency; in Roman law the right which an agent had to be indemnified by his principal (p. 96).

*bona fide*: good faith; honest; honestly (Latin ablative case of "*bona fides*," the ablative case being used in Latin after the preposition "*in*") (pp. 45, 51, 86, 169, 174, 175, 176, 178).
*bona fides*: good faith (pp. 112, 170, 173, 175, 177).
*bonis*: for property (p. 175).

*causa causae causantis*: cause of the cause which causes; remote or indirect cause (p. 77).
*causa causans*: cause which causes; immediate or direct cause (pp. 77, 80).
*condictio indebiti*: literally, action of a thing not due; action for the recovery of a payment which was not due; it justifies a claim based on quasi-contract, for recovery of the amount not due (p. 133).
*corpus*: body; substance; "*corpus* of the bond" means "the bond itself, as distinct from the discharge of the bond" (p. 47).
*culpa lata*: literally, broad fault; extreme negligence (pp. 57, 96).
*culpa levissima*: literally, the lightest fault; the slightest degree of negligence (p. 96).
*curator bonis*: guardian for property, the term used of the guardian appointed to look after the property of an insane person (pp. 171, 173, 174).

*de damno vitando*: concerning a loss to be avoided; in order to avoid a loss (p. 174).
*de die in diem*: from day to day (p. 180).
*de facto*: in fact; actually; as a matter of fact (implying a contrast with the legal position) (pp. 64, 117, 168).
*de novo*: anew; all over again (p. 149).

*delegatus non potest delegare*: a person to whom a thing is delegated cannot delegate; an agent cannot delegate (p. 51).
*dicta*: statements; remarks; observations made by judges in decided cases (pp. 1, 117, 130).

*esto*: literally, let it be so; assuming; supposing; on the assumption; supposition or hypothesis (pp. 33, 70, 123).

*factorio nomine*: in the capacity of agent; as agent (pp. 97, 113, 114, 116, 169).
*funditus*: utterly; completely (p. 16).

*hinc inde*: on the one side and on the other side; on both sides (pp. 100, 109).

*ibid.*: abbreviation of "*ibidem*"; at the same place (p. 23).
*in bona fide*: in good faith (pp. 175, 177).
*in globo*: in full (p. 131).
*in gremio*: within it; as one of its terms (p. 123).
*in hoc statu*: literally, in this state; in the present circumstances; for the time being (p. 176).
*in toto*: in its entirety; in full; completely (pp. 63, 173).
*inter alia*: amongst other things (pp. 6, 69, 70, 80, 103).
*inter se*: amongst themselves (p. 127).

*jus quaesitum tertio*: right acquired by a third party, *i.e.* by a person who is not one of the two contracting parties (p. 133).
*jus tertii*: literally, right of a third party, *i.e.* of someone other than the person who is claiming it; the phrase implies a negative — if it is said of a person, X, that a right is "*jus tertii*," this means that X is not entitled to the right, because it is a right which arises out of a contract between A and B, with the result that A or B is entitled to the right; if something is "*jus tertii*" to a person, the effect is that the person is not entitled to concern himself with the matter (p. 28).

*lucrati*: enriched (plural of "*lucratus*") (p. 11).

*mala fides*: bad faith (p. 173).

*non compos mentis*: not of sound mind (p. 171).
*non sequitur*: thing which does not follow; erroneous conclusion (p. 146).

*onus*: burden; burden of proof (pp. 3, 34, 117).

*per*: (said) by; in the words of; according to the opinion of (pp. 1, 23, 151).
*persona*: person; legal personality (p. 12).
*praeposita negotiis mariti*: placed in charge of the affairs of her husband (p. 29).
*praeposita rebus domesticis*: placed in charge of domestic affairs (p. 29).
*praepositura*: position of being placed in charge; authority; management (pp. 26, 28, 29).
*praepositus negotiis*: placed in charge of business affairs (pp. 30, 31).
*praesumptio juris*: presumption of law (pp. 113, 114).
*prepositor*: person who places (another person) in charge; principal (p. 177).
*prepositura*: alternative spelling of "*praepositura*" (p. 175).
*presumptio juris*: alternative spelling of "*praesumptio juris*" (pp. 113, 117).
*prima facie*: at first sight; until the contrary is proved (opposite of "conclusive") (pp. 11, 47, 60, 76, 86, 120, 124, 135, 155).
*pro rata*: for a proportionate share; in proportion (the word "*parte*" is to be understood as following "*rata*") (p. 156).
*pro tanto*: for so much; as far as it would go (p. 181).

*quantum*: amount (p. 53).
*quantum lucrati*: as much as (they) have been enriched; the amount of the profit of (plural of "*quantum lucratus*") (p. 53).
*quantum lucratus*: as much as (he) has been enriched; the amount of the profit of (p. 76).
*quantum meruit*: as much as (he) has earned; amount based on services rendered (pp. 53, 74, 75, 76, 89).
*quantum valeat*: for as much as it would be worth; to the extent of its value (p. 106).
*quasi*: literally, as if; supposed; in the position of (a *quasi* principal is a person who is treated as if he were, but who is not, a principal) (p. 150).
*quoad*: to the extent of; as regards (p. 30).
*quoad ultra*: to the extent of anything further; as regards the rest (p. 27).

*secundum subjectam materiam*: according to the terms which have been laid down (p. 173).

*sibi imputet*: it must be imputed to himself; the responsibility rests on himself (p. 30).

*sponsio ludicra*: sportive promise; undertaking made in jest (and therefore not worthy of the court's consideration) (p. 92).

*sponsiones ludicrae*: sportive promises (plural of "*sponsio ludicra*") (p. 92).

*sua natura*: by its (*or* their) very nature; on its own; automatically (pp. 172, 173).

*sub nom.*: abbreviation of "*sub nomine*"; under the name of (p. 57).

*summa diligentia*: highest (standard of) care (p. 2).

*uberrima fides*: the utmost good faith (p. 62).

*ultima thule*: land furthest away ("Thule" being the name given by the Romans to the land which they regarded as being at the edge of the world (Shetland? Iceland?)); "ends of the earth" (p. 173).

*ultra fines mandati*: beyond the bounds of the agency; outside the scope of the agency (p. 178).

*unoquoque*: with anyone at all; with anyone whomsoever (p. 175).

*ut res magis valeat*: in order that the matter may preferably take effect; a shorter form of "*ut res magis valeat quam pereat*": in order that the matter may rather take effect than perish, *i.e.* than be held to be a nullity (p. 8).

*vox signata*: literally, a marked word; a word having some special legal effect (p. 89).